The SELF
in SOCIAL PSYCHOLOGY

Edited by
DANIEL M. WEGNER
TRINITY UNIVERSITY

ROBIN R. VALLACHER
ILLINOIS INSTITUTE OF TECHNOLOGY

New York / Oxford
OXFORD UNIVERSITY PRESS
1980

Library of Congress Cataloging in Publication Data
Main entry under title:

The self in social psychology.

Includes bibliographical references and indexes.
1. Social psychology. 2. Self. I. Wegner,
Daniel M., 1948-   II. Vallacher, Robin R., 1946-
HM251.S4223   301.1   79-15325
ISBN 0-19-502647-0
ISBN 0-19-502648-9 pbk.

Printed in the United States of America

Preface

Have you ever wondered why people read books on psychology? Judging by the popularity of such books, it seems that many people—perhaps yourself included—look to psychology to provide insights into the principles underlying their emotions, motives, thoughts, and actions. The fact that people are interested in these matters suggests that a concern with self-understanding is itself a very important principle of psychology. Of course, the public's interest in psychology is not the only indication that self-reflection is an important human preoccupation; indeed, an interest in our assets and liabilities, our values and desires, and even our thought processes is evident in much of our everyday behavior. It should come as no surprise, then, that psychologists have developed and tested theories about how people come to know and evaluate themselves. This book is intended to acquaint you with what experimental social psychology—the science of interpersonal thought and behavior—has to say about these processes.

You should not expect, though, to come away from this book with one perfectly integrated theory of the self in social psychology. This might have been possible a dozen years ago when social psychologists still looked primarily to a few theoretical masters—C. H. Cooley (1902), G. H. Mead (1934), or William James (1890)—for enlightenment on the key aspects of self-reflection. But in the recent history of social psychology, a curious event has taken place. Researchers and theorists in a variety of distinct areas of inquiry, working separately on different problems, have all found it useful to invoke ideas about the self to explain what they have found. These ideas often have strong connections with the writings of the early theorists, but more often than not, they go on to establish new perspectives that are only beginning to be explored. So, instead of giving complete closure on the topic of the self, you will find that this book conveys what is most exciting about any scientific venture—the complexity and diversity of the search for new knowledge.

In the first chapter, Vallacher introduces self theories. The basic principles of self-reflection held in common by otherwise diverse points of view are outlined, as are some of the implications of these broad principles for social thought and behavior. The next four chapters offer detailed introductions to specific self theories that have achieved current prominence in social psychology. Wicklund and Frey (Chapter 2) summarize the basic tenets of self-awareness theory, a theory that synthesizes classic social psychological ideas with contemporary cognitive psychology. In Chapter 3, Enzle discusses self-perception theory, a theory originally advanced to account for certain counterintuitive findings in social psychology, and shows the recent refinements of that viewpoint. This discussion is particularly useful in showing how people identify their motives in everyday life. Pennebaker (Chapter 4) outlines a theory that explains the experience of emotions in terms of self-perception principles; the extension of this analysis to the experience of other internal states, such as pain and illness, is also discussed. Markus (Chapter 5) examines the self in the context of the operation of thought and memory; it is demonstrated how events in daily life are processed in terms of their relevance to one's particular self-view.

The next three chapters show how the self theories discussed in the first five chapters, as well as new perspectives drawn from yet other sources, are useful for understanding topics of enduring interest in social psychology. Wegner (Chapter 6) considers the problem of the "selfishness" of the self by examining the role of self-reflection in altruism and helping behavior. Arkin, in Chapter 7, and Archer, in Chapter 8, demonstrate how one's self-view influences and is influenced by social interaction and social relationships. Arkin focuses on the strategies people employ in establishing and maintaining a certain impression of themselves in the eyes of others; Archer examines the factors that promote honest self-disclosure as opposed to calculated impression management in social relationships.

Since one person's self-view is necessarily different from those of others, the concept of self has implications for the understanding of personality and individual differences; the last three chapters explore these implications. In Chapter 9, Pryor investigates the factors that underlie accuracy and inaccuracy in reporting about one's own personality. The matter of the limits of self-knowledge is taken up here, since the extent to which people know their own attitudes, traits, and behaviors is treated in depth. Individual differences in how people see themselves are discussed by Scheier and Carver in Chapter 10; such differences seem to account for many of the important "personality" differences among people. Finally, Vallacher, Wegner, and Hoine (Chapter 11) abstract several of the central ideas from the preceding chapters to show how self theories may be applied to clinical problems and issues of personal adjustment common among young adults.

As you can see from this brief preview, this book addresses a wide range of topics in social psychology in terms of a potentially unifying concept—the self. For this reason, the book is a useful supplement to traditional texts in social psychology that typically offer far less integration. And, because the concept of the self is intimately related to issues of personality, adjustment, and abnormal psychology, this book is also appropriate as a supplement to courses in these areas. Though *The Self in Social Psychology* is intended primarily for undergraduates, the particular combination of material offered is at the forefront of social psychological research and theory. It is likely, then, that the book will be of interest to advanced students and to professionals as well.

A common complaint about edited books is that the various chapters differ not only in content but also in readability and level of difficulty. In preparing this book, we were very sensitive to this potential problem and took great care to ensure evenness among the chapters. Each contributor has written with the undergraduate in mind. As a result, jargon is kept to a minimum, principles are established in the context of everyday examples, and the major points are summarized at the end of each chapter. Perhaps more important, the authors have communicated with the editors, as well as among themselves, in preparing their respective chapters. So, redundancy has been avoided, and each author has been careful to reference other chapters when this is appropriate. In short, because *The Self in Social Psychology* is integrated in presentation as well as in substance, it is more than a collection of readings and can rightly be considered a unified text.

We wish to thank our contributors for putting forth this careful effort, and for the spirit of industry and cooperation they all displayed in fashioning their chapters. We express our appreciation, too, to those who helped this project in other ways. Shalom Schwartz made detailed and helpful comments on many of the chapters; Alan Appelman, Bill Gabrenya, June Ross Enzle, Mike Enzle, and Bob Wicklund each read and commented on one or more chapters; Randy Evans, Toni Giuliano, Sherry Hoy, Meg Laird, Maureen McGee, and Pete Rodriguez, all members of a seminar at Trinity University, gave us an important preview of student reactions in their comments on the manuscript; Mary Beth Rosson assembled references and indices; and Marcus Boggs, our editor at Oxford, lent us encouragement and sound advice.

San Antonio   D.M.W.
Chicago   R.R.V.
July 1979

Contributors

RICHARD L. ARCHER
Department of Psychology
University of Texas at Austin

ROBERT M. ARKIN
Department of Psychology
University of Missouri-Columbia

CHARLES S. CARVER
Department of Psychology
University of Miami

MICHAEL E. ENZLE
Department of Psychology
University of Alberta

DIETER FREY
Institut für Psychologie
Universität Kiel

HASKEL HOINE
Department of Psychology
Trinity University

HAZEL MARKUS
Institute for Social Research
University of Michigan

JAMES W. PENNEBAKER
Department of Psychology
University of Virginia

JOHN B. PRYOR
Department of Psychology
Ohio State University

MICHAEL F. SCHEIER
Department of Psychology
Carnegie-Mellon University

ROBIN R. VALLACHER
Department of Psychology
Illinois Institute of Technology

DANIEL M. WEGNER
Department of Psychology
Trinity University

ROBERT A. WICKLUND
Department of Psychology
University of Texas at Austin

Contents

The Self in Social Psychology

1

An Introduction to Self Theory

ROBIN R. VALLACHER
ILLINOIS INSTITUTE OF TECHNOLOGY

The concept of the self has enjoyed a long but somewhat rocky history in psychology. Always in fashion in certain circles—most notably, clinical psychology, psychiatry, and personality theory—the self has not always inspired a great deal of esteem among researchers concerned with social psychological phenomena. It is not that the notion of self-reflection had no inherent appeal; even the most strident behaviorist would admit, off duty, that people do seem to reflect on themselves, develop a sense of who they are, and even act on the basis of their self-perceptions. But as a young and uncertain science, experimental social psychology in the 1940s and 1950s was careful not to rely too heavily on unobservable, "mentalistic" constructs—a category that clearly includes the self. To many, the self conjured up an image of a little being inside the person's skull who directed the person's behavior, much as an executive controls the actions of a corporation. This was not only an embarrassing metaphor for a discipline trying to achieve status as a serious science, it also seemed doomed to an infinite regression; what controlled the little executive? A little vice-president?

Concerns about the scientific legitimacy of the self—indeed, about mentalistic constructs in general—have waned somewhat in recent years. In part, this change reflects the dramatic advances that have occurred in computer technology over the last two decades. If a computer, a mere hunk of metal, can operate on the basis of "internal" programs, selectively encoding and systematically transforming raw data, then surely it is not unscientific to suggest that a human being can selectively encode and systematically transform environmental events in accordance with internal programs, producing "output"—behavior—that reflects such programs. In this light, computer programs provide an apt metaphor for mentalistic constructs (see, e.g., Miller, Galanter, & Pribram, 1960). Some of the more intriguing human "programs" involve the selection and transformation of data concerning the self.

With this new lease on legitimacy, the concept of the self has recently become central to social psychology. A wide variety of phenomena—person perception, morality, reactions to success and failure, cognitive consistency, and many others—are considered by theorists to reflect the individual's attempt to achieve or maintain a particular self-view. Because the scope of self-relevant phenomena is so broad, theorists have necessarily addressed numerous questions concerning the concept of the self. It is possible to group these questions into four general categories of inquiry about the self. First of all, just what *is* the self? What are the *defining characteristics* of self-reflection? What capacities or motives does it involve? Is it uniquely human? A second set of questions concerns the *process* of self-reflection; how do we come to understand and evaluate ourselves? In what ways, if any, are self-reflection processes unique, distinct from other mental processes? Third, psychologists are concerned with the *structure* of the self. Given that we have a somewhat distinct understanding and evaluation of ourselves in different roles and situations, and that at different times we use different criteria for self-judgment, how do we organize all these self-perceptions into a coherent self-concept? The final set of questions, perhaps the most relevant from a social psychological perspective, concerns the relation between self-reflection and *behavior*. What difference does the self make in our everyday actions? Just how important is the self to social psychology? These sets of questions are discussed in this chapter and provide the point of departure for each of the subsequent chapters.

THE SELF: DEFINING CHARACTERISTICS

Though we may not like to admit it, most of us think about ourselves a great deal of the time. Words like "self-consciousness," "self-pity," "self-doubt," and "self-respect" are as familiar to everyone as are common household objects. Of course, the content of self-directed thought can be quite varied; we may be concerned with our values one moment, only to be obsessed with a facial blemish the next. The feelings or affective states associated with self-thought are also quite diverse; we may smugly reflect on a recent triumph or we may anguish over our inability to pronounce polysyllabic words. Despite the diversity in content and affect, however, the various manifestations of self-reflection have much in common, and this commonality is quite revealing about human functioning.

SELF-REFLECTION AS SOCIAL PERSPECTIVE

Though various accounts of self-reflection differ in important ways from one another (see, e.g., Cooley, 1902; Duval & Wicklund, 1972; Goffman, 1959; James, 1890; Mead, 1934; Rogers, 1951; Sullivan, 1947), they do agree on one basic point: You are aware of yourself as an object in the world only because other people are aware of you or have been aware of you in the past. If you were unable to adopt the perspectives of other people toward yourself, you would be unable to reflect on yourself; you would have no self-view. This may sound strange; certainly we can think about ourselves in a private way, independent of how others perceive us. But this is only because, over time, we have *internalized*—adopted as our own—the perspectives of others. If you reflect on your physical attractiveness, for example, this is because other people in your past have evaluated you in terms of your looks, and you have adopted their criteria as your own. Even in private self-reflection, then, there is always an implicit audience.

It should be clear from this idea that self-awareness is a product of social interaction. It is often argued, in fact, that perspective-taking generally, and self-awareness in particular, represent the essence of social interaction (see Biddle & Thomas, 1966, for a review of relevant theories). Quite simply, you experience success in your dealings with others to the extent that you can anticipate their actions and reactions. Such anticipation would be impossible without some degree of empathy—the ability to see things from another person's point of view. The better you understand others' attitudes toward objects, events, and people, the more confidently you can predict their behavior toward these things. Of course, one of the "things" about which other people develop an attitude is you. Thus, knowing others' attitude toward you enables you to anticipate their likely behavior toward you, as well as their likely reactions to possible actions on your part. If you feel that someone considers you untrustworthy, for example, you would not expect the person to ask you to watch his or her wallet for safekeeping, nor would you waste your time trying to sell this person a plot of land in Arizona. Sensitivity to others' perspectives is central to social interaction; sensitivity to others' perspectives toward oneself is especially important.

Through repeated interactions with others, a residual self-awareness develops; the individual remembers certain perspectives toward the self and comes to adopt these as his or her own. Not surprisingly, this development of a *self-concept* begins in childhood, when the individual is exposed to social perspectives for the first time. Without prior perspectives to provide an anchor, the child remembers and accepts as valid the views of others—especially the views of "significant others" (Sullivan, 1947), such as parents, older siblings, and teachers. These internalized views from childhood provide a link between the present and the past in one's sense of self. Life's experiences are registered not only in terms of their immediate reward-punishment value but in terms of their relevance to one's self-view as well. Thus, we all have a feeling of personal *identity*—continuity of the self despite the passage of time and changes in our circumstances. Though we appear and sometimes even act differently than we did as children, we still identify the jam-covered urchin in old photos as ourselves. In adulthood, the self-awareness experienced in everyday social interaction is less likely to leave a residue. Though we are aware of others' perspectives toward us and attend to them for functional reasons, we do not necessarily accept them as valid, particularly if they are inconsistent with our internalized perspectives.

SELF-REFLECTION AS "HUMAN"

Given the advantage to the individual of perspective-taking and self-awareness, one might expect this tendency to be distributed throughout the animal kingdom, or at least among other social animals. This does not seem to be the case. In fact, self-awareness is considered by many to be the defining human characteristic, that which makes us unique among animals. This is because self-awareness represents more than an adaptive function; it represents sophisticated mental processes as well. Even among human beings, the ability to overcome one's egocentric viewpoint and understand things from different points of view is not clearly apparent until the age of two or so (see Chapter 5). The perspective-taking inherent in self-reflection requires abstraction, the ability to manipulate symbols—words, for example—as though they were concrete objects. You do not literally "see" yourself from others' point of view; rather, you infer their conception of you in terms of abstract qualities like "sincere," "flamboyant," and "perky."

Aside from theories about cognition, how do we really know that animals are incapable of self-awareness? After all, when you put your Yorkshire terrier in a snowsuit for those mid-winter walks, he certainly *seems* self-conscious; why else would little Nugget crawl under the sofa to avoid your gaze and demeaning laughter? Fortunately, the issue of animal self-consciousness has received scientific attention. In a series of intriguing experiments, Gallup (1977) employed mirrors to examine the possibility that various subhuman primates are capable of rudimentary self-awareness. A mirror allows an organism to see itself as it is seen by others; quite literally, it is an audience to its own behavior. Of course, if an organism is not capable of self-awareness, it should not "recognize" itself in the mirror, but rather react to the reflected image as if it were a stranger. Adult human beings certainly demonstrate self-recognition when confronted with their reflected image; people rarely report an intruder to the police when they happen to glance at the hallway mirror. Interestingly, however, this ability to recognize a mirror image of oneself is not apparent until the child is about two years of age—just about the time the child is learning to communicate with language. Chimpanzees are generally considered to possess "human–like" mental capacities—including the capacity for learning nonvocal forms of language (e.g., Gardner & Gardner, 1969). Are chimps also capable of self-awareness? Can our simian brethren learn to recognize themselves in a mirror?

In one study, Gallup examined the effects of social isolation on chimpanzees' self-recognition. Remember that in order for the self to become an object of one's attention, the opportunity to examine oneself from another's point of view is essential. Because a chimp reared in isolation is deprived of such opportunities, it is unlikely to have developed a sense of self-awareness, even if it has the mental capacity to do so. A socially deprived chimp, then, should not recognize itself in a mirror, but rather react to the reflected image as though it were another chimp; it might, for example, threaten the "stranger" with gestures and vocalizations. A chimp with social experience, however, may have developed a sense of self and thus would seem to be more likely to demonstrate self-recognition when confronted with a mirror; it might groom parts of the body, such as the face, that cannot be seen directly. To test this possibility, chimps that were raised with other chimps and chimps that were raised in complete isolation were placed in individual cages, each equipped with a full-length mirror, for nine days. On the tenth day, each chimp was anesthetized; while it was unconscious, Gallup painted one of its eyebrows and one of its ears bright red with an odorless, nonirritating dye. After regaining consciousness, each chimp was observed in the absence of the mirror to determine how often it spontaneously touched the marked eyebrow or ear. The mirror was then introduced for each chimp, and again, the frequency with which it touched a painted area was noted.

As is evident in Figure 1.1, the difference in self-recognition between the social and isolate chimps was quite dramatic. In the absence of the mirror, none of the chimps seemed to realize it had

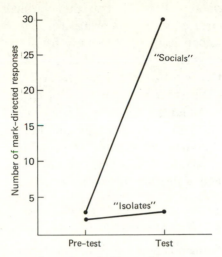

FIGURE 1.1. The number of mark-directed responses among "social" and "isolate" chimpanzees without mirror (pretest) and with mirror (test). (Adapted from Gallup, 1977)

been painted; the frequency of spontaneous touching was practically nil. Among the isolate chimps, this nonawareness was not changed by the presence of the mirror; instead, they responded to their reflection as though it were another chimp (who had a rather innovative approach to cosmetics). But among the social chimps, there was a striking increase in eyebrow and ear touching when confronted with the mirror; they recognized the reflection as the self. In a later study, Gallup provided two isolation-reared chimps with remedial social experience by housing them together in the same cage for three months. When subsequently tested in the manner described above, both chimps showed signs of self-recognition. Taken together, these studies demonstrate not only that chimps have a sense of self but also that social interaction is essential for the development of self-awareness—a finding that is quite compatible with the self theories of Mead (1934), Cooley (1902), and others.

Similar experiments have been performed with other, less "human" primates. No evidence has been found for self-recognition in such animals as rhesus monkeys, spider monkeys, macaques, baboons, or gibbons. It is not that these animals are unable to respond to mirror cues; when looking at a reflection of food, for example, they soon learn to turn away from the mirror to gain more direct access to the object producing the reflection. But even after as much as twenty-one consecutive days of mirror exposure, these animals still show no signs of self-recognition. Apparently the ability to consider the self as an object of one's own attention is a skill confined to human beings and their closest relatives. "Nonhuman" animals are capable of perceiving and evaluating only things external to themselves; "human" animals are capable of perceiving and evaluating themselves as well.

SELF-REFLECTION AS SELF-CONTROL

The fact that human beings can reflect on themselves is more than an evolutionary oddity. As noted earlier, self-awareness and perspective-taking are quite useful in social interaction, allowing the individual to anticipate the actions and reactions of others. Of even greater significance, perhaps, are the implications of self-reflection for motivation and the control of one's behavior. Clearly, a human being—like any animal—develops desires and goals that reflect evaluation of environmental stimuli (objects, events, other people). But because human beings can reflect on themselves, they can also evaluate their desires and goals (Taylor, 1977); in a sense, they have desires about their desires. Thus, a person may be highly motivated to behave in a certain way but inhibit that action if he or she feels it reflects an undesirable desire.

Assume, for example, that you are not doing well in a very important course, one that could affect your career plans. Assume further that on a particularly difficult exam you have an opportunity to cheat, thereby ensuring a good grade, with virtually no possibility of being detected. A simple reward-punishment model of behavior would predict cheating under these circumstances. Quite possibly, however, you would control the urge to cheat, feeling that that means of achieving success is not justified. In short, human beings come to control their impulses and to inhibit their concern with immediate gratification—not out of a fear of punishment (as is the case for subhuman animals) but out of a concern for self-evaluation (see Chapter 2 for a more complete analysis of this point).

Human beings are not born with self-control. Rather, the manifestations of self-control—resistance to temptation, delay of gratification, and the like—are considered developmental variables, characteristics that are acquired in the course of socialization. Central to the socialization process is perspective-taking and its resultant self-awareness. As the individual internalizes the perspectives of others, he or she learns to evaluate privately the desirability of personal impulses, desires, and goals. By adulthood, then, the individual is somewhat exempt from the psychological laws that dictate the behavior of lower animals. Rather than simply behaving in response to rewards and punishments in the environment, the mature person often monitors this natural tendency, expressing it only if it is considered to be appropriate, desirable, or otherwise good.

Although self-control frees the individual somewhat from the control of environmental stimuli and events, this concept does not imply that people have free will, or even that they make rational, well-thought-out decisions. The monitoring and evaluation of impulses and desires is a learned process, and thus can become automatic and habitual in the same way that simple motor behaviors can. In a sense, a person may have no control over his or her self-control. Somewhat ironically, then, a person may behave independently of external rewards and punishments because of his or her self-control, yet not feel in the least bit free. In fact, the perceived *lack* of freedom stemming from rigid self-control may drive a person into therapy. Thus, a neurotic person may feel unable to enjoy even the simplest joys in life—that is, to pursue personal desires and impulses—because he or she experiences intense negative self-evaluation (guilt or shame) when they are contemplated.

THE PROCESS OF SELF-REFLECTION

In our daily lives, we routinely make judgments—about events, other people, and ourselves—and engage in various actions. Quite often, we introspect about the basis for our judgments and the causes of our actions (even without the prodding of a psychologist). How does this attempt at *self-understanding* proceed? Does it represent genuine "insight" into one's mental processes, emotions, and motives? Or is the perception of one's own psychological functioning simply another example of psychological functioning, with no necessary relation to the true state of affairs? A somewhat distinct type of self-reflection involves *self-evaluation*. Once we have knowledge of our thought processes, emotions, motives, and overt behavior, we tend to judge their goodness or badness. How are such determinations made? What sorts of information are attended to, and how is this information processed to yield a self-evaluation?

SELF-UNDERSTANDING

Psychological theory and research are considered important by many people to the extent that such endeavors are personally relevant. For the average person, the motivation to pick up a book on psychology probably centers on this concern with self-understanding. In response to this view of psychology and the concern it reflects, an untold number of "experts" on human behavior have deluged the public with all types of "self-insight" books. Everything from relaxation to screaming has been touted as a means of gaining insight into one's feelings, understanding one's neuroses, and discovering hidden powers locked in one's psyche. The assumption underlying such books, of course, is that there is such a thing as insight. Thus, with a little guidance (in exchange for $5.95), even the most befuddled citizen can come to understand his or her attitudes, emotions, motives—even thought processes—and thus bring them under conscious control. Is this assumption valid? Do people have insight into the workings of their mind and emotions?

Almost all cognitive psychologists would scoff at the suggestion that people are aware of their basic mental processes (see, e.g., Mandler, 1975; Neisser, 1967). They point out that such things as problem-solving, judgment, and memory involve processes that are largely inaccessible to conscious awareness. An examination of contemporary theories and models of cognition reveals how far removed from intuition and introspection our mental processes are. This is not to suggest, of course, that we are ignorant of what goes on inside our heads. But it is the *product* or result of thinking, not the process of thinking itself, that appears spontaneously in consciousness. Suppose someone asks you to name three different kinds of animals. You would have no difficulty in naming three, but are you aware of the rule underlying your selection? You probably have several hundred animals stored in memory; why did you come up with ducks, horseflies, and marmots?

That we do not have introspective access to our basic cognitive processes is not too surprising, perhaps. But what about *social* cognition? Do we have insight into the processes underlying the judgments we make about others, or merely into the products of such processes? It would certainly *seem* that we are aware of how we form social judgments; we spend a great deal of time, for example, explaining why we like some people but cross the street to avoid others. However, contemporary theory and research suggest that the individual is often only dimly aware of the rules underlying his or her inferences and evaluations (Nisbett & Wilson, 1977a; Wegner & Vallacher, 1977). Of course, we *think* we know how we form impressions, make attributions for behavior, and so forth; but quite often these explanations are completely inaccurate.

Consider a study by Nisbett and Wilson (1977b). Subjects observed a videotape of an interview with a college instructor (a male) who spoke with a European accent. Following the taped interview, subjects were to evaluate his accent, physical appearance, and mannerisms, and to indicate his overall likability. For half the subjects, the instructor appeared very enthusiastic, pleasant, and agreeable during the interview; for the other subjects, he acted intolerant, rigid, and distrustful of students. As you might expect, subjects who saw the pleasant version liked the instructor more than did subjects who saw the unpleasant version. In addition, although the instructor's appearance, accent, and mannerisms were identical in both versions, subjects who saw the pleasant version rated these attributes as more attractive than did subjects who saw the unpleasant version; the latter subjects, in fact, considered these qualities irritating. Clearly, then, subjects' liking for the instructor *caused* their evaluation of his accent, appearance, and mannerisms. However, subjects did not see the causal relation in this manner. Instead, when asked about their judgments, subjects expressed the *opposite* causal relation; they believed that their like or dislike of his attributes was the basis for their overall like or dislike of him as a person.

It seems, then, that we often lack insight into our higher mental processes, including the processes underlying social judgment. What about insight into our emotional states and motives? A pervasive theme in the newsstand psychology books referred to earlier is that, with proper instruction, you can "get in touch with your feelings." The implication is that internal states are spontaneous and inevitable responses to events and that the healthy individual has insight into these states; such insight, in turn, allows the individual to express his or her feelings or perhaps bring them under conscious control. This point of view has a certain intuitive appeal. Is it valid?

Psychological theory and research in this area suggest that the nature of emotional and motivational states is somewhat different from what intuition would suggest, and that the self-perception of these states is less than insightful. In fact, it is often argued that emotions and motives *are* self-perceptions; your feelings and desires are what you think they are. Of course, there must be some basis—a state of physiological arousal or a noteworthy action—for assuming the presence of an emotion or motive. Emotions and motives are not the product of pure thought. But contemporary psychology emphasizes that an emotion or motive is not experienced as such until you interpret and label the arousal or behavior. Thus, rather than representing insight, the act of introspection into one's internal state *creates* the emotion or motive that is experienced. A detailed explanation and description of the specific processes involved is presented elsewhere (Chapters 3 and 4). For present purposes, the central point is that the very nature of emotions and motives precludes, logically, the possibility that people can gain insight into them. The fact that people believe that emotions and motives exist apart from their thoughts about them further reinforces the notion that people lack genuine awareness of their psychological functioning (see Nisbett & Wilson, 1977a).

Of course, we are not complete failures as self-observers. Though we may lack insight into the processes of thought and emotion, we are certainly aware of the products of these processes. We may not fully comprehend the bases of our likes and dislikes, for example, but we know what's good for dinner and with whom we'd like to share the dinner. And while quite often we behave rather automatically, without conscious awareness of what we are doing, at other times we are intensely aware of our behavior down to the last detail (see Chapter 2 for a thorough discussion of this point). Self-understanding, moreover, is not limited to awareness of specific attitudes and behaviors. To a limited extent, we have insight into the motives and dispositions that are represented in a variety of our thoughts and actions. Certainly we are in a better position to understand and report on these aspects of the self than is an outside observer who is not privy to our memories and current perceptions (Monson & Snyder, 1977). Self-understanding, in short, represents neither insight nor illusion. We know what we think and do, and we can describe our personalities, but we are blind to the processes underlying our emotions, thoughts, and actions. A complete discussion of accuracy in reporting about the self is provided in Chapter 9.

SELF-EVALUATION

It was pointed out earlier that self-evaluation first occurs when the child learns to adopt the perspectives of others on the self. In interacting with others, the child becomes sensitive not just to the explicit evaluations of the self (e.g., physical rewards and punishments for certain actions) but to the subtle evaluations conveyed by others' tone of voice, gestures, and casual comments. Over time, the child adopts the criteria for evaluation that are implicit or explicit in others' perspectives and may even come to accept their assessment of himself or herself along those criteria. Little Billy, for example, may come to evaluate himself in terms of athletic prowess and be predisposed to feel good in that regard, if he has managed to catch the footballs his parents have been tossing at him since he was two.

It is important to note that people do not necessarily define themselves in only one way on an internalized self-evaluative dimension. Instead, on any given dimension there is likely to be a range of self-evaluations that are considered plausible. Moreover, the extent of the range associated with a particular dimension determines in part how a person will react to social feedback (see Figure 1.2). Along one dimension, an individual may have a very clear, confident self-view that is tied to a specific point on the dimension; such a self-view is much like an *assumption*. In this case, feedback relevant to that dimension may not be processed at all. Compliments and slurs may be reacted to with a yawn if one is utterly convinced of a specific self-view. Imagine taunting Houdini about his magic ("You call that tricky?!"), for example, or questioning Albert Einstein's intelligence ("Pretty fuzzy thinking there, Al"). For most people, however, such definite assumptions about the self are probably confined to fairly observable qualities (e.g., physical appearance) or attributes about which there is objective evidence (e.g., socioeconomic status).

With regard to qualities for which such evidence is lacking— the desirability of one's personality, the correctness of one's opinions, the level of one's abilities—the self-views of most people are probably less rigid, representing *expectancies* rather than assumptions. You probably have a general notion of your social skills, for example, but are unsure about exactly how good you are on this dimension. Social feedback is attended to because it allows one to gain a more specific self-assessment. At the same time, not all feedback relevant to the particular dimension is accepted as valid. The fact that the individual has a general expectancy means that only evaluations within a certain range are considered informative about the self; as depicted in Figure 1.2, information that falls outside one's "latitude of acceptance" (see Sherif & Hovland, 1961) is discounted. If you feel that your social skills are somewhere between average and moderately good (see Figure 1.2), for instance,

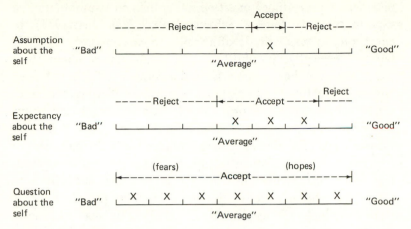

FIGURE 1.2. Self-views and the processing of self-evaluative information.

you may be very influenced by feedback implying that you are indeed somewhere within that range. Thus, a comment or reaction suggesting that you are "OK, but nothing to write home about" may bring about a rather low self-evaluation; the suggestion that you are "fairly adept" socially, meanwhile, may promote positive self-evaluation. But information that falls outside your latitude of acceptance—feedback that suggests you could open a charm school, on the one hand, or that you could close one, on the other —is discounted. Quite likely, such evaluations will be attributed to the evaluator's stable characteristics (e.g., low intelligence) or to his or her motives (e.g., envy or ingratiation). That information about the self is rejected if it is inconsistent with one's expectancies—even if it is inconsistent in a favorable or self-enhancing way—has been demonstrated in considerable research (see reviews by S. C. Jones, 1973; Shrauger, 1975). In this light, what often appear to be defensive or self-serving biases in self-perception may actually represent the acceptance of information that is consistent with one's positive expectancies and the rejection of information that is inconsistent with those expectancies (Miller & Ross, 1975).

Finally, a person's self-view along some dimension may be highly uncertain, representing a *question* rather than an assumption or an expectancy (S. C. Jones & Schneider, 1968; Vallacher, 1975). In effect, the person's latitude of acceptance encompasses the whole range of evaluative possibilities. While uncertainty about some things may not be particularly troublesome ("Which is bigger, Uranus or Neptune?"), uncertainty about the self typically is, since it undermines one's sense of predictability and control. Not knowing whether you are bright or stupid, for instance, makes it difficult for you to predict whether you will succeed in a difficult class or find your way home from the supermarket. If a person is uncertain, he or she is highly sensitive to social feedback and is likely to accept as valid a wide range of evaluations (S. C. Jones & Schneider, 1968; Maracek & Mettee, 1972). This does not mean, of course, that a person reacts calmly and rationally to evaluative information when his or her self-view is uncertain. An uncertain person is likely to be hopeful—or perhaps fearful—about social feedback. Without an expectancy or an assumption, however, the person has no basis for rejecting evaluative feedback from others.

Of course, social feedback is often ambiguous in nature and thus open to alternative interpretations. Suppose, for example, that after meeting and chatting briefly with Brad, Janet smiles enigmatically, excuses herself, and walks away. To predict Brad's interpretation of Janet's rather strange and ambiguous behavior, we would have to know whether Brad's assessment of his appeal to women represented an assumption, an expectancy, or a question. If Brad is convinced that he is quite appealing, Janet's reaction might be seen as evidence of positive feelings toward him ("She'll be back after she regains her composure"); if convinced of his lack of appeal, however, Brad might see Janet's reaction as negative—after all, she walked away. Indeed, research has shown that ambiguous feedback from others is interpreted in terms of one's preconceptions about the self (Jacobs, Berscheid, & Walster, 1971). It could be, though, that Brad has an expectancy rather than an assumption regarding his appeal. In this case, he might have only a rough idea how Janet feels about him; to obtain a more specific evaluation, he might attend closely to Janet's reactions in future interactions with her. Finally, if Brad is in doubt about his appeal to women, he might be totally confused by Janet's reaction. His interpretation at the time, as well as his subsequent actions, would probably depend on whether his hopes or his fears were stronger. If hopeful for the best, he might seek her out ("Maybe she's mad about me!"); if he fears the worst, however, he might avoid future interactions with her ("What if she has me deported?").

It should not be inferred from this analysis that some people have assumptions about the self, that others typically have expectancies, and that still others have nothing but questions (hopes and fears). Most of us are quite clear about some of our qualities, taking them for granted, but have varying degrees of uncertainty about others. And, of course, one's self-view depends in part on the situation one is in. You may be confident about your communication skills when among friends in a casual setting, for instance, but experience considerable self-doubt about those qualities when confronted with a group of people who have no native language. A more complete analysis of various self-views and their implications for the processing of self-relevant information is provided in Chapter 5.

So far, the discussion has centered on the reaction to, and interpretation of, evaluative information that one happens to encounter. Clearly, we are not simply passive recipients of such information; on the contrary, quite often we actively *select* the information that is to be interpreted. One particularly important means by which we create our data is through the process of *social comparison* (Festinger, 1954; Morse & Gergen, 1970). In assessing our behavior and the outcomes we experience, we need some sort of yardstick. Is being invited to two parties in one week a sign of popularity? Is running a 100-yard dash in three days a bad performance? Direct social feedback on such matters is often untrustworthy because of the evaluator's inferred motives (jealousy, ingratiation, and so forth) or judgmental shortcomings (low intelligence or poor empathy). In such cases, the behaviors and outcomes of others can provide the necessary yardstick. The *choice* of comparison others, however, is all-important. After all, you could compare your social popularity with that of international jet-setters, in which case your self-evaluation would be low; or you

could compare yourself with surviving members of the Third
Reich, in which case your self-evaluation would no doubt be more
favorable. Such comparisons do not seem to provide a fair test,
however. A more reasonable yardstick for self-evaluation is provided by others who are perceived to be similar to oneself in terms
of relevant dimensions—such as age, sex, economic background,
attitudes, and so forth, depending on the comparison (see Suls &
Miller, 1977, for a review). This judicious choice of similar others
for social comparison increases the likelihood that evaluative information will fall within one's latitude of acceptance. In this
light, it is understandable why people with objectively poor outcomes (e.g., members of economically disadvantaged groups) do
not necessarily have negative self-evaluations (Coopersmith, 1967);
they are evaluating themselves against others within their own
reference group.

THE STRUCTURE OF SELF-REFLECTION

Each day affords us an abundance of self-relevant information. A
simple interaction, for instance, may generate self-evaluations
along a number of important dimensions—friendliness, wit, sensitivity, intelligence, trustworthiness, dandruff control, and others.
Moreover, evaluative information is often contradictory: the information garnered from one interaction may conflict with similar
information provided by another interaction; today's lessons may
not jibe with last week's; and the self-evaluations generated at
home may differ substantially from those generated in one's work.
Yet, in spite of this seeming overabundance of self-relevant information, most of us have a fairly well-established sense of who we
are and what we are like. How do we organize all the separate
pieces of self information into an integrated self-concept? Discussed below are two ways of viewing the structure or organization
of self-reflection. The first deals with the problem of too many
dimensions; the second deals with the potential conflict among
different sources of self-evaluation.

DIMENSIONS OF SELF-EVALUATION

Although there are numerous dimensions of self-evaluation, many of them tend to reflect common themes. These themes help to organize one's self-perception; in effect, the multitude of individual dimensions is reduced to a manageable few. Two themes in particular—*competence* and *morality*—seem to underlie many of our everyday self-evaluations.

The fact that organisms—not just human beings—strive to affect their environment is central to many otherwise distinct psychological perspectives (e.g., Berlyne, 1960; deCharms, 1968; Deci, 1975; Kelley, 1972; Maslow, 1954; Seligman, 1975; White, 1959). In this view, the motivation to establish a contingency between one's actions and one's outcomes is stronger than the motivation to attain outcomes per se. Play, curiosity, and exploration, for example, occur in the absence of material rewards; the motivation for such behaviors is understanding and control of stimuli in the environment. Among human beings, with their capacity for self-reflection, this concern with establishing and demonstrating competence becomes a basis for self-evaluation. Thus, a person may resist the impulse to accept a highly valuable, easily attainable reward in favor of a less valuable reward, the attainment of which would reflect favorably on his or her ability. A number of specific self-evaluative dimensions would seem to reflect a concern with competence: intelligence, ingenuity, effort, talent, power—in short, any dimension that suggests the capacity for having a significant effect on one's environment.

The other basic dimension—morality—is more explicitly interpersonal in nature. Because none of us live an impersonal existence, we have internalized a number of perspectives pertaining to interpersonal conduct. Thus, we evaluate ourselves in terms of such things as cooperation, fair play, justice, gratitude, reciprocity, courtesy, and altruism. As with competence, a concern with maintaining a self-definition of morality can override simple self-interest or attempts at outcome maximization. For instance, a person may resist the easy attainment of a valuable reward if that attainment involves cheating, deception, or unfairly depriving someone else of the reward. Similarly, altruistic or prosocial action is often motivated by a concern with moral self-evaluation (see Chapter 6).

Competence and morality are closely interrelated. Since morality is the internalization of interpersonal standards, moral behavior is likely to promote effectiveness in one's dealings with others. A person who is seen as cooperative and fair, for example, is likely to engender greater trust than is someone perceived to be competitive and devious. Thus, the former is in a better position to exert social influence—that is, interpersonal competence. Further, as noted earlier, *all* evaluative dimensions reflect the internalized perspectives of other people. Because self-evaluation is inherently interpersonal, the perception by others that you are competent is often enough to promote positive self-evaluation—even if your private self-appraisal is somewhat less flattering (see Chapter 7).

The distinction between competence and morality self-evaluation becomes clear when specific behaviors are considered. Quite often, an act can be considered from both a competence and a morality perspective; in many cases, the two perspectives promote conflicting self-evaluations. Thus, a jewel robbery may be bad in terms of morality (it is illegal and unfairly harms others) but good in terms of the competence required (careful planning, outwitting of authorities, knowing where to shop for gloves). Conversely, an act that reflects poorly on one's competence (slipping on a banana peel and into the shrubbery) may nonetheless promote positive self-evaluation in terms of morality (selflessly providing amusement for bystanders).

It would seem that many conflicts in daily life represent the differing self-evaluations promoted by competence and morality perspectives (Vallacher & Solodky, 1979). To pursue an earlier example, suppose you could cheat on a very difficult exam, and in so doing demonstrate your mastery of the material without any likelihood of detection. Your decision to cheat or not to cheat would represent a conflict betwen appearing competent but behaving immorally (cheating) and behaving morally but appearing incompetent (not cheating). The resolution of this conflict would depend on which basis for self-evaluation was more important for you at the time.

MULTIPLE SELVES

Even when considering a single dimension of self-definition, self-relevant information can be perplexing. Evaluative feedback and the results of social comparison often provide seemingly inconsistent information about the self. You may be seen as considerate and competent by some people (Mom and Dad) but as self-centered and inept by others (everyone else). Assuming that neither point of view is discounted, this sort of inconsistency could threaten the integration of your self-view. After all, you cannot be both fair and selfish, able and inept. Or can you?

In discussing this issue, psychologists have suggested that the individual does indeed hold many different self-perceptions along a given dimension (see, e.g., Gergen, 1971; James, 1890). However, this does not necessarily imply confusion or even inconsistency; in fact, the notion of "multiple selves" represents a means of organizing one's overall self-concept. To understand how, it is necessary to introduce the concept of *role*. A role can be defined as a pattern of behavior that is prescribed (expected or demanded) in a given social relationship. In our daily lives, we occupy a number of different roles—for example, friend, lover, student, employee, and shopping mall patron. Because the demands and expectations for each role are often vastly different, our behavior—and, hence, our self-perception—is likely to show considerable variability. In our "friend" role we may be sensitive and caring, for instance, but in our "employee" role we may be assertive and self-interested. The association of different self-views with different roles thus represents *differentiation* rather than inconsistency. It is only when one has differing self-definitions *within* a role—"Am I a sensitive or an insensitive friend?"—that inconsistency is experienced.

It is easy to see how multiple roles can produce a differentiated self-view. At the same time, it might seem that a role-based self-view would deny one a sense of uniqueness or personal identity. If a role prescribes how one should behave, what distinguishes us from anyone else occupying that role? Indeed, psychologists have pointed out that situational factors, including role-related expectations, tend to overwhelm personality factors as causes of many, if not most, social behaviors (see, e.g., Mischel, 1968). It certainly does seem that certain roles prescribe rather specific modes of action; the roles of military officer, judge, and go-go dancer, for example, even dictate how one should dress. However, many roles are considerably less restrictive, specifying a *range* of appropriate behavior. There are certain broad rules of parenthood, for instance, but certainly people differ substantially in their parenting styles. Individual differences thus can be expressed in a number of informal roles (such as friend or sibling). Roles can be ordered, then, in terms of the degree of personal variation they allow among their respective occupants.

There is another way in which personal identity can be expressed within a role-based self-view. Living as we do in a complex society, there are a great many public and private, formal and informal roles available to us. Each of us, then, can *select* the roles which we feel best express our own sense of who we are. Even critics of a personality approach to understanding social behavior (e.g., Mischel, 1968) suggest that one's choice of roles and situations reflects in large part one's idiosyncratic skills, beliefs, and self-perceptions. By actively choosing the roles which one enacts, a sense of uniqueness, personal control, and self-integration is fostered. Thus, rather than undermining personal identity, the concept of role allows for individual differences in self-perception. (A more complete discussion of this point is provided in Chapter 10).

Figure 1.3 depicts the organization of self-perceptions for a hypothetical person, Edmund, in terms of the two basic self-evaluative dimensions—competence and morality—and a variety of different roles. As is apparent in the figure, Edmund has a highly differentiated self-concept; his role-based self-perceptions reflect different levels of both morality and competence. In his role as Christmas shopper, for instance, he sees himself as moral (he would never shoplift) but rather incompetent; in desperation, he buys everyone an electric fork. Keep in mind, of course, that the specific dimensions underlying competence and morality differ from one role to the next. Edmund's immorality as an

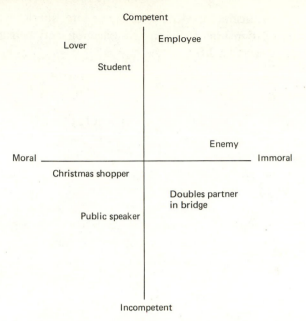

FIGURE 1.3. Organization of Edmund's role-based self-perceptions in terms of competence and morality.

employee, for instance, may reflect competitiveness and ruthless self-interest; his immorality as an enemy may involve deceit, character assassination, and sending live rattlesnakes C.O.D.

SELF–REFLECTION AND BEHAVIOR

Does self-reflection matter? To understand and predict thought and behavior in everyday settings, is it important to consider the process or structure of self-directed thought? Though intuition would suggest that self-reflection is meaningfully related to everyday functioning, there has been surprisingly little research into just what these relationships are. Until recently, most of the evidence that did exist centered on the relation between the self and issues of adjustment. Contemporary theory and research, however, are beginning to investigate more subtle, yet more pervasive, relationships between self-reflection and behavior that characterize everyday life.

ADJUSTMENT

As noted at the outset, the concept of the self has always been popular among those professionally concerned with issues involving adjustment—mental health, deviance, and the like. Many of the principles relating self-reflection to adjustment are quite straightforward, following rather directly from certain of the ideas discussed in this chapter. As you might expect, for example, maladjustment is often associated with a negative self-concept. A positive self-view is not only conducive to personal well-being but promotes positive attitudes toward others as well; hence, it is important for effective and pleasant interpersonal relations (see, e.g., Rogers, 1951).

Positive self-evaluation does not always guarantee adjustment, however. For one thing, people may report that they have a positive self-concept, and even act as though they do, but this may really reflect a desire to impress others about one's qualities rather than a sincere private conviction; Chapters 7, 9, and 10 each provide discussions relevant to this point. Secondly, a highly positive self-view is sometimes associated with biased information processing. There is evidence that people assured of their worth often make self-serving attributions for their failures (Snyder, Stephan, & Rosenfield, 1978) and dismiss unflattering feedback from others (see, e.g., Bramel, 1962). Of course, these reactions per se do not imply maladjustment; the rejection of information outside one's latitude of acceptance is a self principle common to everyone. But the operation of this principle may prevent people with positive self-views—especially those who have narrow latitudes of acceptance—from deriving lessons from life's inevitable disappointments and failures or even from constructive criticism.

There are a number of other self perspectives besides self-evaluation that are useful for understanding issues of adjustment. One contemporary perspective, for example, emphasizes the self-perception of personal control over the events in one's life (see Chapters 3, 4, and 10). In this view, all the positive outcomes in the world—physical comfort and financial security, attention and affection from others—will not instill a sense of well-being if the person feels that these outcomes are independent of his or her actions. There is evidence, for example, that the decline in physical and emotional well-being that is commonly experienced by the elderly who are committed to nursing homes is in part attributable to this effect (Langer & Rodin, 1976; Schulz, 1976). Yet another perspective relevant to adjustment emphasizes the interpersonal nature of the self. Because feedback from others provides important input to one's self-view, sharing personal information about oneself with others and attending to their feedback on such disclosures may be conducive to self-understanding and personal well-being (see Chapter 8.)

In presenting distinct and diverse perspectives on the concept of the self, this book suggests a number of intriguing ways in which self principles may be applied to issues of adjustment. It is possible, in fact, that your appreciation for each viewpoint will reflect an assessment of its implications for personal application as much as its scientific merit. In the final chapter (11), therefore, personal applications distilled from the various perspectives will be made explicit. However, rather than developing all possible applications—a task that would itself require a hefty book—a few representative applications that pertain to common personal problems will be explored.

EVERYDAY THOUGHT AND BEHAVIOR

While early discussions of the self were addressed primarily to issues involving adjustment, present-day theorizing and research regarding the self are intended to shed light on the whole gamut of psychological functioning—the mundane as well as the exotic. Some implications of self theory for everyday thought and behavior have already been discussed. It was argued, for example, that self-reflection is central to social interaction since it allows the parties involved to anticipate one another's actions and reactions. It was also suggested that self-reflection frees the individual from one kind of control—rewards and punishments in the environment—but brings his or her behavior under another kind of control—self-evaluation. As another example, the latitude of acceptance associated with a particular self-view has rather clear implications for the processing of self-relevant information (see Chapter 5); since such information is often provided by other people, the notion of latitudes has implications for interpersonal judgment and social interaction as well.

More generally, the self represents the interface between the individual and social reality, and for this reason it has become a vitally important concept in virtually every domain of social psychology. Social interaction produces self-awareness in the first place, and everyday events provide for continual refinement of one's self-view; in this sense, the self is a product of social reality. But the self is also causal; people perceive and interact with their social reality on the basis of their self-views. Each of the subsequent chapters demonstrates this reciprocal influence, exploring the intriguing and intimate relationships between self-directed thought and many aspects of everyday thought and behavior. In reading these chapters, then, the reader will discover just how central the concept of the self is to social psychology.

The scientific study of the self is far from complete. Future theory and research will quite likely extend many of the ideas to be presented in the upcoming chapters, and may even call for their revision. Each chapter thus not only provides insights into the principles underlying the self but should generate questions for the reader as well. Hopefully this open-ended format will prove exciting rather than frustrating, encouraging the reader to explore personally some of the issues presented. What better way to learn about yourself?

SUMMARY

Self-reflection represents the human capacity for adopting the perspectives of other people. Because we are the object of people's attention when interacting with them, adopting their perspective provides us with a sense of who we are and what we are like. As these perspectives are internalized, we develop a personal frame of reference for judging the goodness or badness of our actions. This process of private self-evaluation frees us somewhat from the control of material rewards and punishments.

Despite our capacity for self-reflection, introspection does not yield perfect understanding of our mental processes, nor of the emotions or motives we experience in a given situation. In fact, the act of introspection is itself another mental process, one that in part creates the emotion or motive we are attempting to understand. At the same time, we are aware of the products of mental processes, including the products of introspection, and can use these products to infer our personal predilections and response tendencies.

Self-evaluation is an important aspect of self-reflection. Feedback encountered in social interaction and the results of social comparison provide self-relevant information that is interpreted in terms of internalized evaluative dimensions. With regard to many of these dimensions, we have preconceptions about our worth and will accept self-evaluative information as valid only if it falls within a latitude of acceptance. For some dimensions, however, we have only an uncertain preconception, or perhaps none at all, so that any self-evaluative information pertaining to such a dimension is taken seriously, though not necessarily accepted as valid.

Though we are rather selective in the information that we encode about the self and tend to interpret such information in a biased fashion, these processes still yield an abundance of potentially confusing self-relevant data. Much of this information is organized in terms of two basic dimensions—competence and morality. Because these organizing themes are often independent of one another, a given act—and, hence, the self—may be evaluated differently, depending on which theme is most salient at the time. Roles provide another organizational principle in self-reflection; potentially inconsistent self-images are differentiated into multiple selves, each corresponding to a particular role.

Principles of self-reflection are considered important in social psychology to the extent that they explain important facets of our thought and behavior. Perhaps the area most often examined from a self perspective is adjustment; the relevant self principles include self-evaluation, latitudes of acceptance, self-perception of control, and the interpersonal basis of self-reflection. Contemporary theory and research have begun to examine the implications of self principles for everyday thought and behavior. Each of the subsequent chapters provides distinct insights into such implications; together, these chapters reveal the importance of the self to contemporary social psychology.

2

Self-awareness Theory:
When the Self Makes a Difference

ROBERT A. WICKLUND
UNIVERSITY OF TEXAS AT AUSTIN

DIETER FREY
UNIVERSITY OF KIEL

In looking at classic and current writings on the self, it is tempting to conclude that the self is involved in the workings of all human endeavors. For instance, the term *self-perception* is to be found in psychologists' descriptions of the way people explain their own behavior. In the realms of fear, rage, and other emotions, it has become acceptable to speak of attribution of emotional states to the *self*. The same applies to public presentations. One is inclined to refer to *self-presentations*, as though there is some discrete entity identifiable as the *self* involved when one tries to impress others through acting, showing off, modesty, vanity, and so on. On a more general level, psychology can even speak of all goal-oriented behaviors as involving the self. It is the *self* which is achievement motivated and strives toward ambitious goals. The *self* is also afraid of failure and shrinks away from striving in special situations. Does the self also walk to school, brush its teeth, and go to bed at night? In short, is the self omnipresent, seemingly involved in every activity? If so, we might as well talk instead of a person's shadow, or personal ghost, that is carried around to accompany us during all our activities.

DOES THE SELF INFLUENCE ALL BEHAVIOR?

It is helpful here to look at an example in which psychologists are especially likely to invoke the self. Suppose that Junior is asked every Sunday morning to go to the neighborhood paper box to purchase the *San Antonio Light* for his parents to read while they recline in bed all morning. As usual, he takes the change and walks to the newspaper dispenser box, expecting to drop in his money. On this particular morning someone is already at the paper box, has just purchased a paper, and, seeing Junior coming, holds the door of the box open so that the young man can take a copy without having to pay. Junior seems to disregard the cues. He drops the change in, reaches for a paper, and walks away. The whole time, the generous man is standing there like a fool, holding the paper box door open.

A self theorist might say that Junior's superego or internalized moral values have dictated his behavior in the situation. The *value* of "Thou shalt not steal" has prompted his decision to pay for the newspaper in spite of the other customer's generosity. This value, needless to say, is part of the system of internalized values that makes up part of the organization of the self.

But let's try suspending that kind of analysis for a moment. Suppose that the lazy couple has trained the pet dog to fetch the paper, rather than Junior. Each Sunday morning the dog marches to the paper box with the change in its mouth, pokes it into the slot, pulls down the door, and bites off one newspaper. This should not be so remarkable, for the lazy couple happen to be smart Skinnerians. Now, it is no surprise when the dog disregards the man's kind offer of a free (and illegal) newspaper. We know that the dog has been conditioned to go through a standard sequence of events (drop in coins, get door open, bite paper) to bring the paper home, and it takes no concept of the self to account for the dog's apparent disregard of the possibility of a free paper.

Retracing our steps, the same kind of reasoning might be applied to Junior. Was he really undergoing an excruciating moral dilemma, having finally resolved it in favor of the appropriate moral about stealing, or was he simply accustomed to dropping money into the machine? The answer here is not forthcoming; it could be either one.

Consider an analogous case, where it is even clearer that the person is not undergoing a moral crisis. A pedestrian in a small town is waiting for a red light at three in the morning. There have been no cars on the street for at least three hours, hence no conceivable danger. Nonetheless this pedestrian waits patiently, and upon the green signal crosses the street. Was this an internalized moral value or simply an overlearned response?

AUTOMATED ACTS AND THE ROLE OF THE SELF

A dog that carries a stick to its master, or fetches the newspaper, and the human being who crosses the street as a reflex to a green light are acting independent of the self. At least, this is so according to the present conception of the way the self works. If some environmental cue, whether a coin slot or a green light, automatically triggers a behavior, it is little more than superstition to speak of the influence of some entity called the self. Recently Abelson (1976) and Langer (1978) introduced the notion of "script behavior," whereby much of human action, including rather elaborate acts, is conceived of as overlearned, and simply "going off" in response to the appropriate environmental cues. These acts, also designated as "mindless" by Langer, are not controlled by elaborate conscious deliberation, conflict, decision making, or anything of the kind.

In sharp contrast to scripted behavior are acts that are not automatic. Normally these are behaviors about which one must ponder—perhaps combinations of actions that are performed for the first time, or for the first time in a given context. For example, someone assigned the task of banker in a restaurant, where one check is presented for a number of acquaintances dining together, must decide how much each person owes as well as the appropriate amount for a tip. None of this is automatic, and it is proposed here that the self will play a deciding role in the individual's behavior in these kinds of nonautomatic instances.

To take another instance: A preacher feels a need to make the Sunday services more "relevant" in order to attract and retain youthful congregation members. Thus he contemplates certain common tactics—replacing the pipe organ with guitar music, introducing dissonant blues sounds into the choir's repertoire, and altering the sermon topics in the direction of sex and modern-day violence. Again, none of the potential changes to be made stems automatically from the situation or from the preacher's previous learning. Each potential outcome is something to be contemplated and decided upon.

What do we mean by the self playing a role in such situations? This is basically quite simple. The person playing banker at the restaurant does not simply divide up the money according to habit. Rather, the way in which the situation is handled is a conscious process of reckoning, governed in part by certain established rules. These rules mediate between the situation (the need to divide up the money) and the final outcome. Accordingly, if the banker is operating on a rule of fair play, or equity, he will be sure that each person present is charged the correct amount and that each person gives a proportional amount as a tip. Thus the chain of events is this: (1) situational demand for a certain kind of behavior (dividing up money); (2) thinking about relevant standards regarding fair play; and finally (3) the behavioral outcome.

Were the same person a Machiavellian or psychopath, an appeal to the self might result in his overcharging all the acquaintances, plus pocketing whatever money was designated as the tip. This is because a different kind of rule would then be dictating behavior—a rule that one should be as clever as possible in the interest of gaining profit for oneself.

The case of the minister is the same. A decision to bring jazz music into the church service is not an automatic behavior. He is first confronted with the problem, then the rule comes into play. If the minister focuses immediately upon a rule of religious propriety and dignity, the outcome would then probably be to retain the traditional church service.

Once the self, by bringing rules or values to bear on behavior, imparts a certain direction to actions, we would probably think that the person would do the same thing when confronted with that situation again. And as the same behavior is repeated over and over (the minister disallows jazz for the fifty-second straight Sunday), the behavioral sequence at some point takes on the character of a script. That is, it becomes automated, and there is no longer a necessity for the contemplation of a rule for action to intervene. At this point, the individual is acting morally but not necessarily thinking morally. That is, there is no active consideration of what is right and wrong, with the rule as a guiding element; instead, the behavior simply goes off automatically.

Thus we see that one should differentiate between two types of behaviors. On the one hand, there are automatic acts, where the self might have played an earlier role during the creation of the habit. But given automation, the mediation of thinking about rules is no longer necessary. On the other hand, there are non-automated acts, requiring the conscious contemplation of rules for appropriate or correct behavior. It is the central purpose of this chapter to show how self-focused attention is important, perhaps often crucial, in determining whether a nonautomated behavior will be guided by a system of rules.

THE THEORY OF SELF AWARENESS

The theory to be described here (Duval and Wicklund, 1972; Frey, Wicklund, & Scheier, 1978; Wicklund, 1975, 1978, 1979a, 1979b) states that the self, as a structure guiding behavior, begins to operate only when the individual's attention is inward-directed. What this means is that the self, a mechanism that brings rules to bear on behavior, works only through conscious mediation. The person must first be consciously aware of that segment of the self which is relevant in a situation; only then will the self mediate behavior in that setting. This means that the self does not function automatically. It plays no role in automatic or "thoughtless" behaviors, and further, it often plays no role in nonautomated behaviors. First, the person must take an inward-directed perspective. How does this perspective come about?

Perhaps the most direct approach is to tell someone to engage in self-contemplation. One of the earliest documented cases of the attempt to instill self-orientation (self-observation) in experimental subjects was reported by Maria Ovsiankina (1928), who was studying at the time under Kurt Lewin, the father of modern social psychology. Ovsiankina was busy in the psychological institute in Berlin, interrupting people in the midst of their tasks in order to determine the impact of interruption on subsequent resumption of tasks. For one of her interruptions, she simply stopped the subject in the midst of his task and instructed him to report his self-observations regarding the previous task. The effect she measured was the number of tasks resumed later, but more important here is what would have happened psychologically as a result of that manipulation. Subjects obviously would have thought about their previous task performance. But not just that. If they possessed any standards or ideals about performance and completion of the task, they should also have thought about them; in turn, those standards should have come to play a role in the interrupted person's self-evaluation and future performance. The details of how this comes about will be described shortly. But first, we must say a bit more about the nature of the onset of self-awareness.

STIMULI TO SELF-FOCUS

When we speak of self-awareness, we are not referring to a general, mystical state in which the individual is aware simultaneously of all aspects of the self. Instead, it is a focused attention directed toward just one facet of the self, much as in the Ovsiankina situation. However, for our purposes, it is by no means necessary to create a self-directed set toward one specific behavior through the Ovsiankina technique. That is, one does not have to tell the subject explicitly what to think about. Rather, it is possible to do something more indirect.

One technique in use since 1971 is that of a common mirror. For instance, in one study by Wicklund and Duval (1971), subjects who were copying foreign prose were confronted with their mirror images. The effect of the mirror was to improve task performance. But why should seeing one's face have anything to do with task performance?

The theory argues that any stimulus forcing the person to become a self-observer has the effect of creating a general inward set—a propensity to examine the self. Once this set is generated, whether by instructions to do so or by a mirror, the resulting self-focusing set becomes more specific. Self-reflection focuses on whatever dimension of the self is most salient, or dominant, in that situation. For instance, in the study by Wicklund and Duval, it would seem reasonable that self-directed attention, which focused first on the face, then moved to a consideration of the self as performer, for it was prose-copying performance that was ultimately affected.

In addition to confronting people with their mirror images, self-awareness investigators have used a variety of other techniques to instill self-focused attention: (1) playing back someone's tape-recorded voice, (2) confronting subjects with a camera, (3) placing subjects in unfamiliar or unstructured surroundings, and (4) giving subjects minority status.

The last two techniques need a bit more explanation. First, it makes sense that unfamiliar or unstructured surroundings would create self-focused attention. This is because one's relationship with the environment is disrupted by such conditions. When there is no free flow of behavior, when disruptions or incongruities are encountered, or when we do not know what to do, self-awareness should occur. By this reasoning, the interruption manipulations of Ovsiankina (1928) should have engendered self-awareness, even without her explicit instructions to become a self-observer. This reasoning is also supported by Shibutani (1961), who thinks that disruptions in social interaction are the root of self-directed attention. Further, and most important, this thesis has been supported directly by Edison and Fink (1976). Some subjects were given highly structured guidelines for interaction with others, such as a listing of topics to discuss as well as the subject's precise role in interacting. Others received only a cursory introduction to what the interaction would be like, and had every reason to enter the interaction confused. Then, using a highly inventive technique whereby subjects' self-awareness was rated by observers, Edison and Fink found that subjects in the unstructured setting manifested considerably more self-awareness symptoms (e.g., fussing with hair, hands, and nails; self-evaluative statements; remarks about one's own body).

Second, we have indicated that becoming unique, or finding oneself in the status of a minority, can bring forth self-awareness. This reasoning comes directly from the Gestalt school of thought (Koffka, 1935): The more unusual the element to be perceived, the more it will tend to be perceived as a *figure*, or as prominent, relative to all other elements in that immediate situation. This thesis is well supported in research by Duval (1976) and Wegner and Schaefer (1978), who placed subjects in the position of a minority in a group and then looked at self-awareness effects.

We can also talk about chronic differences between people with respect to self-focus. A very useful scale, the "private self-consciousness scale," was developed by Fenigstein, Scheier, and Buss (1975) and has been used repeatedly in self-awareness research to differentiate people who are generally high in self-focus from those who are generally low. Just as with mirrors and other stimuli, we may assume that the person who is chronically high in self-awareness will be self aware in some specific way at any given time (see Chapter 10). Thus the chronically high self aware person who is placed in an achievement situation will be attending to achievement needs and values.

SELF AWARENESS AND MOTIVATION

Now we are at a turning point. We have already made the case that the self is not relevant with automatic actions, and also that the self, and the rules the self brings to behavior, have an impact only when the individual's attention is directed toward the relevant part of self. But how is it that self-directed attention then affects behavior? According to the theory it works like this:

The self aware person engages in a process of evaluation, which is defined by the correspondence, or lack of correspondence, of two things. One of these things is the rule, or standard. The other is behavior. The theory has it that a discrepancy between these two elements constitutes an evaluative state. If the discrepancy is negative, the person undergoes a negative evaluation process, which is uncomfortable, and one should thus desire to avoid it. For instance, the subjects of Ovsiankina who looked back at their performance, and whose work was interrupted, probably found that their performance fell short of the standard of completion. Similarly, the minister we discussed earlier would evaluate himself negatively, or experience discomfort, if he had allowed the service to be dominated by jazz, then became self aware and evaluated himself against a standard of religious propriety.

What this means is that falling short of one's standards does not automatically produce discomfort. One must first become self aware—attuned to that aspect of self that is relevant—before a shortcoming will set off the evaluative process. Another way of saying this is that negative self-evaluation consists of two elements: a discrepancy between behavior and some standard about correct behavior, plus focused attention toward that discrepancy.

RUNNING AWAY FROM SELF-FOCUSED ATTENTION

How do we know that these conditions produce discomfort? Several kinds of evidence bear on the issue, all of them concerned with avoidance. For instance, in an experiment with female undergraduate subjects, Duval, Wicklund, and Fine (in Duval & Wicklund, 1972) provided subjects an experience that should have left them with almost no discrepancy regarding their cleverness. They were told that they were in the upper tenth percentile on a test that purportedly assessed the combination of creativity and I.Q. (hereafter defined as cleverness). Other subjects were provided with the basis of a sizable discrepancy, discovering that they were in the lower tenth percentile. Subsequently they were asked to wait in a different room for an experimenter to arrive, and were told that after five minutes, if the experimenter didn't show up, they could leave if they wished. Part of the time the room was equipped with a mirror and a television camera aimed toward the subjects' heads, and sometimes not, thus creating the experimental design indicated in Table 2.1.

TABLE 2.1. Average Latencies for Exit from Experimental Room

	High Discrepancy	Low Discrepancy
Mirror + Camera	6.4	7.8
No Mirror or Camera	8.1	8.2

Source: Duval & Wicklund, 1972.

This process should have involved the following. Subjects who had received positive feedback should have experienced almost no negative affect, independent of whether they were made self-aware in the second cubicle. This is because there was virtually no discrepancy between their standards (to be clever) and actual performance. However, subjects who received negative feedback, and especially those confronted with the self-focusing devices, should have experienced a definite negative affect, consisting of the negative evaluation about the low cleverness feedback. Theoretically there are two ways to deal with this negative affect, considering the two components that comprise it. One is to deal directly with the discrepancy, which here would not be applicable. That is, it would be hard to think of subjects' changing their actual (or imagined) cleverness after such compelling and salient feedback. The alternative is to eliminate, or at least reduce, the self-focused attention; this could be done by leaving the mirror- and camera-laden room. Table 2.1 shows that this is exactly what happened. Of the four conditions, the only one in which subjects left significantly sooner than about eight minutes was the high discrepancy, mirror + camera condition.

There is a very important point to keep in mind here. Subjects' failures, or negative discrepancies, were not impressed upon them directly by the self-focusing stimuli. That is, no one in the Duval et al. study told subjects to "think about your absence of cleverness." Leaving the cubicle in a hurry was prompted simply by looking into the mirror plus confrontation by a camera; thus, the self-focus produced by these devices must have transferred to self-focus on the dimension of cleverness. Similarly, in an experiment by Gibbons and Wicklund (1976), male subjects were either accepted or rebuffed in an initial encounter with an attractive female undergraduate. Prior to this encounter, they had all made a tape recording of their own voices. Then, after the encounter, they were given an opportunity to play back the tapes. Interestingly, those subjects who had been rebuffed were less interested in this kind of self-observation. Again, one must assume that self-awareness provoked by one's voice can carry over to a different self-dimension—acceptability to an attractive woman.

ANTICIPATION OF SELF-DISCLOSURE

Let's carry this theme a bit further. Rather than someone receiving negative feedback on a test or being rejected by the opposite sex, suppose that people are asked to discuss some intimate and potentially unhappy or forbidden aspect of themselves (see Chapter 8). Archer, Hormuth, and Berg (1979) asked subjects to disclose facets of themselves to another person. The disclosure took place while the subject was alone in a cubicle; her remarks were tape-recorded, ostensibly to be disclosed to someone else later. There were two kinds of instructions. Some subjects were asked to relate intimate matters (e.g., "my parents' personalities," "my ups and downs in mood"), while others were instructed to disclose at a superficial level (e.g., "place or places I grew up"). These two groups were further subdivided according to whether or not the subject was face-to-face with her mirror image during the self-disclosure tape-recording session, as shown in Table 2.2. Just as in the Duval et al. (1972) study, the dependent measure was time, but in this case time had nothing to do with leaving the room. Instead, the measure was the subject's latency of beginning to tape-record her self-disclosure.

The combination of intimate disclosure instructions (usually associated with negative self-descriptions) and self-awareness should have been the least comfortable, and in that critical condition we should expect that subjects would have tried hardest to avoid disclosure. The measure taken was how long it took subjects to begin disclosing, and as shown in Table 2.2, the results are in line with this prediction.

TABLE 2.2. Number of Seconds Subjects Hesitated Before Beginning to Self-Disclose

	High Intimacy	Low Intimacy
Mirror	17.1	7.4
No Mirror	9.8	11.7

Source: Archer, Hormuth, & Berg, 1979.

NEGATIVE FEELINGS

The previous studies on avoiding self-awareness say something about the conditions under which we run away from situations that force us into self-focus—and, more generally, about conditions in which we must confront ourselves with something personally negative. An additional result by Archer et al. indicates that these conditions do indeed produce a negative affect. At the end of the procedure, once subjects had made their self-disclosures, they were asked how much they enjoyed the self-description task. As shown in Table 2.3, those with a combination of potentially

TABLE 2.3. Rated Enjoyment of the Self Description Task

	High Intimacy	Low Intimacy
Mirror	4.3	7.7
No Mirror	6.0	6.5

Note: A high number indicates more enjoyment.
Source: Archer, Hormuth, & Berg, 1979.

negative self-disclosure and self-awareness showed the most negative ratings. In short, it would appear that negative affect does stem from these circumstances. Now, let us move on to the major issue dealt with by the theory: Given the impossibility of avoiding these discrepancies, how does the self-aware person reduce them?

THE FOCUS OF THE THEORY:
CIVILIZED AND CONSISTENT BEHAVIOR

If the negative affect-producing self-awareness conditions cannot be averted, the theory then indicates that people will act so as to minimize or reduce the discrepancy. This simple principle has led to a host of predictions in many different areas. Our discussion of the principle is divided into three sections: (1) the impact of idiosyncratic values on behavior, (2) the fitting of self-reports to unique characteristics, and (3) behaviors that stem from generally accepted values.

MINIMIZING DISCREPANCIES:
MAKING BEHAVIOR CONSISTENT WITH PERSONAL MORALITY

The theory leads us to think that self-aware people would be more consistent with their stated personalities. If a man has said, "I am for sexual equality," we should then expect his behavior to reflect it. He should not open doors for women rather than men or use the expressions "girl," "chick," and "wench." To do this would create a discrepancy, the same familiar discrepancy discussed above: On the one hand there is the self-description, which provides a standard for behavior; on the other hand, there is the actual behavior. Thus, under self-awareness-provoking conditions, we should find a reduction in these kinds of hypocrisies or discrepancies.

Evidence for these ideas comes from research by Carver (1975) and Gibbons (1978). In Carver's paradigm subjects were initially divided according to their self-reports of favorability toward using punishment to teach, such that some were quite punitive in self-description and others hardly punitive at all. Later in the semester they had an opportunity to exercise their philosophies by actually teaching students and having the opportunity to punish them with electric shock. Under normal conditions, in which subjects were not stimulated to think about themselves, the initial rated punitiveness was not reflected at all in punishment level. But if the subjects were presented with their mirror images while administering the punishment, their behavior clearly reflected their earlier-stated propensity to punish or not punish while teaching.

A very similar effect was found in research by Gibbons (1978), in which undergraduate females first took a test of sex guilt. In taking this test, they rated themselves on such items as "Obscene literature helps people become sexual perverts." Thus one may assume from a high sex guilt score that the subject would be opposed to sexual matters in general. Later in the semester, subjects were asked to read some pornographic paperback literature and to rate their enjoyment of it. Interestingly, when they rated the literature without any inducement to self-awareness, their earlier-rated sex guilt had almost no impact on their distaste for the pornography. However, when they confronted their mirror images there was a definite relationship. In fact, the correlation between sex guilt and distaste for the passage was .74, in contrast to a correlation of only .20 in the no-mirror condition.

The reader may now want to think back to our opening remarks about the condition under which the self comes to influence behavior. In both the Carver (1975) and Gibbons (1978) research, subjects' values were tapped prior to any self-awareness induction. That is, they were asked about their level of punitiveness in teaching and about their views on sex. These are standards, or rules, which the person might be expected to follow. At the same time, from the present theory we have no reason to think that these standards would mediate behavior unless the person first becomes self-focused and thinks about the relationship between these standards and possible behaviors that they might govern. And this is just what was found in both sets of research. Among subjects in control conditions, where there was only minimal self-focused attention, the values about punishment and sexual matters had little influence on subsequent behavior.

MINIMIZING DISCREPANCIES:
INFERRING ATTITUDES FROM FREELY CHOSEN BEHAVIOR

One area we have not dealt with is the development of the system of values that governs personal functioning. How do these values originate? One answer comes from cognitive dissonance theory (Festinger, 1957) and from self-perception theory (Bem, 1965; 1972), both of which indicate that values grow out of freely chosen behaviors (see Chapter 3). If a child has no special preference for sexually permissive versus sexually repressive literature, a choice between the two will get the value system started. In other words, values develop only when we first behave—and as a result of behaving, we develop a value system that is consistent with these freely chosen actions.

But where does self-awareness theory fit in? As it turns out, the application is easy. If the behavior is already a given, and the person has to characterize the self, that characterization should be especially consistent with the behavior given the induction of self-awareness during the time of self-description or statement of the value.

Take a simple case: A person has to choose among different types of mental games, such as figuring out anagrams (scrambled letters) or finding embedded figures. He is given an opportunity to try different samples of each type of game—in other words, a number of free choices among these different kinds of behaviors. Further, owing to a basic unfamiliarity, there is no special basis for choosing one or another. After several minutes of playing with these mental games, the person is asked to rate how attractive each game is; here we can begin to speak of the formation of values. According to either cognitive dissonance theory or self-perception theory, one should expect a strong consistency between frequency of choosing a certain type of game and later rating of it.

A procedure just like this was used in the third experiment reported by Pryor, Gibbons, Wicklund, Fazio, and Hood (1977). As it turned out, there was virtually *no* correspondence between type of game chosen to play with and later interest ratings of the games (correlation = .13). It is also important to note that self-awareness was minimal during these ratings. However, when self-awareness was heightened by subjects' mirror images, the correspondence was very strong (correlation = .74).

To summarize, the theory is this: Human beings are reluctant to be inconsistent when self-aware. This applies primarily when the behavior stems from an established value. However, when values are being formed (as in the Pryor et al. study), the person tries to make these values consistent with prior behavior. Finally, the cognitive dissonance and self perception theses need to be adjusted. These consistency processes do not necessarily operate without some degree of self-focused attention (see Chapters 3 & 9).

MINIMIZING DISCREPANCIES:
THE OPERATION OF GENERAL SOCIETAL VALUES

It is not only unique or idiosyncratic human aspects that are acted upon when one is self-focused. There are also general societal values that serve as guidelines for behavior when one is self-aware. In this context, we may speak of the self-aware person as being civilized.

For example, Diener and Wallbom (1976) report evidence that college students are supposed to be honest. At least when asked, the vast majority of students are of the high-minded opinion that cheating is morally wrong. Does this mean that they will not cheat when given an opportunity? Diener and Wallbom reported that students cheat to excess (about 70 percent do), at least when given a timed IQ test and a chance to work discretely beyond the time limit. Self-awareness during testing reduced this rate to only 7 percent.

In a study based on a comparable value (Thou shalt not steal), Beaman, Klentz, Diener, and Svanum (1979) set up a situation in which trick-or-treating children could take more candy than was allowed. As a group of trick-or-treaters arrived at a house, they were greeted by the ostensible owner (actually the experimenter). She told them the rules, saying that only one piece of candy per child was allowed. Then the children were left alone in the foyer of the house facing a bowl of candies. Half the time there was a mirror located behind the bowl, allowing the children to see themselves in their dishonesty in case they set out to violate the one-candy rule. The mirror worked just as in the study with college students, markedly reducing the incidence of candy stealing.

By now the reader can see that self-awareness theory is in some sense a theory about the superego. It regards the human self as possessing a complex of values, but further stipulates that these will be acted upon only insofar as attention is directed toward the self. These values are many, and by thinking through his or her list of values, the reader should be able to think of as many suitable experiments as there are values. For instance, we need not stop with cheating and stealing. Provided the members of a community agree that gossip is immoral, an increment in local self-awareness should go a long way toward removing the bite from neighborhood conversations. Also on the neighborhood level, it would be interesting to test the hypothesis that self-awareness should have some impact on behaviors relevant to "Thou shalt not covet thy neighbor's wife" (or husband).

In a less exotic vein, there are documentations of the impact of self-awareness on other general values. For one, the ethic against cruelty has been explored by Scheier, Fenigstein, and Buss (1974), who found that male subjects were less inclined to give painful shocks to a female undergraduate victim when they were self-aware. Again, the theoretical point is the same: Values appropriate to specific behaviors affect those behaviors only when the individual becomes self-focused.

THE LOCUS OF STANDARDS: PERSON OR GROUP?

The Duval and Wicklund self-awareness theory is not the first conceptualization of self-awareness. Credit should be given instead to Charles Horton Cooley, who wrote in 1902 about the self and its relation to the group. The notable feature is Cooley's contention that there is no self apart from the individual's consideration of other people. The reflective self is necessarily self-aware with respect to the points of view of others. Cooley also spoke of mirrors, although for him the mirror had a different meaning. Rather than literally gazing into a mirror, Cooley's person reflects upon the self through the viewpoint or perspective of another. Thus self-awareness does not cause the person to reflect or operate upon idiosyncratic elements, as we have discussed, but instead upon the values or needs of the social milieu.

The Cooley school, as represented subsequently by Mead (1934) and Shibutani (1961), has in fact talked about the onset of self-awareness—usually within the context of social disruptions. For instance, greeting someone by the wrong name, gossiping about someone who happens to be in the next restaurant booth, or finding one's fly to be open are all actions that break down the continuity of social exchange. The result should be self-directed attention. But what is the nature of this attention? For Cooley, Mead, and Shibutani, attention focuses on the values or desires of others; the person's behavior should then come to be controlled increasingly by the immediate social climate.

At least in part, Cooley and his followers have been proven wrong. We have seen that individuals, when made self-aware, act more consistently with their unique, seemingly individualistic values. In Carver's (1975) research, punitive people acted more punitively when self-aware; nonpunitive people became even less aggressive. Similarly, in Gibbons' (1978) investigations, women with high sex guilt tended to increase their aversion to pornography, while women with low guilt enjoyed it all the more. This kind of behavior does not seem as if subjects were acting according to the views of others. Cooley would be quite displeased with these results.

On the other hand, the first self-awareness experiment ever to be run concerned conformity. This was Experiment I of Wicklund and Duval (1971). When confronted with the written opinions of a large majority, subjects who had been listening to a playback of their own voices showed the greatest shift in the direction of *others'* opinions. Complementing this is a result from Hass (1979), in which the subject had to place a large letter "E" on her forehead so that someone else would be able to read it. Self-aware people were more likely to place the "E" so that it was correct from the other's perspective. In other words, these two results (conformity and perspective-taking) imply that self-aware people do sometimes act on the basis of others' perspectives. This would please Cooley, who views the self as defined totally in terms of taking the other's point of view.

But where do we go from here? Let's back up slightly and give some thought to the source of values. Suppose a girl grows up in a sexually disinterested household. The facts of life are never discussed, there is no special issue about nudity, and there is neither approval nor censorship of anything sexual. Thus she grows up treating sex as no different from baseball or any other activity. In other words, there are no special values or standards associated with sex.

At the age of twelve, just as sex comes to be a more salient topic, she moves far away to attend a sophisticated school and moves into the home of a puritanical aunt. The aunt immediately sets out to confiscate the girl's collection of erotic stories for teenagers that she received on the airplane, censor late (suggestive) T.V. programs, and drive boys away from the house.

One day the aunt is not home, and the girl is invited to see a new movie, *Lust of the School Girl*. The case is ripe for a self-awareness analysis. If there is an onset of self-focused attention, which way will the girl turn? Will she respond to the ongoing pressures of her aunt, or will some preexisting value come to the fore?

It might be useful here to recall that until the age of twelve, she had no explicit values about sex; she was surrounded with judgments and standards about sexual matters only upon moving away. Thus, once she becomes self-aware and evaluates whether or not to carry out the proposed behavior, the most imposing standard against which to evaluate that behavior is her aunt's. Obviously seeing *Lust of the School Girl* would be wrong, and self-awareness would decrease the probability of her going.

Further, it shouldn't really matter whether the aunt is physically present when this decision is made. In either case, the only salient standard for evaluation is the puritanical one to which she has been exposed.

Assuming that more liberal influences do not occur, the same girl, continuing to live with her aunt, one day goes off to college and takes part in a psychology experiment in which sex guilt becomes an issue. She fills out her sex guilt scale on the conserva-tive side. Later in the semester, when asked to read a pornographic novel and rate it for enjoyment, all the time seated before a mirror, she writes on her questionnaire that the novel is highly dis-tasteful.

Would this result still be in keeping with Cooley's thinking? By this time our college woman may not even be thinking about her aunt anymore, but would espouse the value anyway. In other words, once she has gone off to college, she may have forgotten the source of this salient puritanical value, or at least, she may not think of her aunt whenever the topic of sex arises. This is probably the stage at which a psychologist would say that the value is internalized. But for the present theory, we are not concerned with whether she has forgotten the initial source of the value. The crucial thing is how salient that value or standard is, as a point for evaluation.

Let's take the example one step further. Suppose she has gone to a progressive college where nearly all of the other women are liberal about sex. After three years she has a chance to sleep with a male student and must now struggle through a moral dilemma. If self-focused attention directs her behavior, through a dominant value, what will be the outcome? Will her aunt's training still be with her, or will the pervasive campus attitude be the value that is acted upon?

At this point, we cannot predict. All that is at issue here is which of two values is going to dominate, and without having further information there is no way to decide. However, there is a general idea that applies to these kinds of conflicts, and we will resume with our example below.

CONFLICT OF STANDARDS: A RECENCY PRINCIPLE

The self-awareness theory has generally been applied to those cases in which the standard, or goal, has been the only salient one available. For instance, in selecting people for his study on aggression, Carver picked those subjects who clearly manifested either propunitive or antipunitive attitudes. In the context of cheating, Diener and Wallbom (1976) were dealing with a norm that was widespread among college students in America. Thus there was little ambiguity regarding what was salient.

A much different case is also important. This was the conformity experiment by Wicklund and Duval, in which subjects were confronted with the opinions of a homogeneous group on each of nine issues, such as federal censorship, the death penalty, and registering firearms. The question here is, why did self-aware subjects conform to others' standards (opinions) rather than their own? The answer, in this instance, is that subjects probably did not have an entirely clear or salient picture of their own attitudes. The point is made by Bem (1972), and even better by Nisbett and Wilson (1977a), that most people do not have a very clear conception of their own attitudes, and that when asked to act on these attitudes, behavior stems only minimally from them. From this reasoning one should think that the subjects of Wicklund and Duval (1971) entered the situation with only vaguely defined attitudes on the nine issues, and that in contrast to this fuzziness, the homogeneous opinion of the reference group was entirely clear.

Let us go one step further: In cases where standards are vague, so that self-awareness leads to guiding behavior or judgments in the direction of the opinions of others, there is one way to keep those judgments from going in the direction of the group—clarify the subjects' own opinions. This was done by McCormick (1977), who confronted subjects with conformity pressure, either under conditions of high or low self-awareness. Some of these subjects had just performed free behaviors that were relevant to those opinions; thus they had a strong and salient behavioral basis for thinking about their opinions. Interestingly, these subjects were not at all influenced by the conformity pressure.

A more general point can be made regarding the conflict between alternative directions for movement. To begin with, it is instructive to examine some remarks of William James (1910) regarding the differences between the various facets of the self with respect to their "seizing" quality. By James' reasoning, such dynamic aspects as emotional states and free decisions have a more captivating quality than do the more static aspects, such as morals or other rules. It is possible to build on James' insight by formulating a recency principle.

When we think about a standard for behavior, or a moral rule, it is not necessarily true that this principle dominates our direction of thinking and/or behavior. This is because the moral rule is a static entity, without the quality of suddenly imposing on our thinking processes. We are not suddenly overcome by rules about behavior in the same way we are overcome by emotions, strong drives, or decisions. Thus a central determinant of the direction taken by the self-aware person, whether in acting on an emotion, acting consistent with a decision, or acting consistent with a moral rule, is *the extent to which that potential source of behavioral influence is already having or has recently had an impact on the person's behavior.*

Returning to the example about conflicting sexual standards, we should be able to predict the effect of self-awareness if one of the standards is based on a recent behavior. For instance, if the student has just taken out a long-term subscription to *Cosmopolitan,* her recent commitment will serve as the basis for behavior. When self-aware, she is then likely to follow the more liberal path. The aunt's training, which has had no direct impact on the college woman's actions for at least three years, will no longer guide her behavior. In short, when self-aware, the woman will follow the direction of her own recent commitment rather than conform.

Conformity versus commitment to one's own decision is just one possible conflict among potential directions to be taken by the self-aware person. Another one, often investigated, is the issue of moral principles versus emotional states. Scheier (1976), as well as Scheier, Carver, and Gibbons (1978), has found that the arousal of emotion overrides the influence that cognitive rules for behavior would normally be expected to have. One might have a rule that aggression is not desired, and in the absence of any other dominant basis for behavior, one would act on that standard when rendered self-aware (Carver, 1975; Gibbons, 1978). However, when anger is generated, an immediate emotional state provides a direction for behavior that opposes the moral principle, and the self-aware person becomes more aggressive rather than less so.

This reasoning brings a new variable to the theory of self-awareness and provides a guide to the direction the individual will take in behaviors that stem from self-focused attention. To the degree that one has recently conformed to a group, self-awareness is then likely to result in conforming to that group again. To the extent that we have just chosen not to aggress, self-awareness will lead us in a continued nonaggressive direction. If an emotional state is leading us to run away from a feared object, and the emotional state is recent or immediate, self-awareness will heighten the tendency to run away (Scheier, Carver, & Gibbons, 1978). In short, conflicts among behaviors for the self-aware person can be clarified using the principle of recency: Those potential influences·that have had the most recent (or current) impact on behavior are the ones to which the self-aware person will be subject.

SUMMARY

This chapter has shown how the self comes to enter into the workings of behavior. The self plays no function in automated behavior; in behaviors that are not automatic, the self becomes relevant only insofar as the person is self-aware. The self-aware condition, defined either as an individual difference or as a state marked by special self-focusing cues, is one of self-evaluation. The person compares his or her current or potential behavior (or traits) against a standard—some goal or value that is relatively salient for the person. Self-aware people are inclined to be more honest, less arbitrarily punitive, often more helpful, and more industrious than those who are not self-aware. Sometimes the standard is nothing more than one's own behavior; in this case, the person tries to minimize any disparity between current and prior behavior. For instance, self-awareness prompts more accurate self-descriptions when the individual is asked to describe his or her own sociability or aggressive tendencies. Often the standard will be a cognitive rule, or moral, which may or may not be shared by most other people, and sometimes it will be something new to the person, posed in the self-awareness-provoking situation by a reference group. If there is no other guide for behavior of sufficient recency, the person will then abide by the values of the immediately present group.

This discussion has two major ramifications for the condition of self-focused attention: (1) It is often aversive, since human beings are so easily dissatisfied with themselves when they engage in evaluation; thus running away from self-awareness is not uncommon. (2) Self-focused attention, if it cannot be escaped, is generally a civilizing state. It is a condition in which the person has self-doubt, shows consistency in thoughts and behavior, and is responsive to those values that society tries to inculcate.

3

Self-perception of Motivation

MICHAEL E. ENZLE

Each of us can easily list a variety of activities we enjoy and go out of our way to pursue. Likewise, each of us is aware of many activities that we consider to be distasteful, immoral, or simply boring. Not surprisingly, our lists would differ. In fact, one person's delight could easily be another's anathema. This chapter examines prominent theoretical models of how such preferences are developed and changed.

The major focus of the chapter is Daryl Bem's self-perception theory. The core of this theory is that people infer their own attitudes and motivations by observing their behavior and the context in which it occurs. In the first section of the chapter, Bem's theory will be presented as it relates to the self-perception of interest and motivation. In succeeding sections, several lines of research relevant to Bem's model will be considered. We will see that his theory leads to some rather counterintuitive predictions. Consider a few examples: Trivial rewards for saying that a boring task is fun will produce increased interest in the task; threats of severe punishment will be less effective than threats of mild punishment in reducing the attractiveness of an activity; highly valuable rewards will reduce the enjoyment of an interesting activity and decrease motivation to become involved in it again.

Theories that emphasize self-perception of competencies will be presented in the remaining sections of the chapter. One model, formulated by Edward Deci, posits a drive for personal control over events in the environment. According to Deci, people enjoy activities that provide them with feelings of competence and control. Finally, two models that have emerged from the field of learning will be discussed. Albert Bandura has proposed that learning processes produce general self-perceptions of abilities to perform activities effectively, and that these self-perceptions, in turn, affect a person's tendencies to approach and avoid various activities. Martin Seligman focuses on the debilitating effects of being unable to avoid painful experiences. He suggests that in some cases people may lose their motivation to exert control over potentially negative events in their lives.

SELF-PERCEPTION THEORY

In 1964, Daryl Bem submitted a doctoral dissertation that quickly had profound effects on social psychology. At a time when this field was dominated by theories that emphasized human drives for consistency among thoughts and attitudes, Bem proposed a model of self-knowledge that was strongly influenced by B. F. Skinner's (1957) behavioristic approach. Behaviorists assert that the science of psychology does not require reference to supposed states such as drives. Rather, the key elements are behavior and the stimulus setting in which the behavior occurs.

SELF-PERCEPTION POSTULATES

Bem's (1967, 1972) self-perception theory adopts the behaviorists' assumption that there are very few internal states that exist independent of the environment and to which people have direct access. He claims that socializing agents (parents, teachers, and others) show children how to recognize and evaluate the majority of their attitudes and feelings. This early socialization relies heavily on direct instruction. Children are frequently told by an adult that they seem to be happy, hungry, bored, and so on. Children learn more, however, than a list of self-descriptive terms. Because of the diversity of events in their lives, they must also learn rules for the continued understanding of their experiences. Bem (1967, 1972) proposes that these rules parallel the procedures that adults use to label the child's feelings and attitudes. Adults usually have two sources of information with which to understand a child's experiences. They can observe the child's behavior (including verbalizations) and the nature of the immediate surroundings. For example, we may observe a child sit in front of a television set and intently watch the screen for half an hour. We may also observe that the main character in the program is a clown. We should be quite ready to comment to the child that she really enjoys the clown. Bem proposes that children learn to use this same strategy in assessing their own attitudes, and will continue to employ it throughout their lives. Bem's (1972) first self-perception postulate, then, is that "individuals come to 'know' their own attitudes, emotions, and other internal states partially by inferring them from observations of their own overt behavior and/or the circumstances in which this behavior occurs" (p. 5).

The logic of Bem's explanation leads to the intriguing conclusion that people evaluate their own experiences in the same way as do outside observers. Bem's (1972) second self-perception postulate formalizes this reasoning: "To the extent that internal cues are weak, ambiguous, or uninterpretable, the individual is functionally in the same position as an outside observer, an observer who must necessarily rely upon those same external cues [behavior and circumstances] to infer the individual's internal states" (p. 5).

IMPLICIT SELF-SELECTION QUESTION

An important aspect of Bem's theory is that people assess their attitudes on the basis of *current* experiences. When we engage in some activity, a clear prior attitude regarding the activity may or may not be present. Bem argues that it usually is not, and that we must therefore ask ourselves the implicit self-selection question: Of the people who do or do not engage in this behavior under these circumstances, why am I one who does? What

must my attitude be? Of course, the theory does not require that
we be this verbose with ourselves. We may simply wonder why
we did what we did, how we feel about it, and rather automatically bring our attention to bear on the nature of our behavior and the situation.

SELF-PERCEPTION PROCESSES

The two postulates and the implicit self-selection question set the
stage for self-perception. The next issue is, how do people use
information about behavior and circumstances to infer their internal experiences? Bem's general answer is that we will perceive
the nature of our behavior toward a stimulus to describe directly
our attitude if the stimulus alone appears to be responsible for
our behavior. If, however, our behavior clearly appears to be under
the control of a reinforcement contingency that is *extrinsic* to
the stimulus, we will not use our behavior to infer our attitude.
Reinforcement contingencies refer to rewards we might hope to
obtain or punishments we might try to avoid by behaving toward
a stimulus in a particular fashion. For example, imagine that one
week you frequently listen to WBOR radio. WBOR specializes in
Gregorian chants, and you have been compiling a list of the se-
lections broadcast by the station. One day a friend asks you how
much you enjoy Gregorian chants. You quickly review your recent behavior and can think of no reason for it other than the
music itself. The nature of your behavior implies enjoyment, and
so you reply that Gregorian chants are your cup of tea. In this
example, you would have construed your behavior to be a reflection of the intrinsically motivating properties of the stimulus,
since there appeared to be no extrinsic cause for it. Your self-
perceived attitude could have been quite different, though, if there
were another justification for your behavior. Suppose you recalled
that WBOR had been conducting a contest. First prize was a
Mercedes 450 SL, an automobile of no small appeal to you. To
win the contest, a listener telephoned at random was required to
name the most frequently played Gregorian chant during the
previous week. You would now be aware of a reinforcement con-

tingency, the conditions for winning the automobile, that could sufficiently account for your listening and list-making behaviors. According to self-perception theory, you would be less likely to tell your friend that you enjoy Gregorian chants.

ACCURACY OF SELF-PERCEPTIONS

Self-perception theory is clearly concerned with how people view the causes of their behavior. But the processes Bem describes do not depend on accuracy in perceiving causes of behavior, or even on objectively verifiable causes. According to the theory, self-perception is a product of *beliefs* about the causes of behavior. People seldom have objective evidence about the causes of their actions and must instead rely on their own powers of observation and memory. Because observational and memorial processes are prone to distortion, selectivity, and error, the beliefs people employ in assessing their attitudes may similarly be erroneous or incomplete. Nonetheless, the effect of believing there to be a sufficient extrinsic justification for a behavior should prevent the inference of attitude based on the behavior regardless of whether the belief could objectively be shown to be correct or incorrect. Similarly, an objectively real but undetected extrinsic cause should not deter people from inferring their attitudes on the basis of their behaviors.

INSUFFICIENT JUSTIFICATION

Reinforcement principles have frequently been adopted by social psychologists to predict how enjoyment of activities and objects can be developed and changed. For instance, a classical conditioning approach would predict that a person's attitude toward an activity should be *directly* affected by the magnitude of the reward or punishment that accompanies the activity. Positive feelings produced by rewards should become associated with the activity so that doing the activity (or thinking about it) comes to produce a similar positive reaction. The greater the reward, the more positive should be the attitude toward the activity. Negative feelings should similarly become associated with activities following actual or threatened punishment. In this section, we shall examine the alternative self-perception hypothesis that the enjoyment of an activity should be *inversely* related to the magnitude of incentives under certain conditions.

INSUFFICIENT REWARDS

One of the first experiments to yield evidence in conflict with learning approaches was conducted by Leon Festinger and Merrill Carlsmith (1959). Each participant initially engaged in monotonous tasks (e.g., repeatedly placing spools in a tray and dumping them out). Subjects in two groups were then asked to convince another person that the tasks were highly entertaining. Half of these participants were paid $1 and half were paid $20 for their speeches. While a reinforcement approach would predict that a large reward for verbal expressions of enjoyment would produce greater attitudinal favorability than would a small reward, Festinger and Carlsmith's (1959) study revealed a reverse incentive effect. Subjects who were paid $1 reported more enjoyment of the tasks than did subjects who were paid $20 (see Figure 3.1).

Bem (1967, 1972) claims that studies such as Festinger and Carlsmith's provide compelling evidence for his self-perception theory. When people receive a large reward (e.g., $20) for expressing an attitude, they should perceive their verbal behavior as sufficiently explained by the reward. Under such conditions, Bem proposes that people will not use the nature of their behavior to infer private attitudes. Their attitudes should be the typical attitude expressed in the population at large. However, people should be unlikely to see a trivial reward (e.g., $1) as a sufficient extrinsic cause for their behavior, and should attribute their actions to the intrinsic properties of the attitude object. In other words, they will infer their attitudes from their behaviors. If people say they enjoy a particular activity or object, and perceive no extrinsic cause for the statement, they will perceive their

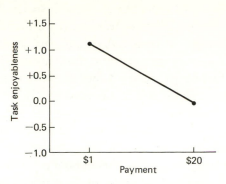

FIGURE 3.1. Effect of payment level on the enjoyment of tedious tasks. (Based on data from Festinger and Carlsmith, 1959)

attitude as being positive. In summary, we could predict that trivial rewards for positive statements should result in the inference of more positive attitudes than should large rewards for the same statements.

Bem's (1967, 1972) explanation of the reverse incentive effect is radically different from the theory Festinger and Carlsmith were attempting to test. Festinger (1957) had earlier formulated a model, *cognitive dissonance theory*, that proposes a motivational basis for attitude change. He asserted that people experience aversive psychological tension when they simultaneously hold cognitions that are in a dissonant relationship. Cognitions refer to mental representations of attitudes, feelings, and behaviors; two cognitions are dissonant when one of them implies the opposite of the other. The theory states that once dissonance is experienced, people will attempt to eliminate it. One way to reduce dissonance is to alter one of the cognitions so that a dissonant relationship no longer exists. Festinger (1957) also proposed that dissonance potentially created by holding two incompatible cognitions could be alleviated by the presence of a third cognition that justifies one of the two dissonant cognitions. Thus, Festinger and Carlsmith reasoned that subjects in their study would hold dissonant cognitions. They would have the initial attitude that the tasks were boring plus the cognition that they had just said that the tasks were fun. Festinger and Carlsmith specifically predicted that subjects who were given $1 would not see the payment as an adequate justification for their verbal statement, and would therefore experience substantial cognitive dissonance. Their attitudes toward the tasks were predicted to become more favorable, since that would reduce the unpleasant dissonance. Believing the tasks were fun would be consistent, not dissonant, with saying they were enjoyable. Participants who were paid $20, however, were expected to perceive that amount as adequate justification for saying the tasks were enjoyable. They should experience little or no dissonance and therefore maintain their attitude that the tasks were boring.

Bem's reinterpretation of Festinger and Carlsmith's (1959) study and many others of the same ilk produced an unusual problem. Bem (1967, 1972) proposes that attitudes are formed by dispassionate observation, while Festinger (1957) maintains that psychological tension accounts for attitude change. Nonetheless, identical predictions can often be derived from both theories. This state of affairs makes it difficult to test the relative validity of the two models. Bem's theory will be emphasized throughout this chapter, though, since it has been extended to areas not anticipated by dissonance theory and provides a somewhat more general account of how people develop self-perceptions of interest in activities.

CHOICE AND CONSEQUENCES

Let's say that you have accidentally wandered into a television studio, thinking it to be your favorite organic dry cleaner. A man rushes toward you, saying that you are just in time to make your appearance. After you have cleared up the case of mistaken identity, he explains that someone was scheduled to make a fundraising appeal for the annual *unguis intracresens* telethon, and apparently will not arrive in time for the speech. "Aha!" he says. "Would you be willing to do it instead? Feel free to say no." You accept, walk onstage, and deliver a two-minute off-the-cuff spot on the need for research into a cure for ingrown toenails.

Suddenly all fifty telephone operators are swamped with calls from enthusiastic contributors who pledge huge sums of money, their life insurance policies, and their children's ponies. Now, how strongly do you feel about *unguis intracresens*? Research stimulated by Festinger and Carlsmith's (1959) study highlights two important elements of attitude inference that are represented in this scenario (e.g., Calder, Ross, & Insko, 1973). You were given free *choice* about whether or not to make the appeal, and your behavior produced impressive *consequences*. Free choice should lead you to discount coercion as a possible cause for your behavior and thus set the stage for attitude inference. You should then use the quality of your behavior as a guide to inferring the favorability of your attitude; since your behavior was obviously effective (was highly persuasive), you should decide that your attitude is correspondingly positive.

INSUFFICIENT PUNISHMENTS

We have just seen that rewards can affect interest and enjoyment in a counterintuitive fashion; small rewards for favorable statements seem to produce more enjoyment of activities than do large rewards. Researchers have also examined the influence of threatened punishment. Suppose that your younger sister frequently smears quantities of grape jelly on pumpkin pie and eats the resulting mess with much smacking of lips and low animal groans of pleasure. The entire scene so sickens you that you can barely manage to finish your peanut butter and avocado sandwich. Everyone knows that if you threaten your sister with every punishment not disallowed by the Geneva Convention agreements, she will cease this behavior pattern, disdain grape jelly and pumpkin pie, and learn to enjoy the really finer things in life (that you will graciously define for her). Despite the obvious nature and widespread acceptance of this approach, there is evidence that threats of severe punishment create neither changes in attitudes nor lasting alterations in behavior. Bem's (1967, 1972) model provides an explanation for these findings as well as a basis for predicting that mild threats are effective in modifying both attitudes and behavior.

A threat of punishment constitutes an extrinsic reinforcement contingency. If we comply with a threat and perceive it as a sufficient cause for our behavior, then Bem's model would predict that we will not infer our attitude from the behavior. On the other hand, if a threat can be employed that actually changes our behavior, but is so subtle that we do not *perceive* it as a sufficient justification for the change, then we should view the resultant behavior as reflecting our attitude. Thus, self-perception theory predicts that mild threats will be more effective in decreasing interest in an activity than will severe threats. Notice that the theoretical effectiveness of a mild threat relies on the deceptive use of such threats and/or on misunderstanding of the objective influence of the threat by the self-perceiver. As mentioned earlier, Bem's model does not deal with objective causality but rather with the perceiver's beliefs about causality.

A study by Aronson and Carlsmith (1963) demonstrates the reverse incentive effect produced by threats. Preschool children were individually told by an adult that he would leave them alone for a short time. He then pointed to an attractive toy (e.g., a fire truck) and issued either a mild or a severe threat of punishment for playing with the toy during his absence. For the severe threat group, he said that if the child played with the toy, he would be very angry and would pack up his toys and leave. For children in the mild threat condition, he also cautioned against playing with the toy but said only that he would be annoyed if the child disobeyed. Surreptitious observation during the experimenter's absence revealed that the mild and severe threats were equally effective in producing immediate control over the children's behavior. Everyone avoided the forbidden toy. Liking for the toy was assessed immediately after the temptation period and then again some forty-five days later. At both times, the mildly threatened children were more likely to derogate the forbidden toy than were the severely threatened children. We now have evidence that another type of extrinsic reinforcement contingency, threats of severe punishment, inhibits the self-perception of attitudes based on behavior. Other research shows that mild threats are superior to severe threats in modifying *behavior* as well as attitudes. For example, Freedman (1965) found that mildly threatened children were less likely than severely threatened children to play with a forbidden toy in a new situation (where there was no fear of punishment) long after the threat had been issued.

A study conducted by Lepper (1973) marks another important advance in our understanding of the scope and significance of self-perception. He suggested that the forbidden toy findings may be due to a more general change than altered interest in a particular toy. Specifically, when children avoid a toy after an adult request and mild threat, they may infer (1) that they do not like it and/or (2) that they are good children (i.e., they comply with adult rules). The first inference would reflect the self-perception effect described by Bem (1972). The second inference is more general. Children may decide that they possess a characteristic of honesty or obedience. Lepper (1973) investigated this latter possibility by having an adult first establish the usual mild and severe threat conditions involving an attractive toy. About three weeks later, a different adult showed the children a game and offered attractive prizes for attaining a very high score. The game was rigged so that they could not win the prize without cheating. During the game, the children were alone and recorded their own scores. Mildly threatened children in the forbidden toy setting were much less likely to cheat on the game than were severely threatened children. This finding indeed suggests that mildly threatened children formed a general impression of themselves as good kids who comply with many kinds of rules and prohibitions. If experimental results such as these generalize to less structured settings, the implications for child-rearing practices are clear. Subtle, though persuasive, threats of punishment may be superior to severe threats in establishing what we generally refer to as a moral code or conscience.

There is an odd footnote to the research in this area. A wire service reporter recently filed a newspaper story that dealt with ethical issues in experimental social psychology. Evidently working from secondary sources, and without an understanding of the research area, the reporter noted in tones of horror that researchers were tempting children to play with "forbidden toys." The mind reels. Thompson submachine guns with live ammunition? Rattle-snakes? Shifty-looking dolls that dispense drugs?

OVERSUFFICIENT JUSTIFICATION

Throughout the discussion of insufficient deterrence, Bem's (1967, 1972) self-perception model served as the explanatory framework. In truth, most of the research in that area was derived from cognitive dissonance theory and can be interpreted just as easily from either a dissonance or self-perception viewpoint. We now turn to an area in which self-perception theory seems to have the upper hand. Specifically, researchers have become concerned with the effects of overrewarding intrinsically motivated behaviors. *Intrinsically motivated* behaviors are those that appear to be performed solely for the enjoyment derived from the activity itself, not for the attainment of rewards or avoidance of punishments extrinsic to the activity. The overjustification hypothesis proposes that intrinsic interest will be decreased if people are explicitly offered and given extrinsic rewards for engaging in intrinsically motivated activities. The self-perception rationale for this prediction should be familiar by now. Imagine yourself at age nine, taking a course in transcendental oboe playing. You have never missed a class and practice the half-lotus playing position in your spare time. One day you assess your interest in oboe playing. You can think of no apparent causes for your behavior extrinsic to the activity itself and hence infer that you really like Zen oboe. Suppose, however, that even though you would have engaged in these behaviors without extrinsic rewards, your parents decide to reward your efforts. They offer you money for going to class, practicing at home, and so on. You agree and are promptly paid for your activities. After a while, you assess your interest in oboe playing. In this case, you could entertain an obvious extrinsic justification for your behavior—you accepted an offer of payment *contingent* on performing the behaviors. According to Bem's theory, you would not use your behavior as an index of your attitude. Instead, you would perceive yourself as less intrinsically interested in the activity and would be less motivated to engage in it if your parents stopped providing extrinsic rewards.

OVERSUFFICIENT REWARDS

Lepper, Greene, and Nisbett (1973) conducted an early test of the overjustification hypothesis. One group of preschool children was offered a contingent reward for playing with art materials (an activity determined to be of high intrinsic interest). The experimenter told the children that they would receive a fancy "good player" award if they would play with the art materials. Children in the remaining two groups were similarly asked to play with the materials but were not offered the "good player" award. After the play session, children in one of these latter groups unexpectedly received the "good player" awards, while the remaining group did not. One to two weeks later, each child was observed during free-play class time, when awards were not available. As shown in Figure 3.2, children spent less time playing with the art materials after having played with them in order to receive a reward than if a reward were neither promised nor given. The comparison between expected and unexpected award groups is also important. Expected award children spent less time playing with the materials than did unexpected award children. Only children who explicitly contracted with the adult for the award presumably perceived their

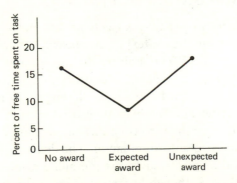

FIGURE 3.2. Effect of expected and unexpected awards on intrinsic interest. (Based on data from Lepper, Greene, and Nisbett, 1973)

behavior to have been caused by the award rather than the activity itself. Later, when given an opportunity to play with the same materials, but with no possibility of receiving a reward, these children chose not to play because they had decided they were not interested in the activity. The unexpected award children should not have perceived a causal connection between the reward and their behavior since a contingency had not been established prior to their behavior.

The overjustification hypothesis includes two preconditions that were not examined by Lepper et al. (1973). One of these is that intrinsic interest in the object or activity *must* initially be high. Calder and Staw (1975) tested this assumed prerequisite by varying the interest value of an activity. Their results showed decreased interest as a result of contingently rewarding participants only when the activity was initially enjoyable. The introduction of contingent rewards actually increased interest in an initially boring activity. A second, implicit precondition of the overjustification hypothesis is that only rewards that can reasonably be seen as a sufficient cause for behavior will result in decreased interest. A study by Enzle and Ross (1978) confirmed this precondition by showing that large financial rewards produced decreased intrinsic interest in a play activity, while trivially small amounts of money did not.

CHOICE, SURVEILLANCE, AND DEADLINES

Perceived choice in pursuing an activity was noted as an important variable within the context of insufficient justification research (e.g., Calder et al., 1973). Folger, Rosenfield, and Hays (1978) have similarly proposed that the overjustification effect implies that people believe they can freely choose to engage or not engage in the activity. If we are simply notified that we must perform an activity and that we shall receive a certain amount of payment, the payment is an irrelevant causal factor. The demand that we do the activity should be perceived as the prevailing cause. If we believe we have free choice, though, we could arrive at the conclusion that we did the activity in order to obtain the extrinsic reward. Folger et al. found that when people were given free choice about playing a game, high payment resulted in less intrinsic interest in the game compared to low payment. For people given no choice, however, high payment produced greater enjoyment of the task than did low payment. Thus, the perception of free choice does seem necessary in order for large rewards to reduce intrinsic interest. The increased interest due to large rewards in the absence of free choice probably indicates that when we *must* do something, it is more pleasant if we also happen to receive a sizable bonus.

The influence of choice on intrinsic interest highlights the fact that we may perceive our behavior to be constrained by forces other than explicit rewards or threats of punishment. A demand that we engage in some behavior may be perceived as a sufficient cause for our behavior when rewarding or punishing consequences are only implicit. Recent research suggests that other factors may similarly influence intrinsic interest. Lepper and Greene (1975), for example, suggested that if people are closely watched while they do something, they may perceive their behavior as at least partially due to the fact that they are under surveillance. The result should be decreased interest in the activity. Children in the Lepper and Greene (1975) study were told that they would be monitored by means of a video camera or believed they were not being watched while they played with puzzles. Later observations of these children revealed that previously monitored children were less likely to play with the puzzles than were nonmonitored children. A word of caution is probably in order here, though. For surveillance to be interpreted as a plausible extrinsic cause of behavior, people must make an assumption about the *intentions* of the observer. They must believe that the observer is prepared to reward them for performing the task or punish them for not performing it. People probably do make these assumptions in many circumstances, but not in all. For example, surveillance in work or school settings (as in the Lepper and Greene study) probably does involve coercive elements that are commonly understood by those surveyed. Surveillance that is interpreted solely as an expression of the observer's interest or curiosity, on the other hand, should not lead to decreased intrinsic interest.

If this chapter is part of a course reading assignment, have you been given a specific date by which to read it? When people are given a deadline to meet, they may perceive the cause of their behavior as successful completion of the activity within the time limit rather than the intrinsically interesting aspects of the activity. The familiar result would be decreased interest after the deadline passes. Amabile, DeJong, and Lepper (1976) have reported research in which precisely this effect occurred. So, if you have a deadline for reading this chapter, kindly disregard it.

DYNAMICS OF SELF-PERCEPTION

The research discussed thus far has been largely directed toward testing hypotheses on the effect of reward and punishment contingencies on intrinsic interest. Another line of research is primarily concerned with the processes that theoretically underlie self-perceptions. These investigations are useful in answering such questions as whether or not self-perception is in fact similar to perception of others.

INTERPERSONAL SIMULATIONS

Since Bem's (1967, 1972) model frequently predicts the same effects as dissonance theory, Bem suggested that support for self-perception could be garnered by investigating peripheral aspects of the theory. Bem (1967) had originally proposed that people often use the same information to evaluate their own attitudes as an outside observer does. This reasoning led him to predict that observers of insufficient reward settings would be able to predict accurately the attitudes of people on the basis of behavior and the surrounding circumstances. The elegance of Bem's reasoning lies in his strategy of separating the self-perceiver from the other-perceiver by having people observe another person rather than themselves. If other-perceivers produced results similar to self-perceivers, Bem could argue that the process of self-perception is indeed like that of other-perception. In several studies, Bem

(1967) successfully showed that observers who were given descriptions of insufficient reward experiments very accurately estimated subjects' attitudes. For example, in one study the task used by Festinger and Carlsmith (1959) was described to observers (Bem, 1967). One group was told that a subject in the experiment had agreed to tell another person that the tasks were fun for a fee of $20, while another group learned that the payment was $1. Estimates of the subjects' attitudes very closely matched subjects' actual attitudes in Festinger and Carlsmith's (1959) study. Bem's (1967) experiment, and many others, show that an aversive psychological state is not necessary to produce inferences of attitudes similar to those expressed by participants in cognitive dissonance research. There is no reason to suggest that observers in these studies experienced cognitive dissonance, since they had no dissonant cognitions. Bem (1972) recognizes, however, that the similarity of results between self- and other-perceivers could occur for a number of reasons other than the possibility that the two types of observers use the same information and processes to infer intrinsic interest. You can get to Chattanooga from either Nashville or Knoxville, but you pass through completely different towns.

FOCUS OF ATTENTION

Wegner and Finstuen (1977) have noted that the results of interpersonal simulations conflict with those of other research. Several studies indicate that self-perceivers (or "actors") are unwilling, compared with outside observers, to make inferences about their attitudes and other internal states (e.g., Storms, 1973). Jones and Nisbett (1971) have proposed that attentional differences may account for these findings. Actors may focus on their environment to the partial exclusion of their behavior due to the necessity of coping with the environment, while observers may typically focus on the actor's behavior since behavior is usually more dynamic than the surrounding situation. But we have seen that people in insufficient reward research express attitudes that are very similar to those estimated by outside observers in interpersonal simula-

tions. This anomaly led Wegner and Finstuen (1977) to suggest
that some feature of self-perception settings, such as concern for
being evaluated by the experimenter, induces people to focus
greater than usual attention on their own behavior—that is, to become self-aware (see Chapter 2) and therefore similar in orientation to outside observers. Their hypothesis is appealing, since self-
awareness seems to promote accurate recall of past behavior and
a general tendency to make self-descriptive statements (see Chapters 2 and 9).

Wegner and Finstuen (1977) evaluated their hypothesis by em-
ploying Bem's (1967) interpersonal simulation approach. Observers were given one of two attention instructions and then
listened to a tape-recorded session representing either the $1 or
$20 condition of Festinger and Carlsmith's (1959) study. Ob-
servers who were simply instructed to listen to the tape (and who
presumably focused on the actor's behavior) estimated the actor's
attitude toward the task to be more positive in the $1 than in the
$20 condition, while those who were told to focus on the situation
judged the actor's enjoyment to have been greater in the $20 than
in the $1 condition. These results suggest that observers, and by
extension self-perceivers, must focus on behavior in order to
produce attitude inferences predicted by Bem's theory.

Perhaps the "implicit self-selection" question is posed only when
people become self-aware. It could be that individuals regularly
fail to make the self-inferences that Bem has outlined because they
focus outward, tracing the changing patterns of environmental
events. The question, What am I like? begs for an answer, and
hence engages self-perception processes when the person focuses
inward, pausing to reflect on the qualities of the self.

PERSONAL AND ENVIRONMENTAL MASTERY

Three models that stress the effects of self-perceived competence
or mastery are presented in this section. We will see that each
model differs from Bem's theory (1967, 1972) in its assumptions
and focus. Although the three models were independently for-

mulated, they arive at similar conclusions. Self-perceived compe-tence enhances motivation to engage in activities, while self-perceived incompetence decreases motivation.

COGNITIVE EVALUATION THEORY

Edward Deci (1975) has developed a model, cognitive evaluation theory, that presents a somewhat more differentiated view of intrinsic interest than Bem's self-perception theory. Deci's (1975) first proposition is essentially the same as the overjustification hypothesis: When people are given rewards contingent on simple performance of an activity, they will perceive their behavior as caused by the extrinsic reward rather than by the qualities of the activity itself, and will consequently become less intrinsically interested in the activity. His second proposition represents a de-parture from the domain of Bem's theory. Deci (1975) hypoth-esizes that intrinsic interest in an activity is directly related to feelings of competence. Factors that make people feel more com-petent at some activity will heighten their intrinsic interest. The third proposition synthesizes the first two in a way that permits us to predict whether a reward will increase or decrease intrinsic interest. According to Deci (1975), a given reward can potentially convey two types of information. One aspect of a reward, empha-sized by self-perception theory, is its capacity to control behavior. The second aspect is the reward's informative value concerning our abilities. Deci (1975) proposes that the effect of a reward on intrinsic interest will depend on which of these aspects is rela-tively more salient. If a person receives a reward following some activity and the controlling aspect of the reward is highly salient, then intrinsic interest should decrease. On the other hand, if the competence-confirming aspect of the reward is highly salient, intrinsic interest should increase.

Early tests of the third proposition were based upon the reason-able assumption that under normal circumstances the controlling and competence-confirming aspects of rewards are differentially salient for various rewards. For example, Deci (1975) summarizes his own experiments as suggesting that positive verbal feedback

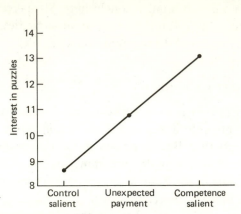

FIGURE 3.3. Effect of control versus competence salience on the influence of reward on intrinsic interest. (Based on data from Enzle and Ross, 1978)

during an activity (e.g., "You're really good at this!") produces increased interest in the activity. Statements that a person is skillful obviously tap the competence-confirming aspect of verbal rewards. Deci (1975) then argues that money is typically perceived as an inducement for behavior per se, and that the controlling aspect of money is therefore normally salient. In previous sections, we have seen that performance-contingent monetary rewards do produce decreased intrinsic interest. By contrasting the effects of money and verbal praise on intrinsic interest, Deci can claim support for the third proposition of cognitive evaluation theory. Monetary rewards (controlling aspect salient) decrease intrinsic interest, while verbal praise (competence aspect salient) increases intrinsic interest.

Enzle and Ross (1978) directly tested Deci's (1975) third proposition by using the same monetary reward to signal either extrinsic control of the participant's behavior or the participant's competence in the activity. In one group, young adults were offered a large monetary payment contingent only on trying to solve puzzles (control aspect salient). In a second group, participants were told that they would receive payment only if their puzzle-solving performance was of high quality (competence information salient). Subjects in a third group were told nothing about the payment prior to working on the puzzles (unexpected payment). At the conclusion of the puzzle-solving period, all subjects in the three groups received identical payment. The results of the study (see Figure 3.3) were in close accord with Deci's (1975) third hypothesis. Intrinsic interest was lower in the control aspect salient condition, and higher in the competence information salient condition, than in the unexpected reward condition.

SELF-EFFICACY THEORY

Albert Bandura (1977) has developed a model of cognitive motivation from his social learning perspective that has interesting implications for the study of intrinsic motivation. Bandura proposes that beliefs about one's ability to perform a given behavior successfully and thereby bring about desired consequences (self-efficacy expectations) are an important source of motivation. People should be more likely to engage and persist in activities for which they have high expectations of personal efficacy than in activities at which they believe they will fail. This reasoning is quite similar to Deci's (1975) hypothesis that self-perceived competence influences intrinsic motivation, but is part of a larger theory that speculates about how people can regulate and change their own behaviors. According to Bandura (1976, 1977), self-regulation of behavior is possible through *self-reinforcement*. By setting personal goals, achieving them, rewarding oneself, setting a slightly higher goal, and so on, a person can develop desired skills at a personally tailored pace. Research concerned with behavior change has shown that self-reinforcement procedures can be at least as effective as the typical procedure in which another person sets goals for the learner and delivers the rewards (see Bandura, 1976, for a discussion of this research). In fact, some investigators have reported that self-reinforcement produces longer-lasting changes than does other-reinforcement after rewards are withdrawn (e.g., Jeffrey, 1974).

Jeffrey (1974) has presented an interesting analysis of the self-perception consequences of self-reinforcement. He proposes that when people learn to self-administer rewards, they indirectly learn that they are controlling their own behavior via the rewards. Self-reinforcement may therefore lead to enhanced perceptions of self-determination which, in turn, maintain previously reinforced behavior even when extrinsic rewards are no longer available. In each of the overjustification studies reviewed in this chapter, the rewards were completely controlled by the experimenter. The experimenter set the reward contingencies (what goal must be reached in order to receive the reward) and physically delivered the reward when the participants reached the goal. According to Jeffrey's (1974) formulation, giving people a measure of control over rewards might moderate the negative effect of extrinsic rewards on intrinsic motivation by preventing the inference that one's behavior is entirely determined by extrinsic factors.

There are two elements of reinforcement procedures which a person may or may not control. One is the establishment of reward contingencies. Lepper and Greene (1978) have suggested that self-determination of standards for receiving a reward may prevent the detrimental effects that externally imposed standards typically have on intrinsic interest, even if the self-set and externally set standards are identical. The second aspect is the actual delivery of the reward once the standard, whether self-set or externally imposed, is met. From an objective perspective, there is no obvious reason why self- and other-delivery of rewards should differentially affect people. Given that a person has satisfied the requirements for receiving a reward, the difference is merely between the person physically taking the reward from its repository and passively receiving the reward from someone else who takes it from the repository. Just such minor differences, however, seem to affect people's perceptions of personal control.

Langer (1975) has shown that nominal control over an unimportant peripheral aspect of an uncontrollable event heightens perceptions of general control over the event. For example, she found that people were more confident that they would win a lottery, a chance event, if they had personally selected their tickets than if another person had chosen the tickets for them. Langer refers to this phenomenon as the *illusion of control*. Illusory perceptions of control over an event, according to Langer (1975), should be most likely to occur when a person performs some action that is typically associated with actual control, even though in the particular setting the action can have no objective influence on the event. Applied to contingent reward settings, it is possible that control over reward delivery may lead to general, though illusory, perceptions of control over the rewarded behavior. Enzle and Look (1979) therefore hypothesized that large contingent rewards should decrease intrinsic motivation in activities when the rewards are externally delivered but not when they are self-delivered. The results of their study replicated the well-established overjustification effect when rewards were delivered by an experimenter. Large rewards resulted in decreased intrinsic motivation compared to trivially small rewards. For self-delivered rewards, however, intrinsic motivation remained high regardless of the magnitude of the reward.

LEARNED HELPLESSNESS THEORY

We have seen that a contingency between behavior and rewards or punishments is a crucial element in self-perception of intrinsic interest and motivation. Seligman's learned helplessness model concentrates on the effects of *noncontingent reinforcement* (see Abramson, Seligman, & Teasdale, 1978, for a recent statement). The major hypothesis of this model is that when people are exposed to uncontrollable aversive stimulation or insoluble problems, they will become less effective in the future when faced with controllable aversive stimuli or soluble problems. In other words, if you have learned in the past that punishment or failure cannot be averted by your coping behaviors, you may be less able to learn effective coping behaviors or to try existing behaviors that would be effective in the future when events are controllable. For example, Hiroto and Seligman (1975) have reported a series of experiments that demonstrate not only the learned helplessness phenomenon but the fact that the effect can generalize across different types of activities. In one experiment, some subjects were exposed to noxious noise that they believed was controllable, but that despite their attempts could not be terminated. Another group of participants were exposed to the same noise but could terminate it. In a subsequent situation in which noxious noise was controllable for all subjects but required a new coping response, subjects previously exposed to the uncontrollable noxious noise learned the effective coping response more slowly than did the other participants. The same preconditions were established in a second experiment, but the subsequent task involved solving anagrams. Subjects who had previously been unable to control unpleasant noise solved fewer anagrams than did subjects who had been able to control the noise.

Abramson, Seligman, and Teasdale (1978) have extended the learned helplessness model to include the consideration of self-perceived causes for failure and ineffectiveness. Most relevant to the models we have considered already is the proposition that the effects of prior helplessness on future behavior will be most pronounced and long-lasting when people perceive prior failure or ineffectiveness as due to their stable, general, personal qualities. Suppose, for example, that try as you might, you cannot establish a running conversation with your Saturday night date. You talk about the weather and draw a blank. You bring up sex and still the ice fails to break. As the evening wanes, you end up in a monologue about the dashboard of the car ("These little knobs are nice"). If this failure is something you find can be explained only by your lack of conversational ability, you will probably hesitate quite strongly in considering future dates with anyone. But if the failure is explained by some external factor—say, you find out your date has not conversed with anyone since 1971—then helplessness will not result.

SUMMARY

Bem's (1967, 1972) self-perception theory provides a simple system for summarizing the effects of a variety of factors on the experiences of enjoyment and interest. The theory states that people often make an initial discrimination of whether their behavior is primarily attributable to the characteristics of the activity in which they are engaged or is sufficiently explained by some extrinsic reinforcement contingency. According to the theory, behavior that is viewed as caused by the inherent qualities of the activity will be used to infer attitudes about the activity. People should then carefully examine the important dimensions of their behavior (e.g., quality, intensity, quantity) in order to understand their experience. However, if people believe their behavior is not caused by the characteristics of the activity, then their behavior should be irrelevant for assessing their feelings. Consistent with this reasoning, we have seen that explicit inducements for behavior, such as promises of valuable rewards and threats of severe punishments, seem to prevent behavior-based attitude inferences.

Deci's (1975) cognitive evaluation theory offers an important qualification of the overjustification hypothesis by recognizing that rewards have different meanings depending upon how they are administered and by proposing that heightened feelings of competence produce increased intrinsic interest. When rewards signal personal competence, intrinsic interest in the relevant activity should increase rather than decrease. Bandura's (1977) theory similarly emphasizes self-perceived competence, but from a somewhat different vantage point. He proposes that successful coping experiences, personally defined standards of performance, and self-administration of rewards should enhance expectations of self-efficacy. Successful coping or mastery is also the emphasis of the learned helplessness model (Abramson et al., 1978). There are strong indications in the research literature that reinforcements that are administered independent of a person's behavioral efforts may result in the belief that the environment is uncontrollable or that the person is incompetent. Such beliefs may lead to subsequent deficits in attempts to exert control.

The phenomena addressed by Bem (1967, 1972), Deci (1975), Bandura (1977), and Abramson et al. (1978) clearly overlap. Self-perceived interest, perceived self-determination and competence, self-efficacy expectations, and perceived environmental mastery intuitively appear to be closely related. They may share common determinants and produce common or interrelated behavioral and attitudinal consequences. A general theory of cognitive motivation may well emerge from the integration of these models.

4

Self-perception of Emotion
and Internal Sensation

JAMES W. PENNEBAKER
UNIVERSITY OF VIRGINIA

Imagine you are reading an intriguing book on the self. Suddenly you become aware of tightness in your chest. This is the first time that you have felt such a sensation. You ask yourself, what caused it, what does it mean? How do you go about evaluating this ambiguous internal sensation? Clearly, you need additional information. Let's assume that one of four things has just occurred prior to the onset of the chest sensation:

> Your date for this evening called and said that you were a repulsive creep because of your vile habits and nauseating appearance.
> Your wealthy Uncle Joe Bob (the family oil tycoon) is mailing you two million dollars because he thinks you are so wonderful.
> You have just returned from a dinner party at your boss's house, where the cook added cayenne pepper to the pumpkin pie instead of brown sugar.
> Your doctor told you this morning that you have extremely high blood pressure and a pathetically weak heart.

Any one of these incidents could account for your chest tightness. However, your appraisal of the sensation and your subsequent behavior would vary depending on which event you had experienced. In other words, the identical internal sensation could be interpreted as two totally unrelated emotions—rejection or elation—or as indigestion or even a heart attack. Bodily information, then, may mean different things to different people at different times.

This chapter deals with how we interpret information pertaining to our bodies. Specific sensations, feelings, and general emotions are evaluated by appraising the state of our bodies within the context of the situations we encounter. The perceptual process by which we study our bodies and internal information is the same process by which we examine our external environment. The chapter begins with an overview of the basic process by which we perceive our world. We will then introduce issues that pertain to the interpretation of various emotions based on bodily information. We focus next on how various emotional and illness sets can influence our perceptions of internal sensations. Finally, implications and practical applications derived from recent work on emotions, health, and sensations will be discussed.

THE PERCEPTUAL PROCESS

Before discussing how we perceive vague internal sensations, we must address the more basic issue of how we perceive anything. For us to perceive stimuli in our environment, we must have sensory data and some way to organize the data. The sensory data may derive from vision receptors, sound waves hitting our eardrums, touch, and so on. The raw sensory data, however, have no intrinsic meaning. Rather, these data are organized within the brain. The organization process allows us to interpret meaningless sensations in terms of higher-order concepts. A jumble of sound waves from an orchestra becomes music. An array of lights, angles, and lines become a scene. The organization of sensory data, then, represents a constructive process (cf. Neisser, 1976).

This is not to say that the perceptual process is passive. Obviously, we do not sit around waiting for stimuli to impinge on our senses. Instead, we actively and selectively seek information from the environment. What sensory information we receive, then, is determined in part by the cognitions that we have already acquired. Sensory data are encoded according to previously encoded percepts or cognitions. Further, these cognitions (referred to as sets, schemas, or hypotheses) partially define which data we will subsequently pick up. Our appraisal of all information, then, represents an ongoing perceptual process (cf. Gibson, 1966; Newtson, 1976). We selectively search our environments to verify or disconfirm these sets. Similarly, information we get from the environment will constantly modify or create new sets or hypotheses. The perceptual process, then, is cyclical. We may start with information about the world which may create a tentative hypothesis— which, in turn, leads to a search for additional information pertinent to the hypothesis. The information we receive may alter the hypothesis, which will change later search behavior, and the cycle goes on and on.

An example of this process would be your search for your shoes when you awake in the morning. You have a specific set which guides your search behavior (i.e., where you look or focus your attention). You will actively search one part of a room, and if unsuccessful, create tentative hypotheses such as, "Did I leave the shoes hanging on the chandelier?" This hypothesis will direct future search behavior. In other words, sets direct search behavior. The information gleaned from the search will alter or create new sets. It should be emphasized that this process can start with information (rather than a specific set). For example, in looking for your shoes, you may discover a body under your bed. This external information will lead to new hypotheses (Is it alive?) and search behavior.

What does looking for your shoes have to do with the interpretation of internal states? As this chapter will demonstrate, we infer emotions, feelings, and illnesses from the perception of sensations. Conversely, we selectively attend to specific sensations if we have reason to believe we are in a situation that may be characteristic of a given emotion, feeling, or illness. That is, the interpretation of bodily state, like the interpretation of the environment, is an ongoing cyclical process.

To the reader unfamiliar with social psychology, the above discussion may appear to be common sense. However, a large part of social psychology's history has not considered the perceptual process. Rather, it has taken an isolated snapshot of behavior and has attempted to construct a simple cause-and-effect world. In reading much of the research in this chapter, you will see that a primary aim has been to establish the fact that perception of arousal sensations leads to a search for an explanation. Other studies have been concerned with the opposite process; an explanation or hypothesis leads to the search for confirming arousal sensations. Both approaches continue to be extremely important. As scientists, we are trying to understand an active and highly complex organism.

EMOTIONS, FEELINGS, AND ILLNESS AS INTERPRETATIONS

As suggested above, the perceptual process involves attempts to explain our internal feelings as well as to confirm beliefs we may have about our bodies. In this section, we will examine half of the perceptual process. We will assume that the individual first becomes aware of vague feelings of arousal, anxiety, or tension. How does the person evaluate these general sensations? In recent years, psychologists have learned that people will often attribute these internal feelings to a variety of emotions and even illness. These findings have radically altered how psychologists have traditionally defined and understood emotions.

We all have an intuitive idea of what an emotion is. If a psychologist gives us a questionnaire, we scarcely need to think in order to rate how happy, sad, angry, or jealous we feel at the time. How do you know what your emotion is? What information, if any, do you use? These questions have baffled philosophers, psychologists, and even physicians for centuries. The fact that emotions may be the result of a cognitive process is a relatively new idea. Historically, emotions have been considered as simple motives, physiological changes, or innate, prewired experiences. In order to understand the current status of the self-perception of emotions, feelings, and even illness, we must first trace the evolution of the various theoretical approaches.

EMOTION AS A MOTIVE

Common sense dictates that an emotion is important primarily in motivating us to act in one way or another. For example, a friend makes a rude gesture toward us; we get angry and punch the friend in the nose. We see a bear, become afraid, and run. In other words, the commonsense approach considers that we perceive the stimulus, then feel the emotion, and finally act on the emotion. Appealing and obvious as this process may be, it is usually not true. In many, if not most, cases we become aware of the emotion *after* and not before we act. The reader can envision a person's almost being hit by a car and immediately jumping out of the way. It is harder to imagine the car's careening toward the person and the person quietly thinking, "My goodness, here comes a car that will kill me. I am afraid. Therefore, I must jump out of the way." Clearly, if actions always followed emotions, the world would have more cars than people.

EMOTION AS PHYSIOLOGICAL CHANGE

One of the first detailed criticisms of the commonsense view was made by William James (1890). According to James, "the bodily changes follow directly the perception of the exciting fact, and . . . our feeling of the same changes as they occur *is* the emotion." In other words, physiological change was considered to be the emotion itself. In physiological terms, activity in various organs due to the autonomic nervous system (which would alter blood flow, heart rate, stomach contractions, etc.) follows immediately from a stimulus. This suggests, then, that we don't run from a bear because of fear. Rather, we are afraid because we run. In addition, the various emotions are distinguishable because each purportedly must have a unique physiological correlate.

The approach of James is quite appealing. It is extremely simple.

One does not have to make inferential leaps about how emotions could cause physiological change since the emotions are themselves the physiological change. Despite these advantages, James' theory suffers from only one problem: It is wrong. For example, injecting a person with adrenalin, or epinephrine (as it is called in the United States), causes physiological changes similar to fear. However, virtually no one reports feeling fear after such an injection. At best, when so injected, people can feel the change and might report that they felt "as if" they were afraid. However, they *know* that they are not experiencing fear (Marañon, 1924). These and other criticisms have seriously weakened the theory of emotion advanced by James.

EMOTION AS BRAIN ACTIVITY

The first viable alternative to James' position was advanced by Walter B. Cannon (1931). According to Cannon, emotion is the result of activity of the central nervous system (i.e., the brain). The emotional experience does not depend on autonomic or other physiological responses. Instead, the person sees the bear, and the image is processed in the brain. The brain dictates the perceived emotion on the one hand, the physiological response on the other. A basic shortcoming of this position is that it is difficult to prove or disprove. In addition, it stops short of explaining when and what emotions will be experienced. For example, *why* does seeing a bear elicit fear and not hunger? If emotions are prewired, as suggested by Cannon's approach, how can we predict which situations will elicit which emotions? Fortunately, a new approach to emotions was to follow which began to answer such questions.

EMOTION AS A COGNITIVE LABEL

In 1962, Stanley Schachter and Jerome Singer reported the results of two experiments which suggested a parsimonious and predictive explanation for emotions. According to their view, the individual first becomes aware of diffuse sensations of arousal, anxiety, or tension. If there is no immediate explanation for this arousal, he or she will label this state and describe these feelings in terms of the interpretations or cognitions available. If, on the other hand, the person does have an appropriate explanation for the arousal, no other explanation will be sought. Schachter and Singer (1962), then, propose that the experience of an emotion is dependent on physiological arousal and an appropriate cognitive label for that arousal.

A clever experiment was conducted to test this cognitive labeling idea. Subjects were told that the study sought to learn how a certain drug—"Suproxin"—affected vision. They received an injection of the Suproxin and were required to wait in another room with an experimental confederate while the drug supposedly took effect. In truth, the bogus drug was either epinephrine—which creates feelings of arousal, including a racing heart, flushed face, and trembling—or an inert placebo which had no physiological effect. Of the subjects receiving the epinephrine, one group was told the actual effects of the drug. That is, the physician injecting the drug explicitly told the subjects what sensations they would feel after the drug had taken effect (epinephrine informed condition). A second group was told nothing about the drug's side effects (epinephrine ignorant.) A third group was told that the injection would result in various irrelevant sensations, such as numbness in the feet (epinephrine misinformed). The placebo condition subjects, like the epinephrine ignorant ones, were told nothing about the possible side effects. In sum, there were four experimental conditions. In the epinephrine informed conditions, subjects had an immediate and reasonable explanation for their arousal symptoms; the epinephrine ignorant and epinephrine misinformed subjects had no clear explanation. The placebo subjects should not have had any arousal sensations and were not informed about side effects.

After receiving the injection together with an explanation (or lack thereof) of internal sensations, subjects were escorted to another room and introduced to an experimental confederate. The confederate had purportedly also received an injection and was waiting for the same vision experiment to begin. In truth, of course, the confederate was hired by the experimenters to make an emotion-related cognition available to the naive subjects. As soon as the experimenter left, the confederate began acting in a gleeful, euphoric manner. During the waiting period, he performed such antics as playing "paper basketball" by throwing wadded paper into a trash can, flying paper airplanes, making and using a sling-shot, and playing with a hula hoop. During the entire escapade, hidden observers recorded how much euphoric behavior each sub-ject engaged in or initiated. Following the experiment, subjects completed a questionnaire assessing their perceptions of their emo-tions during the study.

The predictions according to cognitive labeling theory are clear. Subjects in the epinephrine informed condition could explain any feelings of internal sensations as being due to their injection. Sub-jects in the epinephrine ignorant and epinephrine misinformed conditions, however, could not readily explain their arousal-related sensations. The most available interpretation was the screwball be-havior of the confederate. Consequently, after subjects in these two conditions became aware of their arousal, they would label it as euphoria or excitement. Observers' ratings of subjects' euphoric behavior conformed closely to the predictions. And, as shown in Figure 4.1, subjects' self-reports of euphoria showed the same pat-tern. The major deviation was for subjects in the placebo condi-tion. Theoretically they should not have been aroused and conse-

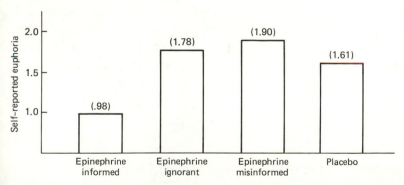

FIGURE 4.1. Self-reports of euphoria. (Based on data from Schachter and Singer, 1962)

quently should not have had to label anything. Apparently, however, their receiving an injection or simply participating in such a study may have produced some anxiety which was later labeled euphoria.

The results of this and other studies support the cognitive labeling view. We first become aware of our arousal and then seek an appropriate explanation for it. The cognitive labeling approach intrigues many scientists because it is simple and makes the assumption that all emotions are physiologically general and indistinguishable. For example, moods of anger and fear, as well as euphoria, have been induced with injections of epinephrine within the contexts of an appropriate emotional label.

As discussed in the first section, the cognitive labeling perspective assumes that in the perception of emotion, arousal is followed by the search for a label. The process is a unidirectional causal sequence. Before discussing evidence that the process may work in reverse as well (i.e., the person first becomes aware of a label and then seeks validating sensations), we will present recent derivations of the cognitive labeling point of view.

EXTENSIONS OF COGNITIVE LABELING

Schachter and Singer's (1962) cognitive labeling theory caught the imagination of several social psychologists. Such diverse emotions or mood states as interpersonal attraction, love, aggression, and crowding have been posited as resulting from the labeling of generalized internal arousal. These lines of research—often referred to as *misattribution*—typically demonstrate that arousal from an irrelevant source can be attributed to any available label.

INTERPERSONAL ATTRACTION

Liking other people or stimuli can occasionally be due to the misattribution of internal sensations. The first demonstration of this was provided by Valins (1966). In his study, male college students observed several slides of attractive nude females. During the slides, the students heard the sound of what they thought was their own heartbeat broadcast over loudspeakers. In fact, everyone heard the same tape-recorded heartbeats that had been synchronized with the slide presentation. For some of the slides the heartbeat accelerated, whereas for other slides the beat did not change. Valins found that students preferred the nudes that were associated with increases in heart rate. Presumably, subjects were attributing their *perceived* (and not actual) physiological change to the pictures. This is a particularly important study for cognitive labeling theory in that it demonstrated that perceived rather than actual physiological change is the crucial variable for the labeling phenomenon to occur. In addition, this and later studies by Valins indicated that the process represented an ongoing perceptual process wherein subjects were actively testing a variety of hypotheses whenever they heard the changes in heart rate. Rather than automatically assuming that they preferred the nude, the subjects would inspect the nude more closely. For example, when hearing a change in the bogus heartbeat, the subject would look more closely and decide, "I like this one because her eyes are so nice." The subjects, then, would now be more motivated to find something distinctive about the nude that was associated with heart rate change.

A recent derivation of the misattribution or labeling of an internal state as it relates to attraction took place in a rather unlikely place. Over the Capilano River in British Columbia, Canada, are two bridges that were the scene of a psychology experiment. One is a narrow, swinging, wobbly suspension bridge which hovers 230 feet over a rocky canyon; the other is a safe, solid bridge only 10 feet above a calm brook. Dutton and Aron (1974) had an attractive female approach male subjects while they walked across one of the two bridges. She asked the subject to complete a short questionnaire pertaining to some pictures of people. In addition, she gave him her phone number in case he ever wanted to know the final results of the study. The authors predicted that subjects who were on the high bridge would be much more aroused than those on the low one. Further, this increased arousal would be attributed to the female experimenter as interpersonal (i.e., sexual) attraction. The predictions were confirmed in two ways. First, subjects on the high bridge more often tended to see sexual themes in the pictures. More important, 50 percent of the subjects on the high bridge later called the woman, whereas only 12 percent of those on the low bridge did so. Arousal from a naturally occurring source, then, can be misdirected (or redirected) to another plausible source.

The adage "I knew I was in love because my heart skipped a beat" has a ring of truth. The cognitive labeling view implies that to promote love, each partner should be arousing to the other. Consequently, on your next date, drink plenty of coffee, run in place, or perhaps have a wreck. With any luck, the arousal will be attributed as love—or at least infatuation.

AGGRESSION

On the other side of the coin is research indicating that arousal from extraneous sources can be directed toward hate, degradation, and senseless violence. In a recent extension of cognitive labeling, Zillman (1978) has shown that arousal from strenuous physical exercise can subsequently be attributed to anger and aggression if the person is insulted by an experimental confederate. This misattribution, or excitation transfer, is most likely to occur several minutes after the exercise. Immediately after running in place, a person typically knows why the heart is racing or the breathing rate has increased. Several minutes later, however, the arousal still exists but the person thinks he or she is now calm. During this phase, then, the person is most likely to be subject to the cognitive labeling phenomenon. A real-world analogue to this can be seen just after drinking a cup of coffee. If you then read a newspaper editorial that disagrees with the way you appraise the world, you will probably assume any arousal sensations are due to the coffee rather than to the editorial. However, if you saw the same editorial five minutes after finishing the coffee, you might attribute your caffiene-caused arousal to the inane editorial. With coffee out of sight, anger at the editor could come to mind.

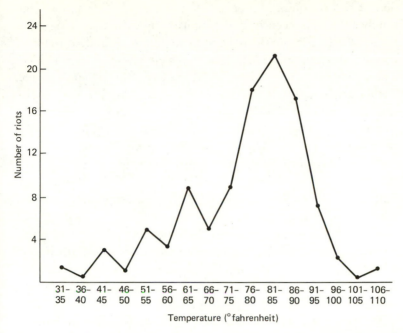

FIGURE 4.2. Frequency of collective violence (riots) as a function of ambient temperature. (From Baron and Ransberger, 1978. Copyright © 1978 by the American Psychological Association. Reprinted by permission.)

Some particularly intriguing work has recently surfaced concerning misattribution and the occurrence of riots. In various laboratory studies, individuals who sit in moderately hot, humid rooms are more likely subsequently to aggress against others if provoked than if they have been sitting in cool, comfortable rooms or extremely hot and miserable ones. In other words, there is a curvilinear relationship between room temperature and aggression. Up to a point (mid- to upper 80s F), the higher the temperature, the more likely that person will be in a foul mood and aggress against others. However, above temperatures in the high 80s, the tendency to aggress decreases. Presumably it is simply too hot, and perhaps any feelings of anger are now attributed to the heat rather than to another person (cf. Baron, 1978). In an extension of this reasoning, Baron and Ransberger (1978) plotted the number the riots occurring at various temperatures in U.S. cities from 1967 to 1971. As can be seen in Figure 4.2, a near-perfect curvilinear relationship emerged, peaking around 86° to 90°F. These findings substantiate the cognitive labeling perspective. Temperatures in the upper 80s are uncomfortable but not oppressive. Because individuals are only moderately aroused, they tend to attribute the arousal to any available external source. Above a certain point, however, the individual can easily discern that his or her arousal is caused by the heat rather than another person. Note that these findings parallel those of Zillman. Misattribution appears to work best when arousal is barely perceptible rather than when its true cause is obvious.

The reader can begin to grasp the expanding scope of cognitive labeling theory and misattribution. In recent years, misattribution models of hunger and eating (Schachter & Rodin, 1974), smoking (Schachter, 1977), crowding (Worchel & Teddlie, 1976), phobias (Nisbett & Valins, 1971), and many other emotions or internal states have been posited. Very simply, each model assumes that the individual becomes aroused for one reason or another. The arousal is then attributed to whatever stimulus provides a good explanation or label for it.

ILLNESS AS AN INTERPRETATION

Although cognitive labeling theory was conceived to explain emotion, it has been applied to several nonemotional body states. One of the more intriguing developments is the idea that perceptions of illness are often labeled in the same way as emotion. People become aware of vague or ambiguous internal sensations and, if they are exposed to an appropriate label, will define the sensations as illness or disease (Mechanic, 1972). Although the labeling of illness has not been directly tested, several real-world occurrences support this view. Two of these—medical students' disease and hysterical contagion—are of special interest.

The first year of medical school is highly stressful and physically exhausting. Students are constantly evaluated, get little sleep, and enter a totally new social and work environment. Consequently, they are constantly physiologically aroused, tense, or drained. An interesting phenomenon among these students is that they sometimes contract the physical symptoms of the diseases they study. In fact, medical students' disease affects about 70 percent of all first-year medical students. As can be deduced from cognitive labeling theory or the principles of misattribution, the students will occasionally overlook the true sources of their tension or arousal. Merely reading about the various obscure illnesses provides an available sickness label. The arousal sensations are then interpreted as the disease.

Another example of the misattribution of illness, called *hysterical contagion*, often affects large groups of people at a time. In one of the first reported incidents, a large textile company was forced to close when about 40 of the 200 workers became ill during the height of the production season. A large number were hospitalized due to symptoms such as dizziness, nausea, and profuse sweating. No physiological evidence for the illness was found for any worker. In a careful analysis of the incident, Kerckhoff and Back (1968) found that the employees were under great stress. Further, after seeing the first person become sick, many others automatically attributed their own stress-induced arousal to illness. In addition, a false rumor in the factory quickly started indicating that the "disease" was caused by invisible bugs that had arrived with the imported raw materials from South America. In other words, seeing people become sick, together with plausible rumors about the bugs (which could not immediately be disproven), provided a suitable illness label for the tense, overworked employees.

Interestingly, hysterical contagion occurs much more frequently than most people think. Factories, prisons, and even grade schools are the scenes of mass psychogenic illness. Recent government studies indicate that the initial arousal can be due to such things as noise, poor lighting, stress from too much overtime work, or poor worker-management relations. The illness contagion will typically start when one worker collapses or perhaps vomits. Those who see the first worker become sick and who may be friends with the worker typically succumb to the disease next. After the first few people feel sick, the illness spreads progressively faster, often appearing to be a virulent epidemic.

Illness can be labeled in much the same way as a variety of emotions. According to Schachter and Singer's (1962) original formulation, the individual first becomes aware of internal arousal and subsequently seeks to label the arousal. The label can be an emotion—euphoria, anger, love—or an illness. Further, the label that will be adopted may come from seeing another person, a unique situation, or even reading about a potential cause of the arousal.

As powerful a theory as cognitive labeling has proven to be, it neglects the fact that individuals do not passively notice arousal and then label it. Instead, they are constantly paying attention to their external and internal environments in an attempt to perceive their worlds accurately. Although individuals do, in fact, often label diffuse arousal, they sometimes *first* become aware of a label and *then* seek out internal information that pertains to the label. The following section deals with this second part of the perceptual process related to the interpretation of emotions and health.

INTERPRETATIONS AND SEARCH BEHAVIOR

As has been suggested, the perceptual process often begins with a given label or interpretation which, in turn, results in a search for information to validate the interpretation. The label can guide our focus of attention and the information we pick out. The Seattle Windshield Pitting Incident serves as a good beginning example (Medalia & Larsen, 1958).

In April, 1954, intermittent newspaper and radio reports indicated that several automobile windshields in Seattle had small pits about the size of a fingernail. Although no explanations for the pits could be verified, various reports implicated such things as fallout from a recent hydrogen bomb test, meteoric dust, vandalism, or simply gravel from the roads. After several days of media reports, the number of people calling the police increased dramatically. Within a two-day period, individuals claimed damages to more than 3,000 cars. The pitting sightings became so frequent that the mayor of Seattle appealed to the governor and to President Dwight D. Eisenhower for help. Within three days, the pitting reports ended as abruptly as they began. What caused this massive destruction to the automobile windows? Later analyses indicated that the windshield pits had been there all along, caused mainly by gravel and road damage. The radio and newspaper publicity caused people to look *at* their windshields for the first time, instead of *through* them. Their search behavior, which had been prompted by the media, led to the acquiring of information supporting the idea that something mysterious was tampering with the city of Seattle.

The Seattle Windshield Pitting Incident is an unusual example of how our attention to and perception of events is affected by the labels we confront. In this section, we will discuss how cognitive labels or interpretations affect search behavior. Specifically, we will examine how this perceptual process is related to our encoding or picking up bodily information and internal sensations. We will then discuss evidence suggesting that the cognitive interpretations we adopt can radically alter the perceptions of the sensations themselves. Finally, the theories and data from both sections of the chapter will be integrated within a larger perceptual model of the interpretation of internal states.

EMOTIONAL LABELS

What sensations are associated with the various emotions? For example, are there any differences in physical symptoms between feeling angry versus afraid? As will be recalled from the research by Schachter and Singer (1962), there *should not* be a physical difference in emotions. People can be made to feel either happy or angry with an injection of epinephrine. The same physiological change has been shown to underlie totally different emotions. From a commensense perspective, these findings seem somehow wrong. For example, when angry, we feel our face flush. When afraid, we tremble. Love is associated with our heart skipping a beat. In our daily lives, then, we usually associate emotions with specific sensations.

Empirically, too, researchers have indicated that emotions are related to the perception of specific sensations. In several experiments, Pennebaker (1979) has demonstrated that various manipulated emotions correlate with specific self-perceptions of sensations. For example, tension is correlated with a racing heart, sore muscles, and shortness of breath. Guilt is associated with an upset stomach and a lump in one's throat. Research by psychophysiologists demonstrates that actual physiological change, too, is related to certain emotional states. A person who feels threatened will evince increased blood pressure. One who is made to feel mistreated and helpless shows changes in skin temperature (Graham, Kabler, & Graham, 1962). Others have shown specific physiological changes with anger and fear (cf. Sternbach, 1966). In sum, there is evidence that unique perceived and actual physiological changes are associated with specific emotions.

How do these findings square with the cognitive labeling view, which implies that all emotions are physiologically similar? The answer lies in the perceptual process. That is, individuals can monitor specific sensations in helping them deduce their emotion. For example, in the Schachter and Singer research, the epinephrine injection brings about gross autonomic activity. If an individual thinks she may be mad, she will attend to her flushed face and racing heart and conclude that she *is* mad. If she has reason to think she is afraid, she may attend to her general trembling and conclude that she is afraid. In other words, we attend to specific bodily sites in order to verify our emotions. At any given time, there is evidence to support our perceptions of any of several emotions. However, we are attending to specific physiological locations and ignoring other sensations which may be irrelevant to the emotion we seek to verify.

This indicates that our perception of an emotion is part of an active perceptual process. In many cases, we confront a special emotional label *prior* to becoming aware of internal sensations. We may tentatively adopt the label or set and then attend to specific sensations to verify or disconfirm the set. An example of this process can be seen with people who are sitting in a classroom just prior to taking a difficult examination. The students are tense and anxious. They may have ingested a great deal of coffee and had little sleep. If a social psychologist asked them why they were aroused, they would respond accurately. According to cognitive labeling theory, then, they should not be motivated to seek additional labels for their arousal. Nevertheless, people in this situation laugh hysterically at the most pathetic jokes, cry at the drop of a hat, and show anger at the slightest provocation. Either these students are abysmally ignorant of the principles of cognitive labeling and attribution theories *or* another process is going on. Whenever the person in this state hears a joke, hears a sad story, or is insulted (i.e., becomes aware of a label), he or she looks inward to see if there is any physiological arousal to verify the emotion. Because the person is generally aroused, confirming information is found. The label, then, leads to highly specific monitoring of internal sensations. The purpose of the bodily search is often to validate a specific emotional label.

ILLNESS LABELS

As would be expected, an illness label or set can also lead to specific bodily search behavior. We are reminded of an illness and then search our bodies to see if we have it. An example of this can be seen when a sick friend visits us. Imagine that your friend remarks that he has a sore throat. Often we will immediately pay attention to our own throats to see if ours, too, might be sore. The label provided by our sick friend prompts us to "check out" our own bodies.

A recent experiment supports this chain of behavior. College students were asked to complete a questionnaire ascertaining the degree to which they were experiencing each of a dozen physical symptoms (e.g., headache, racing heart, itching). Prior to completing the questionnaire, half of the subjects read a statement which noted that "this is the time of the year when we are surrounded by flu and other illness-producing organisms." The other half (the control group) did not read this seemingly innocuous statement. It was found that those reading about the flu season reported many more symptoms than the control group. Further, the increased symptom reporting occurred only for flu-related symptoms (e.g., headache, nasal congestion) rather than for symptoms unrelated to the flu. Merely reading about a specific illness resulted in the monitoring of specific body locations (Burnam & Pennebaker, 1979).

Cognitive labels or interpretive sets, then, are used in evaluating sensations related to emotion or illness. The sets determine where we will focus our attention and greatly restrict the quantity and quality of information that we pick up. One final puzzle must be addressed in examining the perceptual process. How does attending to internal sensations alter our perceptions of them? As will be shown, the answer lies in the nature of the interpretation.

PERCEPTION OF SENSATIONS

At this point, we must stand back and review this process. Our perception of emotions or illness is a cyclical process. We use situational factors from the environment together with sensation information from our bodies in defining our emotional state and health. We alternately use both sources of information. We may first become aware of internal sensations associated with arousal and subsequently attempt to explain or interpret the sensations using whatever cues or labels are available. Schachter and Singer (1962) validated this process in their testing of the cognitive labeling theory. In addition to this process, we may first become aware of a cue or label associated with emotion or illness and then focus our attention on our bodies in order to confirm the label. Because this is a highly active perceptual process, both ways of interpreting internal and external cues are constantly used. The final link in understanding the process deals with the effects of attending to internal sensations. Does merely attending to the sensations alter their perception? Alternatively, must we have a specific set or label when analyzing the sensations before their perception alters? Recent experiments support the second view—that an interpretive set or schema pertaining to bodily sensations can radically alter their perception.

Do various internal sensations seem to magnify when you pay attention to them? For example, if you attend to your nose and nasal passages, does the experience of congestion increase? A recent series of experiments indicates that the answer is no. Rather, it is the *way* you attend to sensations rather than attention *per se* that determines the magnitude and aversiveness of sensations (Pennebaker & Skelton, 1979). For example, in one study people were instructed to attend to their nose and nasal passages in one of three ways: simply focus attention on the nasal passages (attention only condition), attend to sensations associated with difficulty in breathing (nose negative), attend to sensations associated with free breathing (nose positive). A fourth control group did not think about their noses at all. People's perception of congestion did not alter if they merely attended to their noses. However, if they focused on the negative aspects of breathing, they thought their nose was more congested. Interestingly, 30 percent of the subjects in the nose negative condition blew their nose following the study, whereas no one else did so. People in the nose positive condition, on the other hand, reported that their noses became significantly less congested following the attention manipulation. The set by which the people evaluated their nasal sensations, then, radically altered the perception of congestion.

A similar study was conducted on perceptions of heart rate. People were instructed to think about their heart rate's increasing in speed, decreasing in speed, or were simply told to think about their heartbeat. Again, the way people evaluated their heartbeats radically altered perceptions of whether or not their hearts were accelerating or decelerating. Merely attending to one's heartbeat without a given set did not change the perception of the rate. Physiological measures indicated that there were no differences in actual heart rate across the three conditions. These findings are important; they demonstrate that the *way* you attend to a sensation will affect the raw perception.

These findings indicate that a given label—whether emotional or illness related—will dramatically affect any sensations that we expect to be related to the label. Referring back to the example used at the beginning of the chapter, we can see how perceptions of the cause of chest tightness could alter the mere perception of the sensation itself. If we have just received a million dollars and then notice the chest tightness, we might assume that the sensation represents euphoria and is thus benign. However, if we have been told that we have a heart condition and then feel the chest sensation, it will probably be perceived as a painful and threatening event rather than as representing a particular emotion. The important factor to keep in mind is that the label or set that we use at any given time will subsequently affect perceptions of our internal sensations.

SUMMARY

How we evaluate emotions, illness, and internal sensations is not a simple process. We have traced the evolution of several approaches, each of which has aided in our understanding. William James pointed out that emotions are not simply motives that guide behavior. Further, he speculated that the understanding of emotion is tied to physiological processes. Shortcomings of his physiological argument were examined by Cannon. Schachter and Singer added the crucial dimension of cognitive factors in the emotional experience. Their cognitive labeling theory is an ingenious and useful model for our knowledge of the attribution of a variety of emotions, feelings, and even health. Recent advances in cognitive/perceptual psychology and psychophysiology now point to a new modification of cognitive labeling.

Individuals constantly evaluate and act upon their environment. Perception is highly active. Clearly, as the cognitive labeling view has shown, individuals seek to evaluate unexplained internal sensations or arousal. However, they do not passively await changes in internal states. Often they confront an emotional situation—they hear a joke, see a movie or a football game—and *then* survey their bodies to determine if they are indeed happy or sad. Our encoding, evaluating, and selectively seeking information is a constant process. The perception of emotion and internal state reflects this active perceptual process.

A second source of converging evidence for a modification of emotion theories derives from work on the physiological concomitants of emotion and health. It has been established that there are distinctive perceived and actual physiological changes with certain emotions (e.g., anger versus fear). It is difficult to determine how subtle these physiological processes may be. We are not yet at the stage of physiologically separating such similar emotions as guilt versus shame, for example. However, advances in psychophysiology are promising. Ironically, these advances may indicate that modern psychology may have been too harsh on William James. Clearly, there *is* a cognitive component to emotion which James overlooked. However, the physiological-emotional link may be stronger than was recently thought.

Where do we currently stand on the self-perception of emotion and the interpretation of internal sensations? We know that individuals seek to explain their internal sensations. In so doing, they survey their environment to find a plausible label. This label can be a raw emotion such as glee or anger, a feeling such as hunger or crowdedness, or even an illness or disease. We also know that the person sometimes confronts a situation that could be associated with a label; in this case, he or she may attend to internal sensations in order to confirm or disconfirm the label. Finally, this attention to sensations represents a highly selective search for validating information. This would suggest, then, that we may be more likely to encode label-relevant information than irrelevant or disconfirming data. In sum, the perception of emotion, health, and internal sensations themselves is based on the appraisal of information from both the external environmental and internal sensory worlds.

5

The Self in Thought and Memory

HAZEL MARKUS
UNIVERSITY OF MICHIGAN

Our social worlds are tremendously complex; the sheer variety of information available at any time is vastly greater than most people can attend to or even begin to understand. Whether we lead romantic and adventurous lives, haunted by the idea that we "only go around once," or more mundane and plodding existences of too much work, too little sleep, and lost car keys, there is so much information (both about ourselves and other people) potentially available for our attention and organization that we have to be selective. It is impossible for us to make *all* possible inferences, connections, and conclusions. Instead, we focus on those aspects of the social environment that we need to attend to or those that stand out in some way.

Exactly what is seen as distinctive in the social world is, of course, highly variable. It depends on who we are, how we are feeling, and the time, place, and circumstances. Quite frequently the object of our attention is another person or other people, but very often (and some might argue most often) we think about ourselves. Judging from the deluge of popular literature telling us how to pull our own strings, how to be our own best friend, and how to look out for number one, we appear to live now in an age of unprecedented narcissism in which we are thinking about ourselves more than ever. Even the most relentlessly altruistic and apparently selfless among us seem unable to resist information that promises to be self-revealing or relevant to the self in some way.

One of the clearest examples of how the self stands out in our thoughts and memory is known in psychology as the *cocktail party effect*. In a crowded room where many conversations are in progress simultaneously, it is usually possible to make sense only of the conversation you are directly involved in. But should someone say your name, you are virtually certain to hear it, and to orient yourself immediately in that direction, even if it is some distance across the room. This phenomenon has been investigated in the laboratory (Moray, 1959) using a technique known as the dichotic listening procedure; the subject is given headphones and is asked to shadow or listen to a message that is given in one ear and to repeat this message phrase by phrase. This is a very difficult task. Nearly total concentration is needed to repeat the phrase one has just heard, while at the same time listening for the new phrase. While the subject is involved in this task, other information is presented to the unattended ear. The usual finding here is that the subject has no awareness of any information being presented other than the story being shadowed. But if the subject's own name is given in the unattended ear, just as at the cocktail party, the subject can attend to it immediately. Only information that is directly and specifically self-relevant can break through the attentional barrier the subject sets up to perform the shadowing task efficiently. In this case, self-relevant information appears to have unequaled power in grabbing our attention. And, in general, when thinking about the social world, the self is quite likely to be distinctive and of particular interest to us.

This chapter is concerned with thinking about the self—how we organize our own behavior, how we describe it, and how we remember it. It also considers whether thinking about ourselves is special and whether we distort or bias information about ourselves.

SOCIAL INFORMATION PROCESSING

Thinking about ourselves and others is not a simple process; it involves a number of different steps. *Information processing* in the social world involves scanning the social world, selecting certain aspects or features of it to focus on, categorizing, describing, and organizing this information, integrating it with other knowledge stored in memory, using the information to make some kind of decision, judgment, or action, and finally storing this information so that it can be retrieved for use later on. If you are reading this book in a place where there are other people, look across the room, pick out someone, and decide whether you like this person. You probably can do this with very little difficulty and with almost no hestitation. But when you analyze it, you can see that even though the whole process seemed to be quite automatic, in order to make a judgment about whether you liked the person it was necessary for you to perform many mental operations of the type described above. In fact, it is quite remarkable that as information processors we can perform so many operations so quickly. Information processing involves a series of steps, each of which transforms, elaborates, or reduces the incoming information in some way. It is an active, constructive process that involves an interaction of the person (and what is inside his or her head) with the stimulus material. The processes of perceiving, thinking, and feeling are not all-or-none, unitary processes but rather elaborate sequential processes. We may not be consciously aware of all the steps, and we may not be able to describe or talk about them, but it is important to realize that they are occurring and that each of these steps can be influenced by a variety of factors.

When we are concerned with how people process information, we are concerned with *cognitive* processes; it may then be said that we are taking a cognitive approach. *Cognition* means the act or process of knowing; it is often used interchangeably with the words *perception, thinking,* and *understanding.* When taking a cognitive approach to psychology, we are interested in how people think and come to understand their world, and how they use their knowledge to guide their decisions and actions.

COGNITIVE REPRESENTATIONS

Psychologists or researchers who take a cognitive approach are concerned with how information is represented, with the internal pictures or organization of the world. Since the external stimuli themselves obviously cannot get inside the individual's head, it is the internal description or representation of these stimuli that we call information, and it is the nature and content of these representations that concern cognitive psychologists (for a more complete discussion, see Bower, 1974).

The cognitive approach assumes that if we are to understand or predict another individual's behavior, we must first understand how this individual cognitively represents or structures the world. It is not enough just to observe actions; we must understand what these actions mean to the individual and how he or she thinks about them. Two people may engage in what seems to be the same behavior from an observer's point of view, but this behavior may have very different meanings for the two people involved and very different consequences for future actions. And this can be true for virtually all behavior; as one popular song reminds us, "Some dance to remember, some dance to forget." To understand behavior, it is important to understand an individual's frame of reference—the system used to categorize, organize, and understand data from the social world, whether it is about the self or about other people and events.

As information processors, we cannot, at any one point in time, represent everything in the social world; we have to be selective. This selectivity is determined by our past knowledge and experience. We assume that the representations of our past experiences are categorized or organized into structures in our minds that can be called *knowledge structures*. These structures contain conceptually similar or related material, and we use them as a basis for organizing or interpreting new information. They can function as guidelines or maps that tell the perceiver when to look, what to look for, and what it means. These structures can also serve as hypotheses that suggest how the individual should interpret information. In short, knowledge structures are built up from information processed in the past and influence both the input and the output of information. When we look across the library and notice Poindexter, the dumb kid from high school, and wonder how he ever got to college, we are activating a large number of different knowledge structures. In fact, most of the information contained in these thoughts is not immediately provided by the external stimulus itself (Poindexter) but rather by knowledge we supply to the stimuli. Once established, knowledge structures determine whether information is attended to, how it is organized, how much importance is attached to it, and what happens to it subsequently. Thus, if Poindexter comes up with an "A" on the chemistry midterm, it is because the test was easy or because he cheated. There is little chance that the good grade will be seen as evidence for his natural ability or increased motivation.

SCHEMAS

Knowledge structures which we develop to represent the external world provide guidelines about how to interpret incoming data. Without the organization provided by these structures, no perception or thinking would be possible. Throughout the study of cognition and perception, these structures have been given a variety of names. They have been called theories, hypotheses, plans, maps, sets, and expectations, to name only a few, and have been associated with many different theoretical and empirical approaches. But although different in their details, they are similar in that they all involve an organization and integration of past knowledge for use in interpreting future input. One term that is currently being used for these structures which encode and represent knowledge is *schemas*. According to Neisser (1976), a schema is a structure "internal to the perceiver, modifiable by experience, and somehow specific to what is being perceived. The schema accepts the information as it becomes available and is changed by that information; it [the schema] directs movement and exploratory activities that make more information available by which it is further modified" (p. 554). Thus, a schema first operates to specify the nature and organization of information that will fit or be picked up. It also operates like a plan or a guide for directing activity relevant to the schema. Most importantly, however, a schema can be viewed not only as the "plan but also as the executor of the plan. It is a pattern *of* action as well as a pattern *for* action" (p. 56). Neisser asserts that when looking at and thinking about the world, perceivers will "pick up only what they have schemas for and willy-nilly ignore the rest" (p. 80).

THE DEVELOPMENT OF SCHEMAS

The idea of a schema has been very important to Piaget (1954) in his work on how the young child constructs reality and comes to understand the world. Piaget assumes that the infant at first constructs only a few basic and simple images but soon learns to organize these images and to attach meaning to them. For Piaget, the central problem of development is the process by which the very simple structures available soon after birth are combined, elaborated, and modified to become like the complex structures characterizing the adult. He assumes that development does not stop at the conventional age of adulthood but rather continues indefinitely as we form new schemas and integrate and recombine old ones. For both the child and the adult, it is necessary to achieve a harmony with the world. To do this, two processes are involved. The first is *assimilation,* which means acting on the world and changing the available stimuli so that they fit one's schemas; the second is *accommodation,* which means changing one's structures or schemas so they are more harmonious or better representations of the world. These two general processes characterize all structures, whether we are developing a schema for the recognition of words or a schema to understand why we are so hesitant to speak up in class.

Early in a child's life, most of the schemas that are developed are in relation to the self; Piaget calls this *egocentrism.* For the young child it is difficult, if not impossible, to understand that there are other ways to look at things or points of view other than one's own. Egocentrism is not selfishness, merely an inability to take the perspective of another person. Young children assume that everyone thinks about the world just as they do. Piaget observes that children in the egocentric state often carry on whole conversations with themselves in which they do not appear to address their remarks to anyone in particular or to expect an answer. Such egocentrism is found in about 60 percent of speech by three-year-olds but in only about 30 percent of speech by seven-year-olds. Children are not assumed to be capable of logical thought until they can appreciate that others can have types of schemas different from their own, or until they can understand that how they feel and think may not be the same for others.

FUNCTION OF SCHEMAS

As children grow less egocentric, they begin to differentiate the social world more finely and to develop many more structures for thinking about other people. Schemas about the social world are developed as we learn to summarize or generalize about social behavior. Schemas develop from the repeated similar categorization and evaluation of behavior. We may construct, for example, a schema about the social world that says that under most circumstances, "my friend's friend will also be a friend of mine." When we have this schema, we have a theory about the social world that structures incoming social stimuli and allows us to make inferences from scant information and "to go beyond the information given" (Bruner, 1973). It allows us quickly to streamline and interpret complex sequences of events. Thus, contained in this schema about the social world, I have an entire series of organized expectations about a friend of my friend that I'm about to meet. These expectations will direct my behavior with respect to the new acquaintance. My behavior might be quite different if I did not hold this schema, or if I did not have the knowledge that the person I was about to have lunch with was a friend of my friend.

Based on this schema about how the social world is organized, plus my schema that says friends are usually similar in many ways, I can assume that this person will probably laugh at my jokes, like Mexican food as my friend and I do (or at least will be pleasant enough not to make a scene if he doesn't), be relatively easygoing, and no doubt have a number of interesting things to say. These types of expectations and anticipations will shape what I say to this person and will provide me with a frame of reference for interpreting his behavior. Thus when this new person, upon finishing lunch, gets out his calculator and says that we should each figure out exactly how much each one owes, instead of simply splitting it three ways, I will give him the benefit of the doubt. I will chalk up this behavior to the fact that he is a struggling student who needs every penny for tuition. Were he not a friend of my friend, I might be likely to categorize this same behavior as penny-pinching and cheap.

Schemas, then, are the basis of the selectivity that operates in information processing. And although we use words like "generalization" or "theory" to describe these structures, it is probably best to avoid the idea that there is a final, complete product located somewhere in the individual's head. One of the defining features of schemas is that they exist in dynamic interdependence with the environment. This means that schemas direct activity relevant to themselves and are in turn modified by this activity as it occurs. A schema, then, is never the same twice. Schemas are continually changed and updated as they are used as a basis for judgments, decisions, inferences, and predictions.

PROCESSING INFORMATION ABOUT OURSELVES

Many current approaches to personality and the study of the self share the cognitive point of view. Thus, they are concerned with how external events are perceived, how they are structured, how much importance is attached to them, and how they are organized for future use. These approaches all emphasize the active cognitive organization that is characteristic of the developing self.

A COGNITIVE APPROACH TO THE SELF

Many theorists, such as Kelly (1955), Sarbin (1968) and more recently Epstein (1973) and Coopersmith (1977), have explicitly considered the self as a cognitive structure or set of structures that organize, modify, and integrate functions of the person. Viewing the self as a set of cognitive structures or schemas that have an extremely important and powerful role in organizing an individual's experiences helps to demystify the concept of the self. We do not have to think of the self as an ephemeral concept like the soul. A cognitive structure approach helps us to be more specific about the self and allows us to investigate it. Probably the most difficult aspect of the problem of conceptualizing the self is how to represent the *self as a structure* and the *self as a process* within the same description. This problem goes back at least to William James (1890/1968), who noted that there were two distinct aspects of the self—"the self as the *knower* and the self as that which is *known*" (p. 48). More recently, Gordon (1968) has also tried to emphasize these two components of the self. He writes that the self "is a complex process of continuing interpretative activity—simultaneously the person's located subjective stream of consciousness—and the resultant accruing structure of self-conceptions" (p. 162). Theorists who take a cognitive approach try to appreciate these two features of the self; they assume that the self is very similar to a schema as defined by Neisser (1976). The self is thought to be the pattern for action (process) and also the pattern of action (structure). Although researchers hope to understand the process or "knower" part of the self, they focus their research primarily on the "known," or what Gordon calls the "resultant accruing structure." The self is investigated as a set of knowledge structures. This definition not only allows investigators to operationalize the self but helps provide some empirical meaning for the ideas of some of the most influential self theorists. For example, Carl Rogers (1951) takes a cognitive approach, viewing the self as "an organized, fluid, but consistent conceptual pattern of perceptions of characteristics and relationships of the 'I' and of the 'me'" (p. 498).

SELF-SCHEMAS

Central to a cognitive analysis of the self is the idea that people are different because their cognitive structures or schema systems are different. Individuals can organize and describe their own behavior in a variety of ways. We will selectively attend to certain features of our behavior while completely disregarding others. We can, for example, attend to our physical selves and notice hair with split ends, bloodshot eyes, or clothes that need washing. Alternatively, or perhaps simultaneously, we can focus on a variety of abilities and preferences, noting that we like to play racquetball, put in a respectable effort at backgammon, enjoy listening to jazz and eating hot, spicy foods. We can also make some subtle and complex observations about our own behavior—that we become very anxious when speaking in class, that try as we may, we are never quite on time for appointments, or that we are generous, independent, or creative. Thinking about our own behavior involves schemas about the self or knowledge structures that are developed to understand, integrate, or explain our own behavior in a particular area. Self-schemas develop from the repeated similar categorization and evaluation of behavior by oneself and others, and result in a clear idea of the kind of person one is in a particular area of behavior. Such structures enable individuals to understand their own social experiences and to integrate a wide range of stimulus information about the self into meaningful patterns. They also direct attention to behavior that is informative of these aspects of the self.

DEVELOPMENT OF SELF-SCHEMAS

The ability to recognize and differentiate the self as a separate entity is thought to develop gradually as the child masters all of the relevant cognitive activities. Although there is some controversy on this point, a structure of the self is thought to emerge in the child around two years of age (Bertenthal & Fischer, 1978). The development of self-recognition in the infant has been studied with the aid of a mirror. When an infant responds to a rouge mark on his or her nose by immediately reaching for the nose instead of the mirror, we can be fairly certain the infant understands that it is the self that is being reflected. Lewis and Brooks (1978) found, for example, that 75 percent of the twenty-one- to twenty-five-month infants they studied touched their rouge-marked noses when held up to a mirror, but that only 25 percent of the nine- to twelve-month-old infants did.

Following the development of self-recognition, infants will continue to form structures or schemas around those aspects of the self which are regarded as important. Researchers who have studied the development of self-conception find that with increasing age the child's conception of the self seems to become more abstract (Livesley & Bromley, 1973; Montemayor & Eisen, 1977). They assume that some aspects of the self-concept can be understood by asking a child to describe himself or herself. Using a task that asks the child to respond to the question "Who am I?" they found that young children describe themselves in objective, concrete terms, such as their appearance, their address, and their toys. In contrast, adolescents are much more likely to describe themselves in terms of personal beliefs, characteristics and motivations. Montemayor and Eisen (1977), in a study of self-concepts, provide the following examples to illustrate this point. The first description is from a nine-year-old boy in the fourth grade:

> My name is Bruce C. I have brown eyes. I have brown hair. I have brown eyebrows. I'm nine years old. I LOVE! sports. I have seven people in my family. I have great! eye site. I have lots! of friends. I live on 1923 Pinecrest Drive. I'm going on 10 in September. I'm a boy. I have an uncle that is almost 7 feet tall. My school is Pinecrest. My teacher is Mrs. V. I play Hockey! I am almost the smartest boy in the class. I LOVE! food. I love fresh air. I LOVE school. (p. 317)

The next example, from a seventeen-year-old girl in the twelfth grade, illustrates a much more abstract view of the self.

> I am a human being. I am a girl. I am an individual. I don't know who I am. I am a Pisces. I am a moody person. I am an indecisive person. I am an ambitious person. I am a very curious person. I am not an individual. I am a loner. I am an American (God help me), I am a Democrat. I am a liberal person. I am a radical, I am a conservative. I am a pseudoliberal. I am an atheist. I am not a classifiable person (i.e., I don't want to be.) (p. 318)

Exactly how the concrete, somewhat shallow self-concept of the child evolves into more complex and differentiated notions of the self is unclear. We also do not have a good understanding of why people select particular self-structures or categories to define themselves. McGuire and his colleagues (McGuire, McGuire, Child, & Fujioka, 1978; McGuire & Padawer-Singer, 1976) find that people are likely to think about themselves and describe themselves on those dimensions on which they are distinctive or on which they stand out. Thus, young children in classrooms filled with older children were much more likely to mention their age when asked to "tell us about yourself." The kids with red hair (always a relatively small minority) were decidedly more likely to mention hair color. Black and Hispanic children attending a school that was predominantly (82 percent) white were much more likely to mention their ethnic group than were the white students. This research suggests that our self-schemas are likely to be formed around those aspects of the self on which we stand out from other people in some way, or in those areas in which we have had a chance to compare ourselves with others.

CONTENT OF SELF-SCHEMAS

In developing a system of self-schemas, we are likely to include cognitive representations derived from specific events and situations in which we have been involved (e.g., "Last night I spent the entire evening talking to a real bore because I didn't know how to end the conversation"), as well as more general representations derived from the repeated categorization and evaluation of our behavior by ourselves and by others around us (e.g., "I am very talkative in groups of three or four but shy in large gatherings"). Still other components of the self probably consist of very general, traitlike terms ("I am generous," "I am creative," or "I am independent"). These very general schemas come from the repeated similar categorizations of the self across many different situations.

As indicated by the two self-descriptions quoted earlier, the self-concept contains various types of information about the self. There is no reason to think that the self-system is just a set of verbal propositions, however. The development of a schema in a particular area probably gives one the ability to integrate conceptually related information regardless of its form. Thus, a self-schema may well include images and representations that cannot be easily described in words. Some of the information about the self contained in memory may be quite sharp and distinct, while other information is probably much more vague and no doubt changes each time we think about it. Some of the knowledge in self-structures, especially if recent, is probably quite detailed and specific to particular events, while other knowledge may be less structured. Instead, it may take the form of general summary statements or feelings about the kind of person we are. As we grow older and accumulate experiences, and observe ourselves in various situations, we probably cannot keep all the information about ourselves, in all its detailed glory, in mind (nor may we want to). We may begin to generalize or summarize similar behavior. Thus, we do not have to remember every party we have gone to and how we behaved. It is enough to remember that we have gone to many parties where we have met new people and had a good time. And when asked about party-going behavior, we can respond that we are friendly types who usually enjoy parties.

As individuals develop, they may rely more and more on trait adjectives to describe their behavior. Jones, Sensenig, and Haley (1974) found, for example, that when students were asked to describe their most significant characteristics, trait terms like "sensitive," "intelligent," and "friendly" were the most frequent responses. These terms are very general and might be considered so broad as to be essentially meaningless. But this is not the case. Wegner (1977) showed that traits like "friendly" and "intelligent" are associated with relatively fine discriminations in interpersonal judgments. These general characteristics are rich in specific meanings and very useful to an individual in describing either the self or others, precisely because they function as summaries of a variety of detailed behavior that the individual has observed and categorized.

Trait terms also serve as memory aids and tools to help us organize a great deal of conceptually similar material. Recent work by

Cantor and Mischel (1977) indicates that traits function as proto-types or summaries and are powerful organizing concepts in memory. In one study, subjects were first shown a series of statements representing an introverted person (e.g., "Jane is shy"). Then they were given a recognition memory test in which the original statements were mixed with some new introvert statements. Subjects were asked to indicate whether each statement was new or old. Many subjects falsely identified some of the new introvert statements as being old. The fact that these subjects showed a memory bias for new but conceptually related items suggests that in an effort to organize and retain as much information as possible most easily, they formed a model or prototype of the concept of introvert. The result is that specific details are lost, and some inferences and connections are drawn that may not have existed in the original statements. But overall the process is useful because it organizes a great deal of information. One reason trait terms are often used as stimuli for research on the self is that they function as summaries that organize similar behavioral information and thus are assumed to be significant components of our knowledge structures about ourselves and other people.

THE INFLUENCE OF THE SELF ON THOUGHT AND MEMORY

In studying self-structures, investigators have typically made a number of assumptions about these structures. Generally, they have assumed that they are multifaceted structures active in processing a variety of incoming information about the self. More specifically, they have assumed, for example, that if a person has developed a self-structure or schema in a particular area, he or she should (1) process information about the self in a given domain (e.g., make judgments and decisions) with relative ease or certainty, (2) have relatively better memory for behavior in this area, (3) predict future behavior in the area, (4) resist information that is counter to the prevailing schema, and (5) evaluate new information with respect to its relevance for this domain.

SPEED AND CONFIDENCE OF JUDGMENTS ABOUT THE SELF

We do not have schemas about everything. In terms of the self, we have schemas only about those aspects of our behavior that are important to us or distinctive in some way. In a series of studies on self-schemas, Markus (1977) identified people with schemas and those without schemas in a particular area of behavior. These groups were compared for their performance on a variety of cognitive tasks. Individuals with schemas about independence were compared with those who were *aschematic* or *without schemas*. Independent schematics were those who rated themselves at the extreme end on at least two relevant scales (independent/dependent; individualistic/conformist; or leader/follower) and who rated these dimensions as important to their overall self-evaluation. These were people who thought of themselves as independent. Dependent schematics rated themselves as extreme in the dependent direction. These were people who thought of themselves as dependent. Aschematics were those in the mid-range on these scales and low on importance ratings of independence. They were people who probably didn't think much about independence or dependence at all, and who were not concerned with evaluating the independence of their behavior.

A number of different tasks were used to determine if schematics and aschematics differed in how they processed information about the self. On the first task, trait adjectives associated with dependence (e.g., tolerant, conforming, obliging) and adjectives associated with independence (e.g., independent, individualistic, assertive) were presented individually on a screen. Individuals were instructed to press a "me" button if an adjective was self-descriptive and a "not-me" button if it was not. For each word the choice of "me" or "not-me" was recorded, as well as how long it took to make this judgment.

It was assumed that many people would respond "me" to an adjective like "independent," but that they would do so for a variety of reasons. Some would respond "me" because this characteristic is indeed part of their self-structure. Others would do so primarily because "independent" is a good or desirable quality in

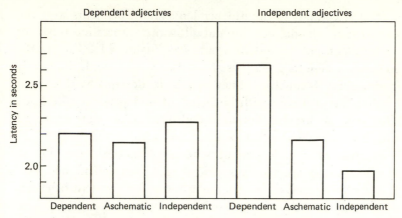

FIGURE 5.1. Mean response latency for dependent and independent adjectives judged as self-descriptive. (From Markus, 1977. Copyright © by the American Psychological Association. Reprinted by permission.)

our society. A measure of how long it takes people to make their judgments allows one to separate these types of individuals. If a particular characteristic is part of the self-structure, the individual will be able to make a "me" decision relatively quickly. If, however, the characteristic is inconsistent or contradicts one's self-schema about independence, but a "me" judgment is made anyway, this will be revealed by a longer response latency.

The individuals who thought of themselves as independent responded "me" to a large proportion of independent adjectives and, as shown in Figure 5.1, took far less time to make their judgments than they did for judgments of the dependent adjectives. The people who thought of themselves as dependent, in turn, responded "me" to more dependent adjectives and responded much faster than they did to the independent adjectives. Dependent individuals are used to thinking of themselves as "conforming" and "obliging," and could make these judgments quickly. In contrast, they are probably less used to thinking about themselves as "assertive" and "individualistic" (even though they might like to); thus, it took them longer to process these words, which were inconsistent with the self-schema.

In clear contrast to the independents and dependents were the aschematics, who did not differ at all in their processing times for independent and dependent words (see Figure 5.1). Clearly the aschematic subjects do not use these two sets of words differently in describing themselves. They appear to be equally at ease in labeling their behavior with independent or dependent adjectives. They have no structure for independence and are not concerned with how independent or dependent they are.

In other tasks, independent schematic subjects were able to supply relatively specific examples of past independent behavior, thought they were likely to engage in future independent behavior, and resisted the acceptance of information that implied they were not independent. A parallel pattern of results was found with dependent stimuli for those who thought of themselves as dependent people. Again, in contrast, the aschematic subjects thought they were as likely to engage in independent as dependent behavior, and were relatively accepting of information about themselves on this dimension. Additionally, the aschematics showed considerable inconsistency across the various tasks, suggesting that their responses were not being mediated by a well-defined cognitive structure.

These findings have also been replicated with respect to schemas about creativity, body weight, and sex role. In a study on sex role self-schemas, for instance (Markus, Crane, & Siladi, 1979), individuals with masculine self-schemas (thought of themselves as stereotypically masculine) and individuals with feminine self-schemas (thought of themselves as stereotypically feminine) were compared with those who were classified as androgynous (thought of themselves as both masculine and feminine or did not think of themselves as either masculine or feminine). Androgynous individuals were assumed to be aschematic with respect to masculinity and femininity, and thus not to have separate, differentiated knowledge structures associated with either of these areas of behavior. Building on the work of Sandra Bem (1974), it was reasoned that the androgynous individual does not partition his or her self-concept, or most other aspects of the social world, into male or female or into the categories of masculine and feminine.

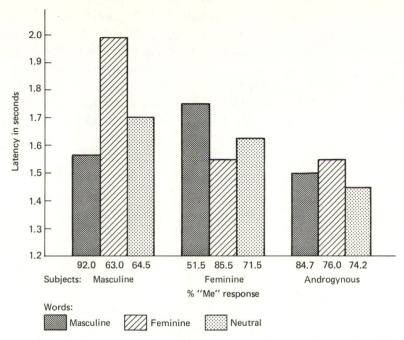

FIGURE 5.2. Response latency and percent of "me" responses for self-descriptive judgments by masculine, feminine, and androgynous subjects. (From Markus, Crane, and Siladi, 1979)

Because they are without schemas in the domains of masculinity or femininity, androgynous individuals are not likely to encode and subsequently process behavior with respect to its relative masculinity or femininity.

To evaluate these assumptions, subjects who were identified as masculine, feminine, and androgynous on the basis of self-rating scales were given the "me/not me" task described earlier. Again, both response and response latency were recorded. The stimuli in this task, however, were the adjectives from the Bem Sex Role Inventory (1974), a scale which includes twenty masculine adjectives (e.g., athletic, competitive, dominant), twenty feminine adjectives (e.g., cooperative, cheerful, gentle), and twenty neutral adjectives (e.g., friendly, happy, helpful). The results of this task are shown in Figure 5.2. The masculine schematics were much faster at endorsing masculine adjectives than they were at endorsing feminine adjectives, although they responded "me" to a large number of feminine adjectives. Thus, these individuals do not seem to object to labeling themselves as "gentle" and "affectionate," but their relative reticence or lack of confidence in these judgments is reflected in the relatively longer time it takes to make the judgments. In contrast, they are quite fast in deciding that the stereotypic masculine characteristics of "competitive," "dominant," and "ambitious" describe them. They are also much more confident that these adjectives describe them than they are about the feminine words. The converse appears to be true for the feminine schematics. In a forced choice, "me/not me" situation, these people are willing to label themselves as "ambitious" or "competitive" but are relatively hesitant about doing so. They are much faster in deciding that the characteristically feminine adjectives are descriptive of them. Among the androgynous subjects, there is no difference in processing time for the masculine and feminine adjectives. These subjects appear to be aschematic and to be equally at ease in labeling their behavior with masculine or feminine characteristics.

MEMORY FOR INFORMATION ABOUT THE SELF

The differential processing of trait adjectives by schematics and aschematics in these studies suggests that a self-structure is important for organizing and processing information about the self. If this is the case, it is also reasonable to expect that we should be able to see the influence of a self-structure on memory. And there are now many studies that suggest a marked effect of the self on memory. A study by Brenner (1975) on the effects of liking on memory found that you may remember aspects of your own performance better than another's performance. In this experiment, subjects (who were dating couples) sat in a large circle and were given a stack of cards, each with one word on it. Proceeding around the room in a clockwise fashion, each subject was required in turn to recite the word on the card on the top of the deck. After several times around the circle, subjects were asked to recall as many words from the task as they could. Recall was best for those words they themselves had recited, second best for those recited by their partner, and third for those recited by a stranger.

A study by Rogers, Kuiper, and Kirker (1977) compared self-reference judgments to three other types of judgments. The individuals in this study were shown forty adjectives, one at a time. For ten of the adjectives, they were asked to decide whether the words had big letters—a *structural* decision. For ten other words, they were asked to judge whether the word rhymed with another word—a *phonemic* decision. For another ten, they were asked to judge whether the adjective meant the same as another word—a *semantic* decision. And for another ten words, they were asked to judge whether the word described them— a *self-reference* decision. Following this task, the subjects were given a surprise recall task; they were asked to write down as many of the adjectives from the task as they could remember. The results reported in Table 5.1 are clear. Subjects recalled on the average 2.84 of the words about which they had made self-referent judgments, compared to only .34 of the words about which they made structural decisions. Thus, recall was far superior for those adjectives used in the self-reference decisions, regardless of whether the answer was yes or no.

TABLE 5.1. Recall for adjectives as a Function of Rating Task and Rating

	Rating Task			
Rating	Structural	Phonemic	Semantic	Self-reference
yes	.28	.34	.65	1.78
no	.06	.34	.68	1.06
TOTAL	.34	.68	1.33	2.84

Source: Rogers, Kuiper, and Kirker, 1977.

Rogers and his colleagues argued that self-reference functions as a powerful coding device to help one process information. It seems that judgments about the self, especially "yes" judgments, activate a self-structure or schema which facilitates recall. A structural decision—for example, about whether a word has big letters—simply involves a perceptual match and probably activates only a few knowledge structures. In making this judgment, there is little need to think much about the stimulus word, to elaborate it in any way, or to connect it with other related words. A decision about whether or not you are friendly, however, probably activates a flood of images of yourself in social interaction with others (e.g., at a party last Saturday night, at the lunch table with the new foreign student, going to the movies alone). These images connect with the stimulus word and help to embellish it. As a result, it is easier to remember this word because of all the associations made to it in a self-reference judgment. In another study, Rogers (1977) also found that if subjects are given instructions to use self-reference to remember certain stimuli, they do much better at the task than subjects receiving no instructions or different instructions.

These studies showing superior memory when the self is involved could lead one to conclude that the self is special in some way. But several other interpretations of this data should be considered. First, in the Brenner study, it could be reasonably argued that the superior recall was due to the fact that subjects said words out loud; this extra attention to, and study of, the word caused it to be remembered better. There is also a problem with the Rogers et al. study. Perhaps recall was enhanced for the self-reference judgments only because this type of judgment was much more personally involving and thus activated a much richer network of images and associations. Perhaps equally good recall would have been obtained if the subjects were asked to make these judgments about any person, say, Abraham Lincoln or their mothers.

To answer this question, Kuiper and Rogers (1979) compared recall of judgments made about the self to those made about a complete stranger and to those made about a person known for some time. They found that trait adjectives used in judgments about the self were better remembered than those made about a complete stranger, but not better than those made about a person known for a while. Somewhat at odds with this finding, however, is the similar experiment by Lord (1978). In this study the same design used by Rogers et al. was employed, except that the four types of judgments were: (1) describes you?, (2) describes your father?, (3) describes Walter Cronkite?, (4) describes a tree?. The self-reference questions produced greater recall than any of the other three questions; this was true for both positively evaluated adjectives (friendly, honest) and negatively evaluated adjectives (fearful, timid). In short, although there is no complete consensus on what is happening in these studies or why, it seems clear that one of the reasons recall of self-reference information is relatively superior is that we have more and better organized information about ourselves than about others. We have more complex and elaborate structures about ourselves in some domains than we have about Walter Cronkite, and this produces differential processing and organizing of self-referent information.

The studies described in the last two sections, which indicate that judgments about the self are made quickly and confidently and are relatively better remembered, provide evidence for a set of structures about the self that allow us to understand, integrate, and explain our behavior in particular areas. In some areas, we are likely to have clear or well-developed structures about ourselves, and it is these structures that are probably frequently activated and used in the processing of relevant social information.

THE UNIQUENESS OF SELF

> To observations which our selves we make
> We grow more partial for the observer's sake.
> **POPE**

Because we have a set of structures or schemas especially suited for processing information about the self in particular areas, information that is relevant or referent to the self is likely to be regarded as different in some way from information about other people or other social objects and events. Although there has been only limited research on this problem, the unique effect of self-relevant information has been used heavily by teachers, politicians, and lawyers. For example, there are reading specialists (although with very little supporting evidence) who claim that if you want to teach Suzy to read, to help her to learn faster, better, and with more enthusiasm, the thing to do is to take her *Dick, Jane, and Spot Go to the Mailbox* primer, and every time Jane's name occurs, replace it with Suzy's. The results of implicating Suzy in the story and having her imagine herself in the thick of the action with Dick and Spot are claimed to be dramatic. Despite the untested nature of these results, it seems to make sense that if Suzy imagines herself instead of Jane as a central character, it is bound to make a difference in the way she understands and remembers this story (see, e.g., Bower, 1978). Attorneys also seem to know the power of making events self-relevant. Jurors are asked to imagine themselves in the defendant's place—to imagine the pain, to experience the fear, to share the uncertainty. And, of course, advertisers mercilessly exploit the self-reference technique. The merchandisers of smoke alarms ask, "If there is a fire in *your* home tonight, will *your* family awaken in time?"

VIVIDNESS AND THE SELF

It is interesting to speculate about some of the factors that may contribute to the power of self-reference. Previously, we suggested that one difference between self-referent information and other-referent information is a quantitative one. We have more information about ourselves than we have about others, even extremely well-known others such as parents or lovers. Consequently we can make more elaborate organizations of stimuli that are relevant to the self, and in turn can make more associations to them and inferences about them. But there are other reasons for this self/other difference which, although related to the quantitative one, merit separation attention. For example, information about the self is often vivid and attention-getting. While we may, as in the Brenner study, attend carefully to the behavior and performance of a good friend, we are in many senses (to paraphrase the popular book) our own best friend, and nothing can rival the attention and concern that are focused on our own behavior. And consequently, from a cognitive point of view, nothing can rival the vividness and salience of the representations of these behaviors. In much of our thinking, it is the salient, vivid information that is likely to be most cognitively available or most ready for use. Recent work on our judgment processes (Nisbett & Wilson, 1977a; Tversky & Kahneman, 1974) indicates clearly that vivid, concrete, easily available information is the most heavily relied upon information, often to the unjustified exclusion of relevant but less interesting information. If, for example, on your first ride on San Francisco's mass transit system BART, your train stalls and you miss your 10 o'clock appointment, you will be hard pressed to extol the virtues of mass transit in this city or pay attention to anything that does, despite the fact that the system transports thousands of riders each day rapidly, efficiently, and without incident. And almost any information you could gather would have great difficulty competing with that vivid image of yourself trapped on the train—bored, irritated, and late.

POSITIVE AFFECT AND THE SELF

Although at this point there is very little specific research or theorizing on the issue, it seems likely that the self-system is in some way connected with the feeling system or the affective system. All judgments about stimuli are likely to involve some discrimination as to their relative goodness or badness (Zajonc, 1979). But this is probably markedly so for self-referent judgments and decisions. Countless studies indicate that the self works to maintain a good image of itself or to maintain high self-esteem. Feelings about the self are probably inextricably bound up with thoughts about the self. Thus, deciding whether Walter Cronkite is fearful is probably accompanied by many interesting images and bits of knowledge, but deciding this about yourself is accompanied not only by these images and knowledge but also by clear feelings associated with being or not being a fearful person. That is, the self-referent response generates a good or bad feeling, or an affective response, that is interwoven with the cognitive response. The association of affect with information about the self is another factor that works to distinguish self-referent judgments and to make them seem qualitatively different or special.

Greenwald (1978) notes that there are still other reasons to expect self-referent information to be special or distinguished in some way from other types of knowledge. The self, he says, "is the least common denominator of experience, meaning that it is the fact shared in common by the largest number of experiences" (p. 15). This fact works to connect many types of knowledge that might be otherwise unrelated and provides a clear basis for organization. The self as least common denominator minimizes inconsistencies, glosses over differences, and helps achieve feelings of self-consistency. And feelings of consistency probably produce good feelings about the self. It is likely that a well-organized self-system, composed of consistent, positively valued self-schemas, will engender good feelings about the self. If, however, one has schemas about the self that are inconsistent or that include a great deal of negative affect, such as "I am a poor math student," or "I am fat," or "I am shy," then one's overall evaluation of the self, or self-esteem, will be influenced. Changes in the structure of the self-system can also produce changes in self-esteem. With the loss of a parent, one also loses the concept of oneself as a child and the good feelings associated with it. If a couple becomes separated, they lose or disturb in some way the concepts of themselves as lovers and partners or as husbands and wives. These changes in the form and content of schemas that have been central to one's self-definition may produce negative feelings about the self or temporarily lower one's self-esteem until the self-structures are cognitively reorganized into a new whole.

THE SELF AS A DISTORTER

> *It is an amiable illusion, which the shape of our planet prompts, that every man is at the top of the world.*
>
> EMERSON

Because we attend so much to our own behavior and endlessly consider its implications, it is not surprising that our personal record of our past events or accomplishments may not be a perfect match with an observer's record of our behavior. Here it is important to note that even though self-schemas are enormously useful in organizing and integrating information, they can also cause us some problems. Thus, we are unlikely to notice things that do not fit our structures, and often we assume that everything that fits is good. The notion that we will go to great lengths to protect our ego or preserve our self-esteem is an old, respected, and when all is said and done, probably one of the great psychological truths (e.g., Freud, 1946). But to what extent this happens, how it happens, and with what consequences is not yet understood.

Greenwald (1978), in discussing how we fabricate and revise our personal history, suggests that if historians were as cavalier about changing and distorting history as we are with respect to our own personal histories, they would be thrown off campus and publicly ridiculed for poor scholarship. We are all aware of how our own interests, attitudes, and values can influence a variety of subtle, and sometimes not-so-subtle, alterations in material to be remembered. Thus, for example, hardly anyone is surprised by the fisherman's description of the dimensions and proportions of "the one that got away."

SELECTIVE FORGETTING

"Looking out for number one" probably begins very early in the information processing sequence. Thus, we are not only more likely to focus on ourselves but also to attend selectively to the *good* aspects of our behavior. We do not yet have evidence on the way self-structures influence the initial categorization or encoding of behavior relevant to the self. However, there is much evidence to indicate that self-structures will influence memory of events about the self, so that our good, correct, responsible, consistent, and successful activities are much more likely to be recalled than the bad, incorrect, irresponsible, inconsistent, or unsuccessful ones.

One of the earliest studies on selective forgetting was done by Zillig in 1928 (cited in Wallen, 1942). The stimuli were quotations from famous authors. Half of the statements were com-

plimentary to females and half were derogatory. Twenty men
and twenty women read the statements and then were asked to
write them from memory. Zillig found that of all the statements remembered by male subjects, only 37 percent were favorable to women. In contrast, of all the statements recalled by
females, 63 percent were favorable to women.

A study by Mischel, Ebbesen, and Zeiss (1973) found that
after completing a personality assessment, people are much more
likely to remember their personal assets than their liabilities. This
result was also obtained in early studies of ego involvement and
selective forgetting done by Wallen (1942). He found that
when subjects were presented with ratings supposedly made about
them by friends, the recall of these ratings tended to change in
such a way as to make them more compatible with the subjects'
self-ratings. Cartwright (1956) also found that adjectives consistent with one's self-description were more likely to be recalled
than inconsistent trait adjectives.

In a fascinating series of studies, Ross and Sicoly (1979)
found that one's own contribution to a group product is more
often and more easily remembered than those of others, and also
that individuals accept more responsibility than others attribute
to them for a product that is a joint effort. Thus, as an example
of this effect, in determining the responsibility for a co-authored
report, both authors are likely to think they did 80 percent of
the work. In a marriage, both husband and wife are likely to
think that they put 75 percent of the effort into the relationship.
Zeller (1950), in reviewing the research on repression, documented a similar phenomenon—the tendency to overestimate
the amount of success achieved in one's pattern of performance
while blatantly ignoring failure.

ASSIGNING RESPONSIBILITY AND TAKING CREDIT

Many studies (Bradley, 1978; Miller & Ross, 1975; Wortman,
1976) indicate that we are often likely to take credit for success
and put the blame for failure elsewhere. Thus, when Suzy suc-

ceeds in school and learns to read, the teacher is happy to accept responsibility and be proud of his teaching technique, but when Suzy has problems and cannot progress rapidly, it may suddenly become necessary to find other reasons for her failure. It becomes important to consider Suzy's unhappy home, the poor quality of the instructional materials, the fact that the class is too large to give each child individual attention, or even that Suzy is just not too bright. The one factor that is least likely to be considered by the teacher is the suggestion that poor teaching is responsible for Suzy's failure. There are, of course, many exceptions to this generalization (see Miller & Ross, 1975). We sometimes do remember our failures or accept responsibility for them, but we are most likely to do so when we can find some way to force a virtue out of the failure. "Yes, I flunked out of graduate school the first year, but I certainly wouldn't want to be the kind of person who would succeed in that academic, one-upmanship, word-game environment."

There are a number of intriguing questions concerned with how these egocentric biases occur. Is it because we pay more attention to our own efforts and thus have more representations concerning ourselves in memory? Or is it because we assign more importance to those aspects of a project we have been personally involved with? Or is it because the people involved in a joint project define the product or the project differently and have differing ideas about what goes into it? Is it correct to label this phenomenon "distortion?" Could it be that both people in a joint project initially perceive and categorize the relevant information in the same way, but that over time each person changes, distorts, or biases this information toward the most favorable picture of the self? Alternatively, it may be that from the very beginning, from the initial stimulus input, information about the self is different from information about others and thus is handled differently throughout the information-processing sequence. Further research on how people think about and remember their own behavior should allow us to understand why we so often see ourselves differently than others see us.

SUMMARY

Thinking about the self, like thinking about any object, involves providing meaning to an incoming stimulus so that it can be represented in memory. Meaning is produced by fitting or assimilating various components of the stimulus to the knowledge structures contained in memory, and then adjusting or accommodating these structures so that they can adequately represent the relevant data. Knowledge structures serve to organize, summarize, or integrate past experience. When we think about ourselves, we use a variety of structures about the self or self-schemas that are developed to make sense of our behavior in a particular area and to guide information processing about the self in this area.

The development of structures about the self begins at birth and continues throughout life as we organize and interpret our experiences. We develop structures about ourselves in those areas that are significant to us or that are distinctive in some way. To examine the influence of these cognitive structures, researchers have used many measures of information processing, such as time to make a decision about the self and the recall of information about the self. Self-structures influence the content of decisions we make about ourselves, how quickly we can make these decisions, and what we remember about them. Because even the most other-directed among us spend so much time thinking about the self, self-structures are frequently used and available for future use in information processing. Thus, we are likely to pay more attention to information about the self and to expend more effort reflecting on it. Often we may even change data so that it fits with our self-concept or ignore or selectively forget information if it does not match our ideas about ourselves.

6

The Self in Prosocial Action

DANIEL M. WEGNER
TRINITY UNIVERSITY

The topic of this chapter is a paradox. To be self-centered, self-interested, or just plain selfish, you see, is to hold the concerns of other people in callous disregard. But *prosocial action* means precisely those behaviors such as helping, kindness, and generosity that have in common a strong regard for the interests of others. How, then, could the self be involved in prosocial action? When is it selfish to share your last cookie, to comb a knee-deep carpet for someone's contact lens, or at the extreme, to risk your life for a stranger's safety? Although such "selfless" actions seem almost impossible to reconcile with the common conception of "selfish" motivation, several streams of social psychological research indicate that there are remarkable links between these apparent opposites. This chapter presents four current views of this curious connection.

In the first section, the possibility that we may consider others as though they were ourselves is introduced; the operation of *empathy* is one way in which positive forms of social behavior may be motivated by selfish desires. Another wellspring of prosocial action is our *experience* of ourselves; that self-perceptions and social feedback suggesting we are helpful may lead us to continuing helpful behavior is the topic of the second section. The third section develops the idea that each person is sensitive to certain *standards* for the self; some of these ideals or expectations incorporate concern for others and thus may serve as guides to altruistic behavior. Finally, a fourth section explores the relationship between *attention* to the self and action that benefits others; as it turns out, self-focused attention provides a common theme for understanding empathy, experience, and standards, and so furnishes a useful way of thinking about the topic as a whole.

EMPATHY: EXTENSION OF SELF

Imagine a child on a snowy sidewalk in a big city. It is early evening, and people are hurrying by as she stands alone, bundled against the weather, her small face illuminated by the shop window that holds a baby doll. She has been there for many minutes, gaze fixed on the tiny toy, and she shivers ever so slightly as she rubs her mittenless hands on her coat sleeves. Do you feel the slightest bit uneasy about the child? Want her to have the doll? Relax. Her family is in a Winnebago parked at the curb, and right now they are foreclosing the mortgage on the shopkeeper as well as on the owner of a mitten market just down the street. The point here is not that the child is in distress, but that you might be—as a result of your empathy with her.

In general, empathy is the feeling of distress or elation that comes when a person observes the suffering or good fortune of another (Stotland, 1969). Shedding a tear at a sad movie or feeling all warm and cuddly at one that ends happily are both examples of empathic emotional responses. Since these responses arise not from our own immediate experiences but rather from the observation of others' experiences, they seem to represent "extensions" of ourselves to include others. That the sharing of emotions in this way can lead to the sharing of favors, kindness, and prosocial action generally, is the assumption held by a number of theorists (e.g., Hoffman, 1976; Staub, 1978) and serves as the theme of this section.

ORIGINS OF EMPATHY

It would be easy to explain the phenomenon of empathy if everyone in the world shared one big body. Emotions would be shared, too, because of the physical connection, and we would just have to be careful not to let anyone hiccup. Since we are separate beings, however, it is necessary to understand how one person may experience the plight of another as though it were a personal experience. It seems that there are two sources of information that allow us to do this. First, we may perceive directly the *emotional expression* of a person and react empathically to it. Second, we may perceive the *emotion-producing situation* a person is in and, by understanding its impact on people generally, develop an empathic response.

Reacting to the emotional expressions of others (crying when they cry, laughing when they laugh) is a form of imitation, and it appears to develop very early in life. There is recent evidence that imitation of facial expression and hand movement occurs in newborn infants (Meltzoff & Moore, 1977), and it probably comes as no surprise to nursery attendants that newborns cry more often when another infant is crying (Simner, 1971). We seem predisposed by our biological inheritance to respond to the behavior of others with similar behavior of our own. It is interesting to note, though, that this tendency may stem in part from a basic confusion between ourselves and others. Hoffman (1976) has proposed, in line with the ideas of Piaget (1965), that the infant's reactions to others' emotions occur because the infant cannot yet distinguish self from other.

A good example of this apparent confusion is found in the research by Simner (1971) on the newborn's crying response. It has frequently been observed that infants engage in repetitive actions —grasping a rattle over and over, kicking the same way several times in succession, and so on. Piaget (1963) calls such repetition a "primary circular reaction" and suggests that it has an important function in the development of complex actions. According to Simner, the infant's tendency to chime in when another infant is crying is traceable to a simple error in this process. The infant mistakes the cries of another for his or her own and then joins in, thinking that the cries are merely being repeated. To test this idea, Simner played a variety of tape-recorded cries and noises to newborns; he found that they were most likely to cry when the recording most nearly resembled their own cry. Empathy at this early age comes from accepting the emotional expressions of others as those of the self.

Unfortunately, this form of empathy with which we are genetically endowed does not really lead us to become concerned for others. If we are concerned, it is for ourselves. Young children who become distressed at the sight of another in trouble often seek out their own mothers rather than trying to find comfort for the person in need. Hoffman (1976) has observed that it is only through an appreciation of the difference between self and others that empathic distress can be translated into action aimed at the other's relief. So, while empathic emotions may occur early in life as primitive extensions of the self, they are not sufficient alone to produce prosocial action.

Developing children come to understand a number of interrelated facts that eventually allow them to grasp the meaning of others' emotional expressions and emotion-producing situations. The facts that self and other are different, that they may have different thoughts, and that they may experience different emotional states, for example, are all understood with increasing age and experience. All of this knowledge can be summarized in terms of what Flavell and his colleagues (1968) call *role-taking ability* —the capacity to understand situations from the perspective of another person. The child who can take the role of his babysitter, then, may understand the sobs coming from behind the refrigerator and loosen the ropes on her wrists. Seeing a situation from the perspective of a person in distress clarifies the nature of the person's emotional expression and often also suggests how the situation might be modified to reduce its discomforting qualities. Instead of seeking solace for the self, the person who has developed the ability to construct a reasonable mental representation of others' emotion-producing situations can be motivated by empathic arousal to provide solace for others.

OPERATION OF EMPATHY

Among adults—who generally have developed the facility to take the perspective of others—the influence of others' emotional experiences can be very dramatic. Experiments in which adults have been exposed to the severe suffering of others—watching a film on sawmill accidents, for example (Lazarus et al., 1965)— show that strong physiological reactions such as increased heart rate and perspiration are often the result. Why, then, don't adults always offer help in situations that allow it? Research on this issue has suggested two possible mechanisms that can short-circuit the "empathic emotion + role taking = prosocial action" relationship.

One process that can dissipate the positive effects of empathy involves the misattribution of emotion. As noted in Chapter 4, there are many cases in which individuals may misinterpret their own emotions, attributing them to causes that are not the real ones. A person may become aroused in anticipation of speaking before a large group, for instance, and then, on meeting an old flame, misinterpret the arousal as rekindled love. In the same way, the arousal that comes from an empathic reaction to another's misfortune may be misattributed to a variety of other potentially arousing events (Coke, Batson, & McDavis, 1978; Gaertner & Dovidio, 1977). The empathic emotion that could arise on seeing an accident victim, for example, might be mistaken for a quite different kind of emotion if Braniff flight 27 roared close over-head just as the victim was encountered. The victim would be less likely to receive help as a result. In the turmoil and potential danger that accompany emergencies and other occasions for pro-social action, there are many distractions that may dampen the influence of empathic arousal in just this way.

Another variable that has special consequences for the effects of emotion on prosocial action is the extent to which the potential helper takes the perspective of the person in need; the fact that adults are capable of role taking does not mean they always do it. In fact, research by Stotland (1969) has shown that people can be instructed to take the role of another and can also be instructed not to. Individuals asked to imagine how a person feels show unusually strong physiological reactions when the person suffers, whereas those who are asked merely to observe the person, noting how he or she reacts, are less likely to evidence such strong empathic responses. Failure to take the role of a suffering person suppresses not only the understanding of the person's situation but also the actual experience of empathic emotion.

When you are walking down the street on a Sunday afternoon and find yourself in a position to offer aid—say, to a person in a wheelchair who needs help to negotiate a curb—no one runs up to you with a freshly mimeographed page of instructions on how to take the role of the person in need or how to avoid it. The variations in role taking studied by Stotland tend to occur naturally in these settings. With close friends, with people you see as very similar to you, or with people in situations you yourself have encountered, it is quite easy to take their roles and to empathize. On the other hand, you might find it easier to take the roles of certain tree stumps than to adopt the perspectives of enemies, people you think are strange, or people whose situations are entirely foreign to your experience. As a rule, you probably understand the perspectives, and hence the predicaments, of only a limited number of people in your life. For this reason, it is likely that the sorrows of many people simply will not move you to action.

What happens in this case, when a person observes the suffering of another but fails to adopt the other's point of view? A study by Aderman, Brehm, and Katz (1974) has shown that those people who are instructed merely to observe a person suffering unpleasant electric shocks, as compared with those who are asked to empathize, are more likely to *derogate* the sufferer. They hold the sufferer personally responsible for the unpleasant experience and conclude that the sufferer is the kind of person who deserves to be shocked. Even when the person being observed experiences no pain, empathy and nonempathy instructions have a similar effect. Asked to report why a person engaging in a conversation behaved in a particular way, observers given empathy instructions answer by pointing out *situational factors* such as the conversation setting or partner, while observers given no empathy instructions more often emphasize *personal factors* such as the person's style and character (Regan & Totten, 1975). With empathy, then, we come to appreciate the situations that impinge on others, both subtle (a conversation partner) and unsubtle (a shock). Without empathy, we see others' experiences as their own doing and view their misfortunes with scorn.

The research summarized in this section indicates that the connection between empathy and prosocial action is a very fragile one. Developing only slowly from the rudiments of empathic emotion present in the infant, the capacity to extend the self to others and thereby to become mindful of their fate can be undermined in many ways. Even if developed properly, empathy can be ravaged by distracting emotional events and is rarely channeled toward those persons whose perspectives are difficult to understand. For this reason, it is fortunate that empathy is not the only path from selfishness to prosocial action. People often engage in kindly and helpful behavior without the strong emotional provocation that is essential to empathic arousal. Thus, although some measure of empathic role taking is necessary for individuals to recognize the needs of others in any setting, there are additional forms of selfishness that may motivate positive social acts when empathic emotion is absent or inoperative.

EXPERIENCE: UNDERSTANDING OF SELF

What if you woke up one morning and found yourself squeezing an otter? Since no one asked you to do this, offering rewards or threatening your life, and since there are few other good reasons for such behavior, you would probably have some explaining to do should people notice. "Why are you squeezing that otter?" they might ask. Because you would look even more ridiculous if you couldn't explain, your response might be to suggest that you like it. You go in for that sort of thing. You are the kind of person who squeezes any otter that becomes available. While this example is somewhat extreme, the fact is that we are often induced to behave in certain ways by causes that we cannot decipher; rather than waking in the morning engaged in an inexplicable activity, we may find ourselves performing it for mysterious reasons at high noon. When this happens, we may attribute characteristics to ourselves as a means of understanding our own actions. This is the process of *self-perception* discussed in Chapter 3.

At the same time, other people may also be baffled by our actions (perhaps even more than we are) and find it necessary to explain things for themselves in a similar way; they attribute a characteristic to us ("This person is obviously an otter squeezer"). When they tell us what we are like, this *social feedback* adds even more to our experience of ourselves. Both self-perception and social feedback, then, are processes by which we come to understand what kinds of people we are, what we like and dislike, and what goals motivate us to action. These processes can contribute to prosocial behavior. When people engage in behaviors that produce no apparent benefits for themselves but have positive effects on others, they may become more likely to engage in similar behaviors on future occasions—either because they perceive themselves as helpful or because others have pointed this out for them. Once a person has experienced the self as a saint, a hero, or a philanthropist, it seems natural to go on doing good deeds.

SELF-PERCEPTION OF HELPFULNESS

A classic experiment by Freedman and Fraser (1966) was the first to suggest that prosocial action might be produced through self-perception. In a study of what they called the "foot-in-the-door technique," these researchers arranged for 156 Palo Alto housewives to receive a phone call from an experimenter who identified himself as a representative of the "California Consumers Group." He asked each woman if she would be willing to allow five or six men from the group's staff to come into her home for two hours one morning to enumerate and classify all her household products; they would need full freedom to go through all the cupboards and storage spaces in the house. As you might expect, the housewives were not too thrilled at this, and when the phone call was the only contact made, only 22 percent agreed to allow it. However, some of the women had been called three days in advance by the same experimenter and asked to perform a relatively less demanding favor. He had requested their help in conducting a survey and had obtained their responses to eight brief questions (e.g., "What brand of soap do you use in your kitchen sink?"). Among these women, the response to the large second request was much more favorable; almost 53 percent agreed to have the squad of nosy men descend on their house. Since this might be explained by suggesting that the housewives had merely become familiar with the caller, Freedman and Fraser also arranged for some of their subjects to receive an initial contact in which the caller only introduced the name of his group and its purpose. The finding that less than 28 percent of these women agreed to the later large request indicates that the act of answering the questions was critical for the occurrence of the "foot-in-the-door" effect.

In a second experiment, Freedman and Fraser demonstrated that it doesn't matter what foot is in the door. When different experimenters made the first and second requests, when they did so on behalf of different organizations, and even when they asked for very different favors, the phenomenon was still observed. Those subjects who granted a small initial favor (of any kind, to anyone, and for any good cause) were more inclined to do a big favor later on. Freedman and Fraser argued that the only satisfactory way to explain such a general phenomenon was to suggest that a change in an individual's understanding of the self followed the granting of a small favor. In essence, the person comes to see the self as one who does that sort of thing; when a later request comes along, the person acts on this new self-view and thus may grant an even larger favor.

Though Bem's (1967) self-perception theory (see Chapter 3) was published after Freedman and Fraser's work, quite a bit of evidence has accumulated to suggest that the foot-in-the-door phenomenon is consistent with the theory. One idea suggested by the theory, for example, is that an initial favor granted for a strong reason should not result in later helpfulness. When one gives help because of a threat or an offer of reward, such reasons alone justify the action and no self-attribution of helpfulness is called for. In fact, research by Batson and his colleagues (1978) shows that when people are paid for helping someone do a task, they see themselves as less helpful and cooperative than when they do it for nothing. Doctors, nurses, police, Red Cross workers, and other professional helpers probably see themselves as "good Samaritans" only when they are underpaid.

Self-perception theory would also predict that the *failure* to give aid the first time, especially if such failure did not seem attributable to strong reward or cost considerations, would lead people to see themselves as *non*helpers and thus to avoid offering assistance at the next opportunity. Precisely this effect has been observed by Snyder and Cunningham (1975). However, Cialdini and his co-workers (1975) have observed an even stronger effect in the opposite direction under the conditions of their own study. What happened was this. These researchers first guaranteed that subjects would fail to help on the initial request by having the experimenter ask each subject to volunteer two hours of time per week for a minimum of two years as a counselor for the County Juvenile Detention Center. Of course, everyone said no. Then, the experimenter made another request, asking subjects to act as chaperones for a group of young people from the center on a trip to the zoo. As compared with a group of subjects who received only the appeal for help with the zoo trip, those subjects who initially rejected the absurdly large request were *more* likely to volunteer. Additional experiments by the Cialdini group and by Cann, Sherman, and Elkes (1975) have shown that this exception to the self-perception reasoning occurs because of an even stronger tendency that appears only under certain conditions—the tendency to bargain. When the same person makes the first and second requests, and when they are separated by only a short time interval, the second request is taken as a concession ("Well, if you won't do that, maybe you'll do this") and therefore is more likely to be accepted. So, if you need to borrow a friend's car for the evening, you might first ask to use it for the harvesting season.

A different kind of variation on the rules of self-perception has been detected by Crano and Sivacek (1978). These researchers conducted a typical foot-in-the-door study by calling people and asking for a small favor—responses to ten questions. While one set of subjects received a simple, courteous call and thanks for their help afterward, another set of subjects got a much more pleasant treatment. They were met by a barrage of compliments as they answered the questions, and on ending the call, the experimenter said, "Thank you very much for your time. Your responses will really help our survey. Thank you again, and have a nice day." Needless to say, the responses of subjects in this second group to a later phone request were more positive than those of subjects in the "neutral" group. At first glance, these findings appear to contradict self-perception theory; presumably a large reward encountered in the initial incident should undermine a subject's tendency to infer that he or she is a helpful person, and hence should lead to decreased aid in the second incident. But, as pointed out by self-perception theorists (e.g., Lepper, Greene, & Nisbett, 1973), an *unanticipated* reward cannot be seen as a good reason for acting, and so does not detract from a self-attribution. In this study, the pleasant first episode probably increased later helping because the unusually thankful experimenter made subjects feel they were exceptionally helpful people.

SOCIAL FEEDBACK

In addition to perceiving ourselves, we often find out about our qualities from communications with others. Such communications may offer us a self-label in a very direct way ("You are helpful"), or they may offer indirect information (like the thankfulness and gratitude of Crano and Sivacek's experimenter) that leaves it up to us to infer our qualities. Whether obvious or subtle, the social feedback we receive acts as another source of self-knowledge and understanding, and therefore may have profound effects on our future behaviors. In one sense, social feedback is merely a supplement to self-perception. Other people observe our actions and may make some of the inferences about us that we fail to draw for ourselves. But since other people can exaggerate, ignore, or even invent information about us, social feedback is not tied as strictly to our observable behavior as is self-perception. Self-labels obtained through feedback from others, because they can be somewhat independent of our previous behaviors, can instill radically new action tendencies. While some of these secondhand labels could have disastrous behavioral consequences ("Mommy, Freddy says I'm the type of person who can eat light bulbs!"), others may plant the seed of prosocial action ("Mommy, Lulu says I'm a good helper").

Studies of the impact of direct social feedback on prosocial behavior have generally shown its effectiveness. Miller, Brickman, and Bolen (1975), for instance, found that children in a fifth grade class who were told that they *were* neat and tidy—by their teacher, the principal, and the school janitor—actually littered less and cleaned up more than children who were told *to be* neat and tidy. In research along the same lines, Jensen and Moore (1977) gave social feedback to boys suggesting either that they were highly competitive ("You don't settle for second best but climb right to the top") or highly cooperative ("You play fair, are willing to share, and don't get pushy with others"). When pairs of boys were later asked to build towers of blocks together, a task in which competition usually leads to a pile of rubble, the pairs in which both boys had received cooperative labels built much taller towers.

The labels others apply to us apparently can be quite sticky, and it is interesting to consider why this is so. In part, the acceptance of social feedback can be explained in terms of self-presentation (see Chapter 7); we find it convenient to present ourselves to others as they would have us be. But since people may accept a label from one person and later behave in accord with it in the presence of others, it appears that social feedback can become a stable feature of self-understanding and is therefore more than a momentary ploy to gain approval. This stability derives from a number of processes, two of which are of special interest. First, social feedback can become internalized because it leads to biased processing of self-information. Because labels are typically very general and abstract ("You are generous"), there are probably several instances of one's behavior that can be brought to mind that are consistent with any label. The label may be accepted over time, then, because the labeled person makes a biased search of self information, both in memory and in ongoing experience, looking for facts that are consistent with the label (see Chapter 5). Told that you are generous, you may agree only casually at the time. But given some time to observe yourself with that label in mind, and to remember past behaviors that could fit, you might adopt the label quite strongly because of all the confirming evidence that becomes available. A second process that tends to multiply the force of social feedback occurs when others behave toward you on the basis of their labels for you. If the people around you believe that you are a helpful and generous person, for example, they may more often ask you for help, and thereby give you more frequent opportunities to observe yourself in prosocial action (Snyder & Swann, 1978).

Despite these processes that encourage the incorporation of social feedback, self-labels are often rejected. Imagine, for example, that the next time your upstairs neighbors organize a roller derby in the bedroom over yours, you decide to use labeling tactics. You take them aside and comment on their unusual quietness and consideration. Unless they take this as a sign of your impending mental collapse and cooperate just to pacify you, it is likely that your strategy will fail. When people hold very definite ideas about themselves, as these neighbors probably do, such assumptions (see Chapter 1) or schemas (see Chapter 5) can lead them to reject contradictory social feedback. It is primarily when people have only vaguely formulated conceptions of their qualities in an area that social feedback about that area is effective.

The self-perception and social feedback processes addressed in this section, in sum, are ways in which people experience and understand themselves; appropriate experience and knowledge can bring about prosocial action. How is it, though, that people know when they are prosocial or antisocial, good or bad, in the first place? For someone confused about these qualities, even the most humanitarian actions could be fuel for antisocial self-labels ("I'm helping this accident victim because I'm the type who loves a good moan"). The way we organize self-information into "good" and "bad" categories, and the way such *self-evaluation* contributes to prosocial action, are treated in the sections to come.

STANDARDS: EVALUATION OF SELF

Do you have a scrapbook? A box of memorabilia? A desk drawer that holds all those snapshots, newspaper clippings, certificates, merit badges, valentines, report cards, ID cards, and other things that your mother began collecting for you? In the years since you first became aware of yourself as an object of thought and evaluation, you have collected much more than just these trinkets. You have accumulated a tremendous store of self-information —facts, ideas, behaviors, labels, interpretations, and very likely, memories of how well or how poorly you thought of yourself in many different episodes. No doubt, you draw on this bank of information in deciding on how to behave in each situation you encounter. Faced with the decision of whether to visit a friend in the hospital or to work on your latest cheese sculpture, you may reflect on particular past events or on general themes in your past self, and end up choosing the activity that this information suggests would produce the most positive future self-evaluation (see Vallacher & Solodky, 1979). But merely saying that people want to be good—to obtain positive self-evaluations —does not tell us whether they will behave in prosocial ways in a particular new situation. It is necessary to know what *standards* of self-evaluation they are using in this instance, and also what behavior would bring the self in line with the standard.

POTENTIAL STANDARDS

When are you pleased with yourself? Clearly, many of the choice pieces in your memorabilia collection represent such moments of self-congratulation, joy, and contentment. That is why you have kept them. The wide variety of objects you may have collected, however, suggests that there are many sources of positive self-views. Your self-concept has surpassed many different standards. Though you probably do not keep mementos of failure (old body casts, photos of people who hate you, etc.), there are many broken standards as well. As an aid in exploring these many standards, it is useful to consider them in terms of a few broad categories. So, based on the work of several theorists (most notably, Kohlberg, 1976; but also, French & Raven, 1959; Haan, 1977; Kelman, 1961; Loevinger, 1966; Wegner, 1975), a handy list is presented in Table 6.1. Although the list is relatively complete, and could therefore be used to evaluate many different qualities and activities of the self, it is designed to be specifically useful in considering the *moral* self-evaluation that underlies prosocial actions.

TABLE 6.1. Standards of Self-Evaluation

1. *The pain standard.* A person views the self more positively when the self is successful in avoiding physical pain, punishment, loss, or other unpleasant experience.

2. *The pleasure standard.* A person views the self more positively when the self is successful in obtaining pleasure, rewards, the gratification of physical needs, or other enjoyable experience.

3. *The approval standard.* A person views the self more positively when the self is liked by others, given approval by them, or incorporated into their group.

4. *The normative standard.* A person views the self more positively when the self compares favorably to others or to tokens of normal, typical behavior such as rules, conventions, and laws.

5. *The justice standard.* A person views the self more positively when the self participates in fair, balanced, and reciprocal relations with others.

One unusual feature of the list is that any one standard could serve as the basis for a prosocial action. Consider, for example, a prosocial act like washing your family's dinner dishes. The pain standard could induce you to do this if everyone in the household filed into your room brandishing weapons while your mother explained that it was your job. The pleasure standard might come into play if your family withheld your dessert until you had put in time at the sink. If you thought they might dislike you because you avoided the dishes, the approval standard would be operating, whereas if you were concerned with breaking the family rules, the normative standard would be involved. Finally, if you realized that it would only be fair to take your turn, you would be accepting the justice standard as a means of evaluating yourself. It is possible that any standard, any combination of standards, or even all the standards could be present and operating in the production of a single prosocial act.

Several additional features of these self-standards deserve comment. First, it should be pointed out that any standard could also serve as grounds for *avoiding* prosocial action. Probably one of the strongest reasons why people fail to help the victims of ongoing violent crimes like robbery, assault, and rape, for example, is that the pain standard guides them to retreat from personal danger. Second, the standards are listed in an important sequence. Those standards near the top of the list are generally more likely to engage a person in activity that benefits the person alone, and are therefore only infrequently sources of prosocial action. Those standards near the end of the list, in comparison, are more often the bases of prosocial action. In this sense, the list represents a sequence arranged in order from personal to prosocial standards. A third feature of the list is that the sequence from personal to prosocial involves a series of steps of increasingly complex thought about the self. Reactions to pain, at the simplest level, seem to require no self-reflection at all. Anticipating pleasure, however, requires some planning and thus depends on the person's ability to extend thoughts of the self into the future. Gaining approval entails realizing that both pain and pleasure can be associated with certain sources—other people—and that others' evaluations of the self are therefore important. Sensitivity to norms and rules, in turn, can occur only when the individual becomes capable of comparing the self and others along a common dimension. Justice, the most complex self-evaluation process, requires the added ability to calculate a balance of resources among the self and others. With increasing complexity in thought about the self, then, the person becomes responsive to standards of self-evaluation that are more likely to result in prosocial action.

STANDARD SALIENCE

When a person enters a particular situation, both the person and the situation determine what standards are most important for self-evaluation. The person enters into the equation because people differ in the importance they attach to each standard. You probably know people who are unusually pleasure oriented, for instance, or others who thrive on "going by the rules." As a person grows up and develops moral maturity and a complex view of the self, he or she moves through stages of moral development that correspond to the sequence of self-standards. So, while young children may be sensitive only to pain or pleasure, moral adults are capable of evaluating themselves in terms of their adherence to more prosocial standards. As people move up through the stages, they become more and more likely to help, share, and become concerned for others (see, e.g., Gunzburger, Wegner, & Anooshian, 1977).

The situation is also crucial in determining the relative impact of the five standards. Certain situations are loaded with opportunities to experience pain, while others may have in store unusual pleasures, strong approval, many rules, or a potential for the pursuit of justice. Although people in lower stages of moral development may have difficulty appreciating higher standards even when the situation makes them stand out, the average adult is probably capable of responding to most of the higher standards. For this reason, situational variations in the salience of standards are usually more important than personal variations in determining the overall importance to an adult in a particular situation. You, for example, could no doubt discern without great effort the likelihood that an act in a specific setting would result in change in self-evaluation on each of the five standards. As one case, consider the act of "clapping erasers" for a professor after class. A slight negative self-evaluation could be produced by this on the pain standard because of the trouble, the chalk dust on your navy sweater, and so on. Pleasure wouldn't enter in at all. Approval could produce a very positive self-evaluation because the professor would like you. Unless your school had strange rules, or the professor had done something to deserve your "repayment," the importance of both the normative and justice standards would be minimal. In short, in deciding whether to do this, you would be deciding on whether the approval was worth the pain.

The salience of standards, as determined by both person and situation, enters into the production of prosocial action in two ways. First, in the self-perception process, a person makes inferences about the self in terms of the standards. Recall Bem's (1967) argument that the self is seen as prosocial when there are no strong reasons for prosocial action. Avoiding pain and approaching pleasure are the strong reasons Bem had in mind. So, when the salience of the pain and pleasure standards is low, but a person does a prosocial act nonetheless, the person infers that the behavior occurred so as to produce a positive self-evaluation on a higher, more prosocial standard. These self-inferences are often bolstered by social feedback, and over time, they make people more sensitive to the potential self-evaluations that could accrue from higher-level standards. In addition to shaping the processes of self-perception and social feedback, the salience of standards also shapes the processes whereby self-understanding is later transformed into action. A person who has observed the self frequently acting so as to produce positive self-evaluations on the approval standard, for instance, will later be most likely to behave prosocially in settings where the approval standard can be met through prosocial action.

This cyclic process leads people to move up from lower to higher standards for self-evaluation. Although people frequently act on an understanding of the self, acting so as to bring the self into line with a salient standard (see Chapter 2), they may occasionally behave in such a way that the sought-after self-evaluation is unclear. When this happens, self-perception and social feedback processes can suggest to them that a positive self-evaluation has been achieved on some new, previously unencountered standard. One who is already sensitive to the pain, pleasure, and approval standards, for example, may find the self behaving in a prosocial way in a situation where none of these standards is salient. The person might then discover, through self-perception or the comments of others, that normative standards underlie positive self-views in this setting. Appreciation of such standards, and behavior designed to meet them, would be the result. We find new standards for the self when the ones we already hold are insufficient to explain our actions.

Standards of self-evaluation, in summary, are implicated in every phase of prosocial action. Beginning with simple standards—pain and pleasure—that are shared with our animal friends in farmyards and forests, we as human beings develop the capacity to view ourselves in terms of progressively more complex standards. These higher-level ideals can then motivate us to behave in more prosocial ways. The standards that are salient in a particular setting, both because of our personal sensitivity to them and because of their prominence in the situation, motivate us toward action. Actions are more likely to be prosocial, in turn, when higher-level standards are salient.

ATTENTION: AWARENESS OF SELF

Suppose you have just finished lunch in a small restaurant. Your party has headed toward the cashier, no one is seated nearby, and the waitress has excused herself to go home because her shift is over. You are alone at the table, and though the service was fine, you hesitate as you count out change for the tip. Why do it? If no one sees, no one cares, right? Just walk away and keep the change. But wait—there *is* someone there. It's you. If, for whatever reason, you are reminded of yourself, you will probably do the right thing and leave the tip. Seeing yourself in a mirror might be enough to remind you; noticing that the local TV news team is crouched under your table, cameras rolling, would do it for sure. That self-focused attention can make people aware of themselves and thus move them to behave in accord with prosocial standards is a possibility suggested by the theory of self awareness (see

Chapter 2). The research devoted to this idea is the topic of this section.

SELF-FOCUS AND HELPING

The notion that people may experience variations in self-awareness is the central principle of self-awareness theory (Duval & Wicklund, 1972; Wicklund, 1975). As the theory has it, when people become self-aware (because of self-focusing stimuli such as mirrors, cameras, other people, or symbols of the self), they become extraordinarily concerned with the discrepancy between their present selves and their ideal selves. They become more likely to evaluate themselves in terms of the salient standards for self-evaluation, and thus they more often behave in prosocial ways when prosocial standards are available.

Several studies of helping behavior published in the last few years have hinted at this connection. Schwartz and Gottlieb (1976), for instance, found that the victim of a violent theft was more often aided when bystanders knew that someone was aware of their response. Enzle and Harvey (1977) showed that people were more likely to give help to another when a third party was to be aware of whether or not help was given, and also when the potential recipient of help was to be aware that a request for assistance had been made on her behalf. These studies are relevant to the relationship between self-focus and helping because, as the theory suggests, people often become self-aware when they know others are watching them. Yet the fact that another person's awareness was the vehicle by which the potential helper was made self-aware in these studies allows for an alternate interpretation. It could be that subjects were merely trying to look good to the others because the awareness of others made the approval standard salient in the situation (see Reis & Gruzen, 1976). Though the effects of self-presentation strategies are interesting in their own right (see Chapter 7), the crucial question of whether prosocial action tendencies are increased when people try to look good to *themselves* cannot be answered by such research.

A study by Duval, Duval, and Neely (1978), however, makes

this point quite nicely. In each of two experiments, subjects' attention was guided toward themselves without the aid of others' awareness. One study used the tactic of showing the subject his or her image on a video monitor; if you've ever seen yourself on TV, you know what a powerful self-focusing stimulus this is. Each subject was made self-aware in this way during a session in which a videotape about the epidemic proportions of venereal disease was also shown. But while some subjects saw their video image either immediately before or after the VD tape, others saw it either four minutes before or four minutes after. When subjects in these groups were later asked to indicate the degree to which they, as members of an apathetic general public, were responsible for failing to stop the epidemic, and also whether they would be willing to assist in the prevention program by donating money and time, striking differences arose between groups. Those subjects who saw their images immediately before or after the tape were more likely to say they were responsible and would help. The subjects who saw their images either four minutes before or four minutes after, in contrast, were less likely to accept responsibility or offer aid; their responses resembled those of a control group that did not see themselves on TV at all. Since the second experiment by these researchers showed a similar effect using a different manipulation of self-focus (subjects were asked to fill out a questionnaire about themselves), it seems fair to say that an awareness of self close in time to an awareness of the needs of others is conducive to prosocial action.

Now, before you decide to solve the problems of the world by outfitting all the needy with cameras and mirrors, it should be recognized that the relationship between self-focus and helping can be aborted or modified in several ways. For the same reason that it is difficult to keep track of activities in all three rings at the circus, for instance, it is often impossible to focus simultaneously on the self and on the other in need. Attention toward the self, aside from bringing standards into view, may make it less likely that the needs of others will be recognized. And, in addition to this "divided focus" problem, there is yet another complication. A recurrent theme in this chapter has been the idea that prosocial action, especially in emergencies, entails some direct danger to the self. Making someone self-aware during such an emergency could cause him or her to burst into flame—in a psychological sense. Extreme self-concern and fear for one's own well-being could often be the result of self-focus because lower-level self-standards are salient in the situation. Needless to say, this would interfere with prosocial action.

Experiments by Gibbons and his colleagues (1978) and by Gotay (1978) have provided clear evidence in support of this possibility. In the five studies Gibbons and his associates conducted, self-focus was often found to *reduce* the likelihood of helping; in the study by Gotay, a similar consequence was observed under certain conditions. Whether self-focus increased or decreased the incidence of aiding behavior in these investigations was a matter of the salience of self-evaluation standards. When Gibbons et al. made the justice standard salient by making subjects feel they had been unfairly overpaid for doing a task, self-focus increased helping; when Gotay highlighted the normative standard by placing signs advocating helping all over the walls of her laboratory, helping was also enhanced by self-focus. But when prosocial standards were not emphasized in these studies, or when more personal standards were featured (as when Gibbons et al. arranged for subjects to fail an exam just before being asked to help), subjects exposed to mirrors became less likely to lend a hand. These studies, in sum, show the central importance of the salience of standards in the link between self-focus and helping.

GROUP SIZE EFFECTS

How can a mugging in a big city go on apparently unnoticed and usually undeterred in the presence of tens and sometimes hundreds of people? Concerned with the all-too-frequent lack of helping in incidents where helping would seem to be a natural activity, Latané and Darley (1968) embarked on a series of now-classic studies designed to find out why. They staged a variety of "emergencies"—apparent fires, possible injuries, and even robberies—both in the lab and in natural settings, and found that the presence of all those potential helpers was itself the root of the problem. The likelihood that any individual would help regularly *decreased* with increases in the number of potential helpers present in the situation.

Latané and Darley argued that increasing the number of bystanders present in an emergency probably did not make each bystander less likely to notice that an emergency had occurred. Rather, everyone noticed, but because others were present who shared responsibility for offering aid, each person took a little less responsibility for self. This *diffusion of responsibility* effect has been interpreted in terms of self-focused attention by Wegner and Schaefer (1978). They point out that the level of self-focused attention experienced by each potential helper in such a setting should decrease with increasing numbers of bystanders. In a typical helping situation, it is the victim who is the focus of attention; bystanders make up an "audience" and spend most of their time staring at the victim. One result of this is that the victim becomes painfully self-aware; the other result, however, is that bystanders in large groups fail to focus on themselves and so fail to offer assistance.

Wegner and Schaefer also suggest that the diffusion of responsibility has a complement—the *concentration of responsibility*. According to this idea, increasing the number of *victims* should increase the likelihood of helping. To illustrate why this should occur, consider what the focus of attention would be if you and several other people saw a man fall to his knees and call out for help. The man, right? Now, consider the focus if you and those same people were standing in the middle as the Mormon Tabernacle Choir fell to its knees and called out. You and your cohorts would be on the spot, the focus of your own attention because the victims were now *your* audience. It is likely that you would try to gather your wits and offer aid immediately.

In an experiment designed to test the self-focus explanation of diffusion and concentration effects, Wegner and Schaefer arranged for subjects to enter a situation in which prosocial standards would be salient. The subject was fitted with an eyepatch and sunglasses, was asked to do an editing task for money, and then was con-

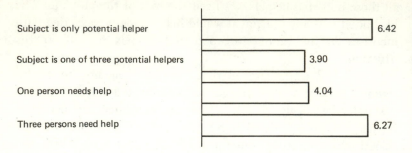

Subject is only potential helper — 6.42

Subject is one of three potential helpers — 3.90

One person needs help — 4.04

Three persons need help — 6.27

FIGURE 6.1. Average number of "work credits" a subject donated to others. (Based on data from Wegner and Schaefer, 1978)

fronted with the information that a fellow subject had failed to complete the task under an even more severe handicap (tiny print to edit) and would not be paid. Some subjects were led to believe that they were the only person who could solve this problem, while others were under the impression that they were one of three potential helpers. Additionally, the plight of either one victim or of three victims was presented to each potential helper. As can be seen in Figure 6.1, each subject was more likely to donate part of his or her own production in the editing task to others under conditions that tended to increase self-focus. Aiding was enhanced with more victims and with fewer potential helpers, so both the concentration and diffusion effects were observed.

In general, group size has striking effects on the self-awareness of individuals in the group, and consequently has similar effects for prosocial action. Zimbardo (1969) and others have noted the *deindividuation* that is often part of membership in large, unstructured groups, arguing that lacking a sense of self, individuals in such groups may not only fail in prosocial action but also succeed in *anti*social action. The finding of Diener and his colleagues (1976), that Halloween trick-or-treaters in large groups are more likely to steal extra candy than those in small groups or alone, is just a mild indication of the thoughtlessness, violence, and anarchy that can result from losing one's self-awareness in a crowd. It is ironic, perhaps, that the only thing that saves us from the extremes of selfishness is an awareness of ourselves.

THE COMMON THEME

No, it's not ironic, it's the theme of this chapter. If there is a unifying thread running through the different research traditions and theories, it is that the person's capacity for self-reflection is uniquely responsible for prosocial action. In the relationship between self-awareness and standards of self-evaluation, this link is quite clear; self-focus makes it more likely that a person will evaluate the self on the salient standards. As a way of tying the chapter together, it is interesting to consider the nature of empathy and of experience (self-perception and social feedback) in terms of self-awareness as well. Although research has not yet been conducted to examine these connections explicitly, there are some findings that hint at what could be discovered.

With regard to empathy, for instance, some recent studies suggest that self-awareness could be involved in the way empathic emotions bring about prosocial acts. Recall that empathic emotional *arousal*—strong emotion similar to that of the person in need—underlies the operation of empathy in the production of prosocial behavior. Research carried out by Wegner and Giuliano (1979) indicates that arousal can cause self-awareness. Subjects in this study who were asked to run in place for a few minutes (as a means of increasing arousal) were more likely than relaxed subjects to refer to themselves (using "I" and "me") when they were asked to supply pronouns to complete sentences. It could be, then, that the arousal that comes from seeing another person in distress acts to produce self-awareness, and so brings on self-evaluation and prosocial action. Although a good start has been made (see, e.g., Hormuth, 1978), more research is needed to determine the extent of the connection between emotional arousal and self-awareness before this conjecture can be accepted.

The influence of self-awareness on the processes by which people experience themselves—self-perception and social feedback—will no doubt also be a topic for future study. However, there is already some consensus among findings to suggest that an important relationship exists. Very simply, it seems that self-awareness is necessary for these processes to take place (see Chapters 2 and 3); for a person to make inferences about the self, it is essential that attention be focused on the self. As an illustration of this, consider a person who does a favor for another—the bag boy at a grocery who stops to help an elderly man pick up some change that has dropped. If the bag boy rushes on to other tasks, taking this incident quickly in stride, he will probably never engage in self-perception. Only if something happens to make him reflect on himself will the correspondent self-inference be made. Someone could ask him a reflective question ("Why did you do that?"); someone could give him a self-label ("I wish my son was as helpful as you"); he could simply come in contact with a self-focusing stimulus (like the group of checkout clerks who gather to watch him help). In these or other ways, the behaviors a person enacts are registered in the store of self-information to become food for thought about the self. An awareness of the self, in sum, is implicated in every phase of prosocial action.

SUMMARY

According to the ideas presented in this chapter, the self is not all that selfish. In the first section, the notion that we may extend ourselves to include others through processes of emotional empathy was considered. It was pointed out that while feeling emotions similar to those of a distressed person is a capacity people develop very early in infancy, the ability to understand the emotion-producing situations of others by taking their perspectives develops with age and experience; this mature form of empathy can then lead to prosocial action. In the second section, self-perception and social feedback processes were examined for their contribution to the development of prosocial action. It was shown that people induced to perform prosocial acts for nonobvious reasons will often repeat such behavior in the future because they have perceived themselves as people who behave in prosocial ways. A parallel process of self-labeling and later positive social behavior can occur when people are given social feedback indicating that they possess prosocial qualities. The third section treated the various standards of self-evaluation that people develop as a means of understanding whether they are good or bad. Self-standards regarding pain, pleasure, approval, normative comparison, and justice were introduced, and the importance of the salience of standards for prosocial action was discussed. The fourth section, both summing up and extending the others, showed that self-focused attention is linked in many ways to prosocial action. Self-awareness increases the likelihood that people will behave in accord with salient standards; self-awareness underlies the diffusion and concentration of responsibility observed in helping and emergency settings; and self-awareness may also be involved in the operation of emotional empathy, self-perception, and social feedback.

7

Self-presentation

ROBERT M. ARKIN
UNIVERSITY OF MISSOURI-COLUMBIA

Even a casual observation of everyday interaction reveals that people often behave in ways that will create a certain impression on others; social psychologists refer to this phenomenon as *self-presentation*. For example, it is difficult for a guest to avoid complimenting a host or hostess about a special dish, no matter how certain the guest may be that a major ingredient was overlooked. People sometimes rehearse their role in a conversation prior to dialing the phone or knocking on a door to help insure that the "right" impression will be made. And when the occasions are more special, that people attempt to control the images others form of them is all the more apparent. People usually put their best foot forward and attempt to make the most favorable impression possible when they are being interviewed for a job; one might even tailor the image one presents to match the preferences of the interviewer, perhaps saying "yes" when one is feeling "no, no, no." Even if you protest that you personally would not adopt these ploys of self-presentation, the phenomenal success of self-help books such as Dale Carnegie's *How to Win Friends and Influence People* surely suggests that many persons would.

The ways in which we attempt to win friends and influence people are seemingly infinite in number. In recent years, social psychologists have provided fascinating and insightful accounts of the intricacies of various "social influence" tactics. For example,

158

we often try to ingratiate ourselves with others by paying them compliments we don't mean ("I really *do* like your name, Hortensia, it's . . . ah, um . . . so unusual!"). Doing favors for people is also a way of influencing them; the recipient may feel obliged to return the sentiment as well as the favor. Conforming to someone's opinions is still another way in which we attempt to stay in his or her good graces ("Oh yes, Professor Malaprop, I also think the theory of happy teeth is fascinating"). One could argue, in fact, that *all* behavior in social interaction is designed in part to influence the thoughts and behavior of the other people present. For this reason, it is necessary to limit the scope of this chapter.

Rather than discussing tactics of social influence generally, this chapter will focus on the strategies and tactics we employ in managing the impressions that others form of us. Termed self-presentation, this aspect of social influence involves the explicit description of one's attributes to others as well as an individual's behaving in a manner intended to imply that he or she possesses certain characteristics. Naturally, we could attempt to convince someone that we are wild and crazy by saying that we are, or by behaving in wild and crazy ways. How and when we go about convincing others that we are intelligent, responsible, honest, fair, and so on, is the core of this chapter. As pointed out in Chapter 1, our self-concept is composed of the residue of interpersonal evaluations encountered during and since childhood. In this chapter, the ways in which we try to bring about positive interpersonal evaluations (by conveying that we possess positive characteristics) and the ways in which our self-concept may be affected by our relative success in this endeavor are discussed.

THE BASIS OF SELF-PRESENTATION

Goffman's (e.g., 1959) engaging theory of self-presentation views every encounter between people as a sort of theatrical performance in which each participant enacts a "line," a complete pattern of verbal and nonverbal acts communicating one's view of the situation and participants (especially oneself). A central feature of the person's line, termed "face," is defined as the positive social value that a participant claims for herself or himself in the interaction. A participant who maintains an image appropriate to the encounter (in the eyes of others) and thus receives information from all participants that this self-presentation is appropriate and that he or she is worthy is said to be "in face" or "maintaining face." In contrast, if one's line breaks down or is rejected, one is said to be "out of face," which is highly similar to the everyday term "losing face." Stepping squarely into the leavings of a Great Dane while on a first date, or joking loudly about the absurdity of the name Melvin—only to hear one of those present referred to as Mel soon after—are examples of how to lose face in short order.

According to Goffman, face-to-face encounters are governed by a set of rules that prescribe what behaviors are appropriate for the situation. Of course, there are different rules and expectations for different role relationships (lover, racquetball opponent, stranger) and for varying circumstances. Among these rules, a fundamental aspect of social interaction is that encounters involve mutual commitment and reciprocity among the participants. Specifically, participants in an interaction are committed to use a variety of techniques to help one another maintain face. This process, termed "face-work," is easily seen in the excuses we help provide others for their social blunders or personal disasters (e.g., "Gee, I ran into that door myself just last week") and our acceptance of others' face-saving techniques ("I agree, it was a tough test; I can't imagine how I pulled an A").

However, the maintenance of face is clearly not the goal of social interaction. Rather, it is a necessary condition for the continuation of social interaction. Face-work is designed to overcome obstacles to smooth encounters and lasting relationships. The goals of the relationship are the multitude of material and social benefits we obtain from affiliating with others. Thus, a basic aspect of Goffman's theory of self-presentation is that self-presentation and certain specified reactions to others' self-presentations are necessary for effective interpersonal relations.

QUEST FOR SOCIAL APPROVAL

It seems clear that face-work is performed in the service of maintaining relationships. What about the "line" that defines the self that the individual brings to the situation? We defined self-presentation as the strategies and techniques used to influence the impressions others form of us during social interaction. Implicitly, it was assumed that people are highly concerned about winning the approval and avoiding the disapproval of others, and attempt to do so by presenting themselves in a positive manner. Social approval is assumed to be a crucial determinant of behavior, especially the "line" one brings to an encounter. But why?

The traditional answer to this question is that people don't like disapproval or that it feels good to gain approval. This answer rests on the assumption of a need for approval or acceptance that all people possess. We could end our analysis here by using this motive as an explanation of why people behave as they do. This would be understandable. After all, that is the way we explain behavior in commonsense terms. We often tend to think that other people behave the way they do because of traits they possess. For example, if we see someone stamping on the toes of every passenger on a bus as he or she proceeds toward an empty seat, we might guess that this person is an aggressive type. And we might generalize that this individual is more likely to be a member of the local chapter of Hitler Youth than of the Friends of Furry Felines. The need for social approval or acceptance certainly appears pervasive, and we may be right to assume that everyone possesses this need to one degree or another. Many psychologists would agree (e.g., Rogers, 1961). Maintaining the social approval of others certainly has survival value for both the individual and the species (those who approve of us affiliate with us and therefore are able to meet many of our basic needs), and it is therefore conceivable that such a need could be transmitted from generation to generation along with the genetic code responsible for our hair color, skin color, height, and other characteristics. But this commonsense analysis, placing the need for social approval within the person, may be premature. The basis of the quest for social approval and the relationship between self-presentation and social approval may be determined more by situational factors than previously imagined.

Specifically, it can be suggested that social approval is sought incessantly because it has instrumental value rather than because it is inherently valuable (Jellison & Arkin, 1977). In other words, social approval may be sought as a means to an end, rather than as an end in itself. Jellison and Arkin (1977) noted that people typically reward those of whom they approve and not those of whom they disapprove. Thus, social approval may be valuable primarily because obtaining other rewards (e.g., affiliation, friendship, sex, money) is predicated upon garnering social approval. From this viewpoint, the quest for social approval may be pervasive solely because of the way our culture has linked social approval with other rewards.

Indeed, it is extremely rare in everyday relations for people to give important rewards to people they dislike (e.g., few people tip an obnoxious waiter generously). This very infrequency may mask the importance of the relationship between social approval and other rewards. To point out this relationship, Jellison and Gentry (1978) conducted an experiment in which the subjects were students invited to a supposed job interview. Shortly after arriving, the students learned that the personnel manager who would interview them either typically hired individuals whom he *liked* personally or usually hired individuals he *disliked* personally (because they typically worked out better for the particular job he needed to fill). Assuming that their subjects would sense intuitively what social psychologists have demonstrated clearly in research (namely, that people like people who express attitudes similar to their own), Jellison and Gentry gave their job applicants an opportunity to learn about the interviewer's attitudes toward some issues and then asked them to complete an attitude survey that would be seen by him. Not surprisingly, the students expressed similar attitudes to the personnel manager when he supposedly hired individuals he liked; however, they expressed dissimilar attitudes when he supposedly hired individuals he disliked. Thus, subjects were willing to incur the interviewer's disapproval if they could gain the rewarding job by doing so.

The implications of this finding are interesting. If social *disapproval* always led to rewards, we would live in a very different social world, one in which disapproval might be sought as much as approval. Children might give up trying to be the teacher's pet and strive instead to be the teacher's wild animal. But this is not the case; in our world, people behave in ways designed to gain approval because such approval is almost always useful in the search for additional kinds of benefits. In fact, the very pervasiveness of this connection often leads us to ignore it and to accept the need for approval as a complete explanation for behavior that results in approval. When someone does something that results in *disapproval*, people usually recognize that other motives may have led to the act. The unruly child who obtains parental frowns, for example, is said to be seeking attention. But when someone does something that produces approval, we seldom stop to recognize the additional goals of such action, and note instead that the person is merely trying to self-present in a positive light.

THE LINK WITH OTHER REWARDS

Although it seems common, even approval seeking may not be quite as pervasive as it appears at first. If the basis of self-presentation is approval seeking, and approval is valuable only when it is tied up with other positive outcomes, then people should present themselves in a positive way largely when influencing the judgments of others will make a difference in obtaining social and material outcomes. This notion was tested in an experiment by E. E. Jones and his colleagues (1965) in which half the subjects were placed in a dependent role where they would benefit by making themselves attractive to a target person. The remaining subjects were not controlled by the target person; therefore, they had little reason to impress him.

Subjects were assigned to be "workers" in a simulated business situation in which a "supervisor" would evaluate their performance. Half the workers learned that the supervisor was free to decide after the worker completed each problem whether or not a solution was correct. The remaining workers were led to believe that the supervisor was committed to a series of specific solutions worked out in advance. When given the opportunity later, workers presented themselves as very concerned about (1) morale, (2) getting along with others, (3) cooperation, and (4) mutual supportiveness (all values that they had overheard the supervisor endorse earlier) when they were interacting with the supervisor, who was free to decide on a performance standard. Subjects interacting with the supervisor who was not free to decide on a standard, in turn, were less likely to endorse these values. In short, subjects were very sensitive to contextual factors when expressing their opinions to the supervisor. They presented themselves as similar in attitudes to the supervisor only when the probability of gaining a positive evaluation, and hence, reward, was high.

It is certainly reasonable to separate situations appropriate for self-presentation from situations where this effort is useless. Indeed, while most people would put their best foot forward during a job interview with a personnel executive, few persons would waste time attempting to impress this person's receptionist. The fluctuation of self-presentation across situations with "important" versus "unimportant" people is a familiar theme in movies, plays, and television, just as it is in everyday life. When people change their self-presentations at the drop of a hat—in situation comedies or in your living room—you might infer that they have been "plotting" or planning their behavior to impress you. But the goals of gaining approval may not always be salient to people prior to their behavior, and the "masks" they wear may not be donned as the result of conscious deliberation. Most likely, some self-presentation strategies are planned and chosen, while others are automatic because they have been used many times before. In either case, though, it certainly seems true that people who maintain face and receive social approval have mapped out a path of least resistance in the social world.

THE EVIDENCE

Traditionally, social (and most other) psychologists have drawn a general distinction between causes of behavior that are *internal* (e.g., attitudes, traits, and values) and causes of behavior that are *external* (e.g., social pressure, threats, or incentives). This distinction can be seen clearly in the achievement motivation literature, where psychologists have theorized that people see their task performance as due either to internal causes (i.e., their ability or effort) or to external causes (i.e., the difficulty of the task or luck). Happily, the theorizing of social psychologists closely matches their subjects' behavior. Research in which subjects are asked to organize their perceptions of various causes of behavior along any dimension they wish (by rating the perceived similarity of various causes to one another) shows that the internal-external distinction is useful to most people. And well it should be. Much of interpersonal relations involves the prediction (and perhaps control) of the behavior of others (Kelley, 1972). It is clearly important for one to be able to decide, for example, whether the person who just stamped on one's toe did so because of internal factors, (aggressiveness, a bad mood, or a streak of cruelty) or external ones (someone tripped him, his shoes didn't fit, or he had no place else to stand). The degree to which someone's behavior is seen as due to internal versus external factors should affect dramatically the way others behave toward this person.

In spite of the obvious value of distinguishing carefully between internal and external causes of behavior for predicting what someone is likely to do in the future, a great deal of research conducted during the last decade reveals that people are not perfect at drawing this distinction. In fact, numerous studies show that there exists a systematic bias in the way people perceive others. People tend to *over*attribute the behavior of others to the person's internal characteristics, qualities, or traits. (This does not apply to peoples' perceptions of their own behavior, however; see Chapter 9). Indeed, this phenomenon is so pervasive that it has been called the *fundamental attribution error* (Ross, 1977). Because psychologists and the public alike are subject to the bias (Wegner & Vallacher, 1977), it would not be surprising to find that both the commonsense thinking of the average person and the theorizing of the psychologist converge on an overly internal view of the causes of behavior. In fact, it seems that on a semiannual basis this fundamental attribution error reappears in social psychology courses everywhere. Students and professors alike are surprised (and undoubtedly somewhat dismayed) to see in topic after topic (e.g., conformity, bystander intervention, obedience) how easily people forget their attitudes and values and conform to the more salient and pressing demands of the situation (see Milgram, 1977).

SELF-PRESENTATION APPROACH

Most social psychologists assume the presence of internal dispositions as causes of behavior but study the effects of the social context instead (consistent with the accepted definitions of the purposes of social psychology). The situational factors that make up the social context are studied, in part, because they appear to be in conflict with internal, dispositional forces. The self-presentation approach also assumes that the social situation is remarkably influential in affecting behavior; however, it also asks, To what extent is behavior that appears at first to reflect internal dispositional factors actually a response to external forces as well?

According to the self-presentation perspective, some behavior that is commonly assumed by psychologists and nonpsychologists alike to reflect internalized values, dispositions, or attitudes is highly (if not solely) dependent upon situational contingencies of social approval and disapproval. To provide evidence for this viewpoint, researchers have adopted the strategy of selecting a behavior that conventional wisdom assumes to be a reflection of internal dispositional influences and then investigating whether individuals express the behavior to a greater extent when they are likely to receive social approval for it than when they are not. If people stop behaving in a particular manner when they no longer receive social approval for it, it seems reasonable to conclude that the expression of the behavior is dependent upon the social approval itself, and that the behavior is not caused by internal dispositional factors. A second research strategy involves demonstrating that people have a working knowledge of the subtle factors influencing whether or not others approve or disapprove of a particular behavior.

This section of the chapter discusses three areas in which these self-presentation strategies have been employed. For each topic, a good place to begin is by discussing briefly the conventional (dispositional) view of the causes of behavior. Following this, the evidence supporting the self-presentation perspective will be presented. As an aside, the reader should bear in mind that rigorous research on self-presentation began only recently. Self-presentation has long been viewed by social psychologists as a nuisance, and not as a research topic. Despite the relative infancy of research on self-presentation, what follows is a good beginning.

SEX ROLES

The differences between the sexes are commonly thought to stem from basic biological differences, perhaps hormonal or genetic in nature (Frieze et al., 1978; Tavris & Offir, 1977), or from basic personality differences deriving from differential socialization (e.g., Horner, 1972). Women are often characterized as more emotional, sensitive, compassionate, affectionate, and compliant than men, but less competitive, aggressive, analytical, ambitious, or intelligent. Although the differences between the sexes may be fewer and smaller than sex-role stereotypes suggest (e.g., Tavris & Offir, 1977), there are real and clear behavioral differences between men and women (e.g., Cooper, 1979).

Perhaps because cross-sexed behavior has been so systematically suppressed in our culture (Costrich et al., 1975), counterexamples ("masculine" women or "feminine" men) have been few and far between. Possibly for this reason, it has been easy for psychologists and nonpsychologists alike to assume that sex differences are inherent and immutable. Recently, however, theorists have viewed sex differences in a larger perspective, as socialized behavior patterns and therefore as potentially changeable. Horner (1972), for example, has argued that many women have internalized (i.e., privately accepted) the belief or expectancy that "success in achievement situations will be followed by negative consequences"; she has labeled those persons high in the "motive to avoid success." Persons with this personality disposition, or motive, are said to have an *internal, psychological* barrier to achieving success rather than a barrier based on physiology.

In contrast to this traditional approach, the self-presentation view of sex-role-related behavior would predict that most people conform to the traditional sex-role stereotypes because attractive others approve of such conformity. Both men and women undoubtedly sense, consciously or not, that others hold well-articulated expectations for gender-appropriate behavior. They may simply conform to different sets of expectations about what is appropriate. The implication of the situational viewpoint is that the behavior of men and women could change dramatically from one moment to the next if the expectations that others held and communicated to them were to change. Zanna and Pack (1975) have shown just how changeable sex-role-related behavior can be when the expectations that others hold for the individual are varied and he or she is motivated to impress the other.

In this study, female undergraduates were given an opportunity to describe themselves (on a questionnaire) to either a highly desirable male (a six-foot tall, twenty-one-year-old senior with no current girlfriend, a desire to meet female college students, and a car!) or to a less desirable male (a five-foot five-inch, eighteen-year-old freshman with a girlfriend, no desire to meet college women, and no car) just prior to a get-acquainted conversation with him. Because they had seen a questionnaire completed by the man earlier in the study, the women had either learned (through manipulated information) that his image of the ideal woman conformed to the traditional feminine stereotype (i.e., emotional, deferent, soft, passive, etc.) or to its reverse (i.e., independent, competitive, ambitious, dominant, etc.). When the partner was highly desirable, the women described themselves in ways that conformed to his ideal, portraying themselves as more conventional in terms of sex role when his ideology was traditional and as less conventional when his ideology was liberated. When the partner was generally undesirable, however, the effects of his ideology on the women's self-presentation was nil; they portrayed themselves as neither traditional nor liberated.

Zanna and Pack tested an additional hypothesis with even more far-reaching implications. In addition to completing a questionnaire, their subjects were asked to complete a test that purportedly assessed their intelligence (the scores from which would be included in the information given to the partner). Remarkably, when the prospective partner was desirable, the women's performance on this test was much lower when his ideal woman was traditional than when she was liberated. When the prospective partner was undesirable, their performance was unrelated to his ideology.

Apparently, subjects faced with the desirable traditionalist moderated, or reduced, their performance on the intelligence test in order to present themselves to him in an attractive way. Thus, it may be that the occasional finding of lower performance by women than by men on certain kinds of tests is attributable to the existing (but changeable) relationship between performance and social approval in our culture and does not reflect lesser abilities among women or even a dispositional fear of success. This viewpoint is supported by the finding that women usually score much lower than men on the mathematical aptitude portion of the College Entrance Examination (math analytic abilities are not *supposed* to be the province of women) but improve dramatically if the same problems are reworded to deal with cooking, gardening, or other activities normally thought to be within their domain (Milton, 1958, 1959).

So as not to leave the male reader wondering, we should add that Jellison et al. (1975) have repeated Zanna and Pack's findings for men as well as for women. They found that men also lower and raise their intellectual performance and adjust their sex-role identity to match the preferences of attractive others.

Indeed, men apparently go to great lengths to ensure an appropriate sex-role self-presentation. In two clever experiments, Holmes (1971) instructed half his male subjects that they would be asked to suck on several objects, including a rubber nipple on a baby's bottle, a pacifier, and a breast shield. The remaining subjects were told that they would be asked to feel various objects, such as sandpaper and cloth. All the subjects were then informed that in the second half of the study they would be asked to experience some electric shock (or to squeeze a hand dynamometer measuring strength of grip) while their physiological responses were recorded. As the experimenter busied himself with setting up the equipment, subjects were told to indicate on a questionnaire how great a shock intensity they would be willing to accept (or how many times they would be willing to squeeze the dynamometer). Subjects who anticipated the embarrassing experience reported that they would be willing to accept a much higher shock intensity (or squeeze the dynamometer more times) than did subjects who did not anticipate the embarrassment. Presumably subjects' willingness to endure higher shock intensities or to expend great effort was meant to show that they were tough, courageous, masculine types and to avoid fostering the embarrassing impression that they enjoyed the sucking task, were infantile or immature, or perhaps were even homosexual.

EXCHANGE

Lerner (1971) and others have argued that people possess an intense desire to believe in a just world. Injustice deeply upsets people. Learning that someone has attained a reward through deceit, avoided a prison term by receiving an unwarranted clemency, passed an exam without studying, or found happiness without even searching for it can madden even the most well-adjusted and realistic person. People seem eager to believe that "people get what they deserve and deserve what they get." This motivation is supported by a great deal of research (see Berkowitz & Walster, 1976).

Perhaps the most dramatic evidence supporting the view that people have well-defined and deep-seated values or standards about the importance of justice is that they will behave in ways that are very costly to themselves in order to restore justice. The term *equity* is usually used by social psychologists to refer to fairness in the exchange of work for money. Not surprisingly, research shows that when people feel they are being underpaid for their work, this perceived *inequity* causes feelings of unhappiness, disgust, anxiety, and a desire to escape the situation. What is more surprising is that people also seem to experience distress when they are *overpaid* for their work. Research shows that people attempt to restore equity when overpaid by working harder, if that is possible (Adams & Rosenbaum, 1962; Moore & Baron, 1973). After reflecting for a moment on this costly way to restore equity, it is not hard to see why the popular belief among most people is that the desire for equitable relations must stem from internal, personal standards.

In contrast to this view, much research suggests that conformity to the norm of equitable exchange is, at least in part, a strategy designed to win the approval of relevant others. Support for this self-presentation view of exchange behavior can be found in several experiments in which subjects were asked to make allocations of payment for their own and others' work. For example, Reis and Gruzen (1976) arranged for subjects to allocate $5 among themselves and three work partners. Each allocator was told that the four workers in his or her group had performed at different levels on a task, and the exact input of each worker was specified. The main experimental variable was whether or not the subject's allocations would become known to others, and, if so, to whom they would become known. Thus, for some subjects, it was noted that the experimenter would be aware of their allocations, while for others, the experimenter would not know this. And for some subjects in both groups, it was made clear that all the co-workers would learn of the allocation pattern, while for others, it was emphasized that the co-workers would remain unaware of this and would not even be told the total amount divided.

The most equitable allocations—in which payment was proportional to performance—occurred when subjects thought the experimenter alone would know of their decision. Since all participants were working for the experimenter, this adherance to an equitable distribution rule probably reflected the "reward for productivity" relationship implicit between employer (the experimenter) and employees (the subject and co-workers). In contrast, when subjects believed that only the co-workers (and not the experimenter) would learn of their decision, they allocated money equally among workers (about $1.25 each) regardless of levels of productivity. This equal distribution of rewards suggests that the meaning of "fairness" changes depending on who is aware of the distribution.

Apparently when only one's peers are aware of one's values, it is best to share and share alike. What is fair when no one is aware? As you might expect, when neither the experimenter nor the co-workers knew of the distribution, subjects allocated more to themselves than to their co-workers; self-interest was paramount when they thought their decisions were private. It should be noted, however, that subjects still were not completely self-interested in this condition; they didn't just pocket the $5 and slink off into the night. The other participants still received some of the money, although less in this condition than in others. This lack of total self-interest may mean that even when their actions are completely private, subjects' allocations reflect a concern for internal standards regarding justice (see Chapter 6). It could also mean, though, that experimental subjects may remain unconvinced that their behavior is completely private and will bring about no repercussions.

In a different context, Kidder, Bellettirie, and Cohn (1977) also tested the idea that reward allocations are heavily influenced by social approval and disapproval. These authors predicted that reward distributions by men and women would reflect traditional sex-role stereotypes when their allocations were to be made public but would deviate in the direction of the opposite sex role when anonymity was assured. Kidder et al. (1977) felt that the traits associated with the masculine sex role—competitiveness, independence, achievement striving, and the like—should lead men to distribute rewards in public according to a norm of equity. The traits linked with the feminine sex role—cooperation, concern for others, dependence, and so on—should lead women, in turn, to distribute rewards equally when their behavior is public. The researchers found that public allocation decisions indeed followed sex-role stereotypes quite closely, with men dividing rewards more equitably and women dividing them more equally. However, if subjects could supposedly keep their decisions secret, they were partially relieved of the burden of sex-role expectations and their allocations departed from the cultural stereotype. In short, it seems that the apparent differences between male and female standards for justice stems from the concern with self-presentation.

A basic tenet of the internal standard view of equitable exchange is that people experience distress when norms or standards of equity are violated. Rivera and Tedeschi (1976) provide evidence, however, that the expression of such distress may be attributable in part to self-presentation concerns. In a work setting, a supervisor distributed $1 between two subjects with equal production contributions. Some subjects were equitably paid 50¢ for their work, whereas others were overpaid, receiving as much as 75¢ or 90¢. Rivera and Tedeschi measured subjects' feelings of guilt and happiness in one of two ways: by means of the typical paper-and-pencil questionnaire used in social psychological research or a technique called the "bogus pipeline" (Jones & Sigall, 1971). The bogus pipeline technique is designed to separate self-presentation from sincerity. Subjects are led to believe that a sophisticated-appearing apparatus can detect their true feelings, much like an advanced lie detector, through muscle responses recorded by (bogus) electrodes placed on their hands and arms. Because the equipment can allegedly detect lies, the subjects feel obliged to tell the truth and not feign attitudes and judgments that they do not really hold.

Rivera and Tedeschi found that subjects who responded via the paper-and-pencil format reported feeling more guilty and less happy if they had received 75¢ or 90¢ than if they had received the equitable 50¢ payment. However, subjects who responded via the bogus pipeline reported feeling happier and no more guilty if they had received 75¢ or 90¢ than if they had been paid equitably. Apparently the individual who is paid inequitably, but favorably, is secretly happy but must publicly feign guilt and unhappiness because he or she has benefited unfairly at someone else's expense.

ATTITUDE CHANGE

Traditionally social psychologists have conceptualized attitudes as predispositions to evaluate and behave toward something in a certain way. In this view, any given attitude is said to reflect some combination of the available information the person has about the positive and negative aspects of the attitude object. This conceptualization suggests that the more information the person has about something, the more stable his or her attitude should be across circumstances and over time. Your attitude toward being in an automobile accident, for example, is probably quite stable and enduring, presumably because you have weighed the clear draw-backs (pain, expense, and so on) against the meager benefits (sympathy from friends, a chance to meet doctors and lawyers).

In apparent contrast to this view, there is evidence that people seem to change their attitudes quite readily to fit the demands of new social situations. In fact, the evidence suggests that attitude change occurs so readily that it must often *precede* rather than fol-low any detailed information processing. For example, there are numerous studies showing that individuals interacting in a group adopt a more polarized (more extreme) attitude than they would if they were responding alone. Quite often, the polarization effect occurs before the group members have had an opportunity to discuss the issue (Jellison & Arkin, 1977). The net effect of this tendency is that the average position of the group is more extreme than the average position of each individual responding alone. This finding was quite surprising when it was first demonstrated in the early 1960s. Until then, most people had supposed that people's behavior in groups would be more conservative (moderate or neu-tral) than their behavior when alone. Because the polarization effect went against conventional wisdom, and because it had such obvious implications for a culture like ours—in which important decisions are made by committees (e.g., juries, boards of directors, the National Security Council)—it quickly became a hot topic among social psychologists.

Current views of this phenomenon suggest that individuals adopt a more extreme position in a group setting out of a concern for self-presentation (Jellison & Arkin, 1977; Myers, 1978). One inter-pretation is that people like to demonstrate their uniqueness and therefore act in ways that will create an impression of their individuality or independence (Myers, 1978). The way of creating such an impression is by adopting a position slightly more extreme than that of others. A somewhat different interpretation is that people sense, consciously or not, that endorsing a position slightly

more extreme on the preferred side of an issue will help convey
the impression that they are knowledgeable, authoritative, expert,
or well-informed (in short, competent). In support of this interpretation, Jellison and Davis (1973; also, Jellison & Riskind, 1970)
demonstrated that people who endorse a position on the preferred
side of an issue are (up to a point) seen as more intelligent. Thus,
it appears that people may endorse fairly extreme group judgments
in order to demonstrate that their ability equals, if not surpasses,
that of the other group members. Research has also shown that for
polarization to occur, subjects' judgments must be public and
other group members must be important and open to influence
(Baron & Roper, 1976; Jellison & Arkin, 1977).

There is also evidence that individuals often present themselves
in the *opposite* fashion, changing their attitudes toward a more
moderate position. This effect occurs primarily in situations where
people anticipate hearing a persuasive speech designed to change
their attitude. It was originally proposed that subjects adopted a
neutral position when they anticipated hearing a persuasive appeal
in order to convey an impression of themselves as broadminded,
flexible, and so forth. However, it might be that individuals adopt
a neutral position when they anticipate an attempt to persuade
them, not to convey a positive image but rather to avoid disapproval. By appearing to have no attitude at all, one can avoid appearing to have the wrong attitude. Supporting this possibility,
Turner (1977) found that individuals high in social anxiety (fear
of disapproval) endorse neutral judgments prior to hearing a persuasive message, but that those low in social anxiety do not.

OTHER TOPICS

In addition to the three topics discussed above, social psychologists
have offered self-presentation analyses of several aspects of social
behavior that are usually interpreted from other perspectives.
These other topics include: aggression; helping behavior; performance at tasks in the presence or absence of others; assignment
of responsibility for performance at certain tasks; self-disclosure;
attitude-behavior consistency; and styles of delivering persuasive

appeals. The research on sex roles, exchange, and attitudes was presented in some detail merely to illustrate the self-presentation point of view.

SELF-PRESENTATION AND IDENTITY

Up to this point, self-presentation has been discussed as though any individual entering a given situation would behave in pretty much the same way. Clearly, this is not so; people differ greatly from one another in the self that they present to others. Though it is reasonable to assume that everyone is concerned with being perceived positively, there are many specific self-presentations that can achieve this general goal in a given situation. Consider two participants in a tennis match, for example, both of whom want to make a favorable impression on observers. One person may self-present as highly moral by adhering closely to the rules, giving her opponent the benefit of the doubt on close calls and resisting the temptation to execute an aggressive shot when her opponent gets tangled up in the net. The other participant, meanwhile, may be more concerned with being perceived as a winner—not simply competent but also persistent, tenacious, and even aggressive. More generally, positive self-evaluations can be achieved in different ways in the same situation (see Chapter 1). A person's choice of self-presentation, therefore, may reveal a great deal about his or her sense of personal identity. In this section, some dramatic and surprising implications of this point are demonstrated.

STATUS AND SELF-PRESENTATION

One important aspect of identity is status or social power. People of different status tend to behave differently, in part because of the respective images they are attempting to cultivate or maintain. To some extent, a person's status—and hence, his or her self-presentation—is dependent on the situation. Jones, Gergen, and Jones (1963), for example, demonstrated how individuals holding different positions in a status hierarchy employ different modes of self-presentation when interacting with one another. In this study, two ROTC cadets, one of whom was much higher in rank than the other, exchanged opinions on a number of issues. Some of the issues concerned their own branch of the service, while others were peripheral and unimportant. During the discussion, high-status cadets held firm on issues directly related to the military, presumably to maintain their position of power, but conformed to the low-status cadets' ideas on peripheral issues, presumably to demonstrate friendliness and approachability. The reverse pattern, however, was demonstrated by low-status cadets. It appears, therefore, that one's status in a situation can affect what self-presentation is considered most appropriate and acceptable. Sensitivity to cues such as status can help smooth the course of interpersonal relations.

Status is not always a function simply of the objective power relations between people. Krantz (1978) has argued that some people consistently view themselves as low in status or social power. In particular, Krantz argues that the "slim is beautiful" value in our culture leads obsese people to define themselves as deviants, to feel excessively self-conscious, and to be preoccupied with their physical appearance. He suggests that the obese, who appear to follow standards of social appropriateness more than do others, often devote considerable time and energy to overcoming the low status that they perceive derives from their physical appearance.

STIGMA

Personal characteristics (like obesity) that tend to lower one's value in interpersonal relations are often referred to as *stigmas*. The term "stigma" comes from the ancient Greeks, who at one time identified slaves, criminals, and traitors by burning or cutting some symbol onto their bodies (Goffman, 1963). Today the term is used in a more general sense to connote a variety of characteristics that are considered culturally undesirable—physical and mental handicaps, social factors that make one undesirable (like being unemployed, homosexual, or a convict), and demographic factors that tend to imply low status (like being old, poor, or ethnic).

Goffman (1963) has argued that an interaction between two people may be very difficult if one of them is stigmatized. Part of the problem rests with the "normal" party to the interaction. You can probably recall some time when you have felt uncomfortable being around someone who was stigmatized in some way. Mental instability provides a classic example. Farina and Ring (1965) found that individuals who were informed that a member of their group had once been hospitalized for mental illness judged him to be less adequate and less likable, and treated him less well than did another set of individuals who thought the very same person behaving the very same way was reasonably well adjusted.

But the "normal" party to the interaction is not completely responsible. Farina et al. (1971) found that mental patients who thought a partner knew about their mental status felt less appreciated, found the interaction more difficult, and actually performed more poorly on a cooperative task than patients who thought their partner didn't know about their mental status. Furthermore, the behavior of the first group led them to be perceived as more tense, anxious, and poorly adjusted than the second group—even though in neither condition did the partners know about their mental status.

People who are stigmatized may not only accept their status but may sometimes even prefer to retain their stigma as a "self-handicapping strategy" (Berglas & Jones, 1978; Jones & Berglas, 1978). Specifically, people may sometimes cultivate handicaps (e.g., poor eyesight, weak nerves, an old football injury) that supposedly make adequate behavior less possible. Social psychologists have written a great deal, often humorously, about the enormous array of justifications, excuses, and explanations individuals offer for inadequate behavior in order to externalize others' judgments about its causes (Goffman, 1963; Jellison, 1977; Jones & Wortman, 1973). Jones and Berglas (1978) went one step further, arguing that persons with an uncertain view of their abilities or achievements may engage in self-handicapping behavior in order to ensure that their failures cannot be taken as evidence of their incompetence. For example, they argue that, for some people, underachievement, in which an individual exerts less than total effort, thus inviting probable (but not certain) failure, may be preferable to exerting as much effort as possible. Maximum effort enhances the probability of success, but it also implicates one's ability more irrevocably as a cause of failure, if failure should occur. Thus, exerting effort is a risky strategy if failure seems at all likely. In a similar manner, Jones and Berglas propose that alcohol provides an excuse for marginal performance and thus serves a similar self-protective function. Perhaps you remember feeling more free to say or do something wild after a few drinks, partly because you could point to the alcohol later as a reason for your strange behavior. In sum, Jones and Berglas argue that the life style of the alcoholic, the underachiever, and other self-handicappers may reflect the adoption of a very useful self-presentation strategy (see Chapter 11).

SELF-CONCEPT

In reading this chapter, you may believe that self-presentation has little or nothing to do with the "real self." Many social psychologists, too, have characterized self-presentation this way in the past, perhaps because they first became acquainted with self-presentation phenomena as a methodological problem to be overcome, not studied. Although it may seem that self-presentation has little to do with the real self, it does. In a variety of ways, self-presentation can blur the distinction between public appearance and private experience.

As you have already learned in Chapter 3, people form their attitudes in part by observing their own behavior (Bem, 1972). It follows from this principle of self-perception that public appearance can have a dramatic influence upon private self-concept. This is especially likely if the public self is met with consensus or agreement from others (or at least not disagreement). Gergen (1965), for instance, found that when an attractive interviewer subtly agreed with subjects' positive statements about the self and disagreed with their negative statements, the subjects experienced

greater self-esteem and described themselves more positively following the interview than they did before it. Similarly, Gross et
al. (1973) found that subjects showed greater change in their
private beliefs toward an attitude position advocated in a speech
they were assigned to deliver if they learned later that the audience
had rated them "sincere" as opposed to "insincere." In a very
real sense, then, people may become what they say they are—as
long as no one disagrees.

Furthermore, as indicated earlier, the ulterior motives underlying
self-presentation are not always in one's conscious awareness. It
is not uncommon for people to seek approval and avoid disapproval
naturally, without pondering the reasons why. Thus, when people
present themselves in a certain way, there may not be an obvious
external reason for having done so. In accordance with self-
perception theory, the lack of an obvious motive may promote the
general tendency for people to feel they are what they claim to be.
Therefore, as Braver et al. (1977) point out, "an affectation
adopted to enhance the general impression one makes on others
could easily become part of the person's self-concept" (p. 575).

Appearance can create reality in still another way. If others
attribute an individual's behavior to personal characteristics rather
than to some feature of the environment, they should be likely to
treat the individual as if he or she really is what he or she appears
to be (see Merton, 1949; Rosenthal, 1969). For example, if you
act warm and friendly toward Joe (whether you "feel" it or not),
Joe is likely to respond in a warm and friendly manner toward you.
As a result of Joe's good spirits, you would probably like Joe—
whether or not you did before you behaved toward him in that
warm and friendly way. Appearance becomes reality. Snyder and
his colleagues (Snyder, Tanke, & Berscheid, 1977; Snyder & Swann,
1978) have provided some interesting empirical accounts of how
social perception can become social reality in just this way.

As discussed in Chapter 1, self-concept formation and self-
evaluation are social processes based essentially upon the individual's interaction with others. Many social psychologists view a
person's self-concept as solely a reflection of the impressions of significant others. Manis (1955) found strong support for this view-

point. He measured the self-concepts of university freshmen living in a dormitory at two different times, six weeks apart, in order to see how much the behavior of others would influence self-concept. He found that each individual's self-concept tended to converge over time with the concept of him held by others. The convergence was due almost entirely to changes in the individual's self-concept rather than to changes in the way he was viewed by the others.

In sum, then, the self-concept may be a transient, ever-changing entity, no more stable than the contemporary conceptualization of the self that a person has adopted as his or her own (Jellison, 1978). If so, to penetrate a person's public self and gain a glimpse of the "true" self may not be possible. As Tedeschi and Lindskold (1976) put it: "Thomas Wolfe once likened the person to an onion. As you peel off one layer after another and finally reach the center, he said, you find . . . nothing! Perhaps the person is nothing more than all the presentations he makes of himself. There may be no true self or attitudes to discover" (p. 209).

SUMMARY

There are numerous ways in which individuals attempt to "win friends and influence people." Among them, self-presentation is perhaps the most interesting and important because of its influence on the individual's self-concept. Although social approval of the self is often sought for its link to other rewards, people are not always conscious of this connection. Because of this, and because others often treat the individual's self-presentation as sincere, what the individual does and says to make a favorable impression on others is likely to be incorporated into the individual's self-concept.

The presentation of the self in a favorable light often provides the basis for behaviors that are thought—by both psychologists and others—to reflect a person's stable, internal qualities. Much of the research reviewed in this chapter reveals that these apparently internal dispositions are heavily influenced by the subtle and sometimes fleeting demands of social situations; sex-role stereotypes, values regarding justice, and attitudes were all found to vary in accord with self-presentation strategies. When confronted by people who have social power, who hold or control desirable rewards, who may be open to influence, and who are available for communication, individuals may change many of their values to gain social approval.

People are not wholly at the mercy of situational variables in the search for approval, though; they may choose among different strategies for managing impressions of themselves. They may, in fact, attempt to engender the immediate disapproval of others (through self-handicapping strategies) to gain other rewards or greater approval in the future. Rather than behaving to maintain a positive self-view in our eyes, we may more often act to achieve a positive image of ourselves in the eyes of others. We do this not because of a need for social approval but because of the instrumental value of approval in maintaining social interaction and the rewards it can bring.

8

Self-disclosure

RICHARD L. ARCHER
UNIVERSITY OF TEXAS AT AUSTIN

> Come now again thy woes impart,
> Tell all thy sorrows, all thy sin;
> We cannot heal the throbbing heart,
> Till we discern the wounds within.
> > GEORGE CRABBE,
> > The Hall of Justice,
> > Pt. ii, l. 1.

This chapter is about *self-disclosure*, the act of revealing personal information to others. Often, when we think of self-disclosure, we visualize a scene in which someone haltingly confesses to some weakness or transgression, as advocated in the quotation above. But self-disclosure can also take the form of a joyous declaration of love or triumph. And in addition to the different kinds of self-information that may be disclosed, such a revelation has both personal and *inter*personal implications. In other words, disclosing intimate information may affect the discloser, the listener, and the relationship between them.

ORIGINS IN SOCIAL PSYCHOLOGY

Since self-disclosure has such interesting implications for social interaction, it should come as no surprise that it has a long history as a topic for social psychology. Georg Simmel, the great sociologist, and Kurt Lewin, the father of social psychology, were quick to recognize the importance of self-disclosure in relationships. Lewin (1935) developed a theory in which self-disclosure was the key to unlock the structure of personality (Lewin, 1964). Later he used his concept of personality in his classic description of differences in openness between relationships in Germany and the United States (Lewin, 1948). Lewin noticed that Americans were more intimate in their day-to-day encounters but that Germans revealed more within their friendships. Simmel (1950) also considered the role of revealing and keeping secrets in the different types of relationships that exist between strangers, acquaintances, and friends. He is perhaps best remembered for his astute observations concerning the surprisingly intimate exchanges between people thrown together by chance, probably never to see each other again—the "stranger on the train" phenomenon.

The insights of Lewin and Simmel sound the familiar note of truth, so undoubtedly these social psychological theorists must have been the first to organize a program of research to investigate self-disclosure, right? Wrong. Social psychologists must sheepishly concede this honor to Sidney Jourard, the well-known humanistic psychotherapist. On the basis of his experiences with patients, Jourard (1964) argued that disclosure was crucial for mental health and criticized the traditional masculine sex role for creating men who were afraid to reveal their true selves to others. He created a questionnaire to measure individual differences in disclosure and examined self-disclosure exchange in both laboratory and natural settings (Jourard, 1971a).

Now that we have taken a brief look at the intellectual roots of self-disclosure, let us return to what disclosure is and what it does. After identifying the *dimensions of disclosure*, we will focus on the *feelings* of the revealer and the *functions* disclosure serves. The chapter will conclude with a consideration of the role of disclosure in *close relationships*.

DIMENSIONS OF DISCLOSURE

Defining self-disclosure as the act of revealing personal information to others will not take us very far until we identify what personal information is. Perhaps you may think this self-evident; if so, then you are not unlike the early researchers in self-disclosure.

THE SUBJECTIVE APPROACH

When Rickers-Ovsiankina (1956), one of Lewin's students, and Jourard (1971b) set out to construct the first scales to measure individual differences in disclosure, they relied primarily upon their own experiences and intuitions. For example, Rickers-Ovsiankina (1956) reports that she selected items ranging from clearly superficial topics to those of presumably personal and intimate character. But in addition to their intuitions, the early disclosure researchers show by their interpretation of responses to the scales that *reluctance to disclose* was their other definition of intimacy. They argued that it's what you *don't* say that is central to the self. If Sam refuses to tell you about his date with Shirley, or you have to drag it out of him with promises, threats, or trickery, then you can be sure he considers what happened personal. Jourard and Lasakow (1958) found that people are less likely to tell others about their personal finances, their personalities, and their physical characteristics than about their attitudes, tastes, and work experiences.

DESCRIBING DISCLOSURE

Later disclosure researchers became a little more sophisticated. Rather than settling for their own intuitions, they decided to sample the intuitions of larger numbers of people. Taylor and Altman (1966) asked naval recruits and University of Delaware freshmen to decide how intimate each of 671 statements was and in what topic category each belonged. Some subjects sorted the statements into one of thirteen categories: (1) Religion; (2) Own Marriage and Family; (3) Love, Dating, and Sex; (4) Parental Family; (5) Physical Condition and Appearance; (6) Money and Property; (7) Government and Politics; (8) Emotions and Feelings; (9) Interests, Hobbies, Habits; (10) Relationships with Others; (11) Personal Attitudes, Values, and Ethics; (12) School and Work; and (13) Biographical Characteristics. Others rated the entire list of statements for the degree of intimacy or personal character of the information. Besides telling us how many ratings a college student or sailor can make before he runs out of the room screaming, the results of the study serve as a road map to intimate disclosure. That is, conversation will turn intimate when college students talk about their own marriage and family or their parental family, their emotions and feelings, and especially love, dating, and sex. On the other hand, conversation becomes more superficial when students turn to government and politics, interests, hobbies, or habits, and biographical characteristics ("By the way, what's your major?"). By determining which statements produced the widest range of ratings, Taylor and Altman were able to pinpoint the topics for which students had the most disagreements about intimacy. Interestingly enough, people seem to be more certain about what isn't intimate than about what is. College students agree very closely in their ratings for biographical characteristics and interests, hobbies, and habits, for example, but disagree on information about parental family and even love, dating, and sex.

The work of Taylor and Altman (1966) and the earlier studies of Rickers-Ovsiankina (1956) and Jourard (1971a) are useful because they describe the kinds of self-information people consider personal. They show that people can pinpoint the things they call intimate, and these are often the things they are unwilling to share with just anyone. But these descriptive studies still leave us without a concept of self-disclosure. In the next section, some generalizations will be offered about what self-information tends to be filed under "confidential—for your eyes only."

THE CONCEPTUAL APPROACH

Before concentrating on a recipe for intimacy, it is helpful to develop a special language to talk about self-disclosure. The notion of personality structure conceived by Lewin (1964) and elaborated by Altman and Taylor (1973) is useful here. As shown in Figure 8.1, the self may be represented as a series of concentric circles, like the layers of an onion. *Depth* or intimacy of self-disclosure is like an arrow or a knife plunged deep within the onion. But this

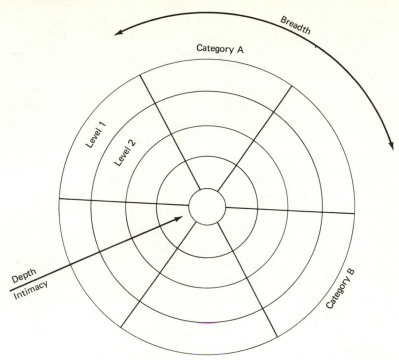

FIGURE 8.1. A self-disclosure model of personality structure. (Adapted from Altman and Taylor, 1973. Copyright © 1973 by Holt, Rinehart, & Winston, Inc. Reprinted by permission of Holt, Rinehart, & Winston.)

onion is also sectioned like an orange. The sections are *categories* of self-information, such as the love, dating, and sex and biographical categories of the Taylor and Altman (1966) study discussed earlier. These categories radiate outward from the center of the self and appear as wedges, like the pieces of a pie. The *breadth* of self-disclosure depends upon how much information about a particular category is revealed, or how many categories are covered in the revelation. To get back to the onion analogy, breadth is like stripping away part of a layer of onion skin. Thinking about disclosure in terms of both depth and breadth serves as a reminder that the statement, "Cynthia told me a lot about herself," doesn't

have to mean that she revealed her deepest sexual desires. Instead, it may mean that she described her interest in jogging down
to the last detail or that she flitted from one topic to the next
all evening.

Altman and Taylor (1973) have identified several key properties
of the depth dimension of personality. Each of them is a kind of
definition of intimacy. The decreasing diameter of the circles in
Figure 8.1 graphically depicts the assumption that there are fewer
intimate than superficial aspects of the self. Furthermore, the
way in which the categories extend across both the outer and inner
layers points up the one-to-many relationship that is assumed to
hold between things on the inside and things on the surface. It is
more intimate to reveal an all-embracing personality trait ("I have
a streak of cruelty in me") than to relate some action taken on a
particular occasion ("I remember when I needlessly embarrassed
Jack in front of all his friends"). In the examples, the cruel behavior could be derived or predicted from the trait, along with
many other things about the discloser. This suggests that the
greater the generalization about the self, the greater the intimacy
of disclosure.

Altman and Taylor (1973) also list *uniqueness* as a property
of depth. Things that distinguish a person from others are more
intimate than things held in common with others. It would be
more intimate for you to disclose, say, that you are psychic and
can bend forks through the power of your mind than to disclose
that you are a psychology major and want to become a psychotherapist. The psychokinetic disclosure identifies you as someone special.

Low visibility aspects of the self are also associated with
depth. Recently, Runge and Archer (1979) tested the notion that
naturally *private* self-information such as motives, feelings, and
fantasies would be perceived as more intimate, when disclosed,
than more *public* forms of self-information such as behaviors and
events (see Fenigstein, Scheier, & Buss, 1975). As expected, Runge
and Archer found that a woman's disclosure of a romantic day-
dream about her professor was seen as more intimate than her disclosure of an incident when she was picked up by the police for

driving while intoxicated. The drinking charge was an event and a matter of public record, but the romantic fantasy was private until the woman revealed it.

High depth disclosures often involve *perceived vulnerabilities*, too. When we reveal to others some weakness we think is our Achilles' heel, the information is experienced as intimate. Jones and Archer (1976) found that male subjects viewed a self-description made by an experimental confederate as much more intimate when it included an admission that he was seeing a psychiatrist for depression and that his father was an alcoholic than when it did not.

In addition, *socially undesirable* aspects of the self, regardless of whether or not we view them as negative, are considered more revealing. Jaynes (1978) showed that a female confederate who disclosed that she could be nosy, gossipy, and selfish was seen as more intimate than one who disclosed that she could be humorous, trustful, and enthusiastic. An even better demonstration can be found in an experiment by Derlega, Harris, and Chaikin (1973) on deviant disclosure. Their subjects, to no one's surprise, judged the tale of a woman confederate who told of being caught by her mother in a sexual encounter as more personal than the same woman's sketch of a summer vacation with her family. Of greater interest, however, is the fact that the confederate's sexy story seemed slightly more intimate to subjects when she was caught with another woman than when she was found with a man. Homosexuality is still considered especially unacceptable by many people.

Last but not least, Altman and Taylor (1973) note that disclosures that carry strong *affect* or feeling have greater depth. Morton (1978) has pointed out that disclosures have some level of *evaluative* intimacy as well as some amount of *descriptive* intimacy. That is, they may reveal personal emotions and feelings as well as facts about the self. In a study by Berg and Archer (1978), a woman who showed concern or sympathy for another who was depressed about alcohol consumption was considered to have been more intimate than a woman who responded with factual information about her own problem—breaking up with her boyfriend.

CONTEXT ALTERS CONTENT

So far, intimacy has been treated as if the content of the self-information revealed is all that matters. But most readers will agree that intimacy is also a matter of context. To decide how personal a revelation really is, it helps to know who made it, when, and to whom. Research has supported a number of our intuitions about which contextual factors are actually conducive to self-disclosure. Chaikin, Derlega, and Miller (1976) found that a nice, cozy room with pictures on the wall, soft cushioned furniture, a rug, and soft lighting led subjects to disclose more intimately than a harshly lit room with bare cement-block walls. Rohrberg and Sousa-Poza (1976) found that subject pairs who drank screwdrivers, a shot of alcohol with an orange juice mixer, had more intimate discussions than pairs who received just the orange juice laced with a taste of alcohol. Brundage, Derlega, and Cash (1977) found that more intimate self-descriptions were given to physically attractive partners. Putting together the results of these studies, one comes to the conclusion that dinner for two with candlelight, wine, and an attractive date will indeed be a pretty intimate affair—at least in terms of what is said.

Since certain aspects of the situation seem to invite intimacy, people have developed *expectancies* about when disclosure *should* occur that match their observations about when it *does* occur. Obviously it is seen as more appropriate to disclose to a friend than to a mere acquaintance or a complete stranger (Chaikin & Derlega, 1974c). But even intimacy with a stranger is all right as long as he or she discloses first and you are simply returning the compliment (Chaikin & Derlega, 1974a). As a matter of fact, holding out on someone who reveals intimate self-information is considered inappropriate. People believe in a disclosure "generation gap" too, feeling that disclosure between persons of roughly the same age is more acceptable (Chaikin & Derlega, 1974c). There is even evidence that the infamous "double standard" pertains to disclosure. Given a problem that could be disclosed (guilt over having caused a fatal car accident or concern for a parent who had suffered a nervous breakdown), a woman is seen as being better adjusted when she reveals it and a man as better adjusted when he keeps it to himself (Derlega & Chaikin, 1976).

These expectancies about appropriate disclosure enter into our perceptions of intimacy in two ways. The first, called an *assimilation effect*, is fairly straightforward. People see a disclosure as more personal because it occurs in an intimate context. For instance, Rubin (1975) observed that the same disclosures led to perceptions of greater openness when the discloser was female. The expectancy took precedence over the behavior. But preexisting notions of appropriate disclosure can also alter perceptions in a more complex fashion called a *contrast effect*. Suppose that two people are conversing. One person reveals something intimate, but the other discloses something superficial. Since the disclosures occur side by side, each will be judged in the context of the other. That is, the intimate revelation will seem even more personal and the superficial remark even more trivial. Berg and Archer (1978) reported just such a contrast effect. In their study, a woman's disclosure that her parents were splitting up over her mother's alcoholism was seen as particularly intimate when a second woman followed it with a disclosure about her interest in becoming a journalism major. Further, the future reporter's statement appeared especially superficial following the first woman's blockbuster. So, intimacy is something that must be taken in context. The perceiver's experiences coded as expectancies can alter the depth of disclosure. Now that the dimensions of disclosure have been identified, it is time to look into the personal and interpersonal dynamics of disclosure.

FEELINGS AND FUNCTIONS OF DISCLOSURE

How does it feel to unveil intimate things about yourself to another? It's a pretty serious business. Jourard (1964) recognized that self-disclosure was a kind of double-edged sword. On the one hand, disclosure brings to mind some things about ourselves that we would rather forget and puts us in the risky position of trusting the listener with confidential, sensitive information. On the other hand, confession sometimes makes us feel better about ourselves and may even help us figure out who we are.

SELF-AWARENESS

One sure thing about self-disclosure is that it makes a person more self-conscious. Duval and Wicklund (1972) have developed a theory that predicts some important consequences of self-awareness. The theory posits two alternative directions for the focus of attention. We may focus attention on the environment, away from the self, and be concerned for what is happening "out there." Or, we may focus attention on the self. In the state of self-awareness, a person is said to compare the *actual* with the *ideal* self. This kind of self-evaluation usually leads a person to find the self wanting. After all, ideals are aspirations for the future rather than achievements of the past. Thus, self-awareness is usually a negative state. According to the theory, self-aware people are motivated to bring their real selves into line with their ideals when possible and to avoid or escape the state of self-awareness when it is not. Self-awareness is created by the presence of an audience or a camera. Hearing a tape recording of your own voice or seeing yourself in a mirror will also focus attention on the self. (The theory of self-awareness is discussed in greater detail in Chapter 2.)

Archer, Hormuth, and Berg (1979) reasoned that self-disclosure, insofar as it consists of self-information and takes place before an audience, typically involves self-awareness. These investigators designed an experiment to compare the feelings and behavior of subjects disclosing under conditions of heightened self-awareness to those of subjects for whom self-awareness had been reduced. Half the subjects were asked to talk on fairly intimate topics, like "My ups and downs in mood." The other half talked on more superficial topics, like "My favorite ways of spending free time." All subjects were isolated in cubicles and told that no one would hear them, although their statements would be recorded via a hidden microphone. But in the heightened self-awareness condition, subjects also found themselves face-to-face with a large mirror. The reactions of the subjects exposed to the mirror should be similar to the reactions people experience for disclosure before an audience. So, it is interesting to compare them to those in the reduced self-awareness condition—in which subjects were in a position somewhat akin to that of a person who locks himself in a closet and talks to his winter coat. Results showed that subjects found the task less enjoyable in the heightened self-awareness condition when the topics were intimate. Subjects in the heightened self-awareness condition also seemed to avoid discussing intimate topics. They waited longer to begin than subjects in any of the other conditions. Finally, self-aware subjects reported that they felt worse about themselves when the task was over than less self-aware subjects. These results suggested that some of the more extravagant claims about the joys of instant intimacy in encounter groups are in error. Self-disclosure to a perfect stranger or group of strangers may only enhance negative feelings about the self. Self-awareness may explain why revealers often tend to focus upon their weaknesses rather than their strengths.

THE RISK OF REBUFF

It is difficult enough to cope with the feelings of self-consciousness produced by disclosure to another. But in addition to enduring their own self-criticism, revealers must run the risk of criticism from others. The self-information a person offers may lead to rejection from others, particularly if the content is unusual or deviant. In the study by Derlega et al. (1973) comparing reactions to homosexual and heterosexual disclosure, discussed earlier, the researchers also collected impressions of the discloser. The impressions of the woman who mentioned her homosexual involvement were markedly more negative than those of the woman who reported a heterosexual incident. It is not surprising, then, that people who score high on measures of *need for approval* consistently clam up when they are paired with another person in an intimate setting and invited to disclose (Burhenne & Mirels, 1970; Cravens, 1975).

When a revealer is rejected, his or her response is twofold.

Taylor, Altman, and Sorrentino (1969) set up an experiment to examine disclosure itself as an indicator of a person's reactions across time to receiving positive or negative evaluations from another (a confederate). In one condition, the confederate's evaluations were consistently positive, while in another they were consistently negative. There were also two hybrid conditions. The confederate either turned from positive to negative or vice versa. As you may have guessed, subjects disclosed less when the confederate ended on a negative note (negative-negative and positive-negative). But even the hybrid condition that ended positively (negative-positive) produced much less disclosure than continuous positive feedback. Even a mild put-down can turn a gushing revealer into a clam.

Although rejection will block disclosure, the situation may not end there; the rejected discloser may also retaliate. An experiment by Green and Murray (1973) provides an illustration. Female undergraduates wrote letters to their confederate partner that were either superficial (courses, vocational aspirations, etc.) or intimate (including relations with men and concerns about physical appearance). Later the confederate sent back to the subject a neutral commentary, a commentary criticizing her writing skills and reasoning ability, or a commentary impugning her genuineness and personality. The second part of the experiment was set up to look like a study of the effects of punishment on learning. Apparently, but not really, by chance the confederate was chosen to be the "learner" and the subject the "teacher." The teacher had to give an electric shock to the learner whenever she made a mistake. It was the women who had received some type of negative feedback and who had disclosed intimately during the earlier letter exchange who delivered the most shock.

Clearly, self-disclosure can be an unpleasant experience both because of the way it makes a person feel and because of the way it is taken by others. However, this is only half the story. Disclosure has a number of important functions. People would hardly be themselves without it, and social intercourse would never be the same.

DISCLOSURE AND MENTAL HEALTH

In his book *The Transparent Self*, Sidney Jourard (1971b) argued that self-disclosure is both a cause and a result of psychological adjustment. Jourard claimed that "every maladjusted person is a person who has not made himself known . . . and in consequence does not know himself" (p. 32). For Jourard, self-disclosure has *motivational* properties. A need to disclose to at least one significant other exists and must be met. Of course, a person may suppress the need to reveal the self, but "in the effort to avoid [disclosure], a person provides for himself a cancerous kind of stress . . ." (p. 33). Jourard believed that not only psychological but also physiological problems like ulcers could result from failure to self-disclose.

There is little doubt that communication about the self plays a role in satisfying needs. People certainly cannot expect others to help them obtain a goal unless they reveal what they desire. In order to get help with an emotional problem, for example, people must first reveal to a psychologist facts about themselves that they usually regard as strictly personal. Festinger (1954) went beyond this general focus on the function of communication in hypothesizing that individuals are led to exchange information about their attitudes and abilities to meet their needs for social comparison. The drive to compare is said to arise in the absence of objective standards of acceptability. People often want to know how they are doing in some area for which no score card or grading scale exists. When no one knows what "good" is, then they want to know how others are acting and thinking. (A lengthier discussion of social comparison appears in Chapter 1.) Mowrer (1971), too, has argued that the disclosure of certain self-information— transgressions committed against others—is necessary to reduce guilt and eventually eliminate neurotic worries and fears. But Jourard has gone further than anyone else. He postulates a general motive to communicate intimate information and states that frustration of this motive is associated with maladjustment.

Unfortunately, in fifteen years of research on this issue, very little evidence to support Jourard's contention has emerged.

Many studies have used the Minnesota Multiphasic Personality Inventory (the MMPI), perhaps the most widely used test of personality and adjustment. The only consistent finding in these studies is that low disclosers are more introverted (see Goodstein & Reinecker, 1976). Some studies using questionnaires (Pedersen & Breglio, 1968; Pedersen & Higbee, 1969) and clinically diagnosed psychiatric patients (Mayo, 1975) have also found a weak link between neuroticism and disclosure. Low disclosers do tend to be somewhat more neurotic. But overall, the evidence for a strong relationship between disclosure and psychological adjustment is just not there.

Another view of self-disclosure and mental health may be more useful. Jourard (1964) conceded that too much disclosure is probably just as much an indicator of personal problems as too little. Whether or not disclosure or lack of it produces stress, disclosing too much or too little will certainly have a deleterious effect on interpersonal relationships. According to Chaikin and Derlega (1974b), neither personality extreme can disclose *appropriately*. One *over*does it, while the other *under*does it. Neither attends to the expectations that are held by others about the proper degree of intimacy within a given social context. Consequently, both will have few satisfactory relationships. We usually think of a person as either a blabbermouth or a clam, but not both. But Chaikin, Derlega, Bayma, and Shaw (1975) reasoned that neurotics, because of their emotional overresponsiveness and high anxiety, may be viewed as blabbermouths in some situations and clams in others. One of the most obvious cues that intimacy is appropriate in a situation is the depth of disclosure of the other person. If one person talks about his or her deepest secrets, then it is okay, even expected, that the other person in the conversation will be intimate too. Chaikin et al. demonstrated, however, that male neurotics do not follow this simple rule of interaction. They seem to disclose at about the same level no matter what their partner does. Ironically, the preoccupation of neurotics with their own problems may interfere with appropriate response intimacy. As a result, they may experience rejection and ridicule—and more problems.

SELF-PERCEPTION

A further aspect of Jourard's (1964) thinking has especially interesting implications for social psychology. Jourard wrote that people who disclose to others would know themselves better as a consequence. This might be true in at least two ways. First of all, by revealing feelings to others, we make them more concrete. Remember from the earlier discussion of the dimensions of intimacy that feelings are originally private, known only to the person who has them. Feelings are also changing all the time, often without our awareness. Research (e.g., Festinger, 1957) has shown that private feelings are often distorted to make them appear consistent with public behavior. Reading some interviews with famous politicians will probably lead you to the same conclusion! It is harder for us to play this little game with ourselves where behaviors are concerned, because unlike feelings, they have been witnessed by others. By disclosing information to another, people turn their private feelings into public behavior and make them more difficult to deny or distort—even to themselves. In short, disclosure *commits* people to their feelings (Kiesler, 1971).

The notion of self-disclosure as a commitment brings us to the second way in which disclosure can lead to self-knowledge. Self-disclosure is a social act that involves risks. It's one thing to feel that you don't know where your life is going, but it's another to disclose that information to someone else. If a person is willing to take these risks and reveal sensitive information to another, then considerable trust in the listener is implied. The revealer must surely like and respect the listener to behave so intimately. Many people would grant that *receiving* intimacy often leads to liking a revealer because of the trust it implies. But it may also be that the very act of *giving* intimacy leads to liking the listener for the same reason. Daryl Bem (1967, 1972) proposed a theory of self-perception that makes just such a prediction. According to Bem, when people find themselves taking action in a situation and no clear-cut external causes for the behavior are present, they attribute the cause to themselves (see Chapter 5). So, if a person who is neither drunk nor in love makes an intimate disclosure to another who is not a close friend or a paramour, and about whom he or she knows little, then the behavior will be attributed to his or her own feelings. The revealer *must* have liked the listener to have placed such trust in that person. It may seem as though this theory puts the cart before the horse, but remember how confused and murky things can be in a first encounter. It's very hard for people to determine why they are acting as they do. Only later, when more information has passed between them, do persons begin to see their actions clearly as responses to what they have learned about the other person.

Archer and Berg (1979) conducted a study to show how self-perception may operate in first encounters. Female subjects disclosed on a topic of their choice to a confederate partner; the confederate also disclosed to them. The experimental variable was whether the subject or her partner went first. When the subject went first, she knew almost nothing about her partner. They had been introduced, but that was all. In this condition, the intimacy of the subjects' disclosures correlated positively with their attraction toward their partner at the end of the study. The more intimate the subject had been, the more liking she reported for the confederate. When the confederate disclosed first, the relationship between behavior and feelings vanished. In this condition, attraction for the confederate depended only upon what the confederate had disclosed. Apparently the confederate's going first led subjects to attribute their own disclosure to reciprocity (something external) rather than to their feelings about her. These results are consistent with the notion that one's own self-disclosure serves as an indicator of attraction for another when no better information is available. Perhaps along the lines proposed in self-perception theory, disclosure tells us how to feel in first encounters rather than the other way around.

PRIVACY

To disclose or not to disclose? When considering the decision to reveal self-information, it is impossible to ignore the issue of *privacy*. Altman (1975) has defined privacy as follows:

> *Privacy is conceived as an* interpersonal boundary process *by which a person or group regulates interaction with others. By altering the degree of openness of self to others, a hypothetical personal boundary is more or less receptive to social interaction with others. Privacy is, therefore, a dynamic process involving selective control over a self-boundary, either by an individual or a group.* (p. 6)

Clearly, self-disclosure is one of the major mechanisms people use to regulate privacy. Derlega and Chaikin (1977) have described the role of disclosure in privacy maintenance in greater detail. They view disclosure in a *dyad,* or couple, in terms of an opening and closing of boundaries. As shown in Figure 8.2, there are two types of boundaries: the *self boundary,* separating one member of the dyad from the other, and the *dyadic boundary,* separating what passes between the two from everyone else. When the dyadic boundary is closed—that is, when no uninvited third party is present—people are more likely to open the self boundary through disclosure.

Individuals seem to maintain the degree of intimacy with one another at a level that is appropriate to the time, place, and length of the relationship. Argyle and Dean (1965) claim that if a sudden shift in intimacy takes place due to the actions of one person, the other will attempt to restore the balance in some way. This seems to be particularly true of men. In experiments in which the listener, who was a stranger, sat very close to the subjects (Skotko & Langmeyer, 1977) or maintained a lot of eye contact (Ellsworth & Ross, 1975), the intimacy of male subjects' disclosures decreased. But female subjects in these experiments apparently regarded the stranger's familiarity as more of an invitation than an invasion. The intimacy of their disclosures actually went up. These sex differences are quite consistent with Jourard's (1964) observations on the male role.

One reason that men tend to reject intimacy from strangers in these studies may be that they perceive it as a threat to their freedom. Jack Brehm's (1966) theory of *psychological reactance* states that people feel they have specific freedoms to engage in various behaviors. Freedoms may be relatively unimportant things, like

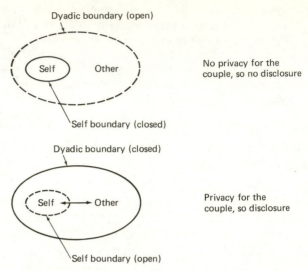

FIGURE 8.2. The relationship between privacy and self-disclosure. (Adapted from Derlega and Chaikin, 1977. Copyright © 1977 by the Society for the Psychological Study of Social Issues. Reprinted by permission.)

the right to tie your shoe, or very important ones, like the privilege of picking your own friends. When someone threatens some important freedom, people are said to experience a negative motivational state called reactance. The motive is directed toward the goal of restoring the freedom.

Archer and Berg (1978) predicted that receiving intimacy from another may sometimes generate reactance. For example, when strangers tell their troubles to a person who just happens to occupy the next bar stool, the listener may feel threatened. Besides having to serve as a captive audience, listeners in this situation may feel called upon to disclose feelings and experiences, things they consider private, embarrassing, or even potentially damaging to complete strangers. They may even get stuck in a relationship they never bargained for. Of course, freedoms are important to both male and female listeners, and both may experience these kinds of feelings. But because of traditional sex-role training, men may well feel more threatened by unsolicited intimate conversation than women.

Many studies have demonstrated the operation of a disclosure *reciprocity effect* (see Chaikin & Derlega, 1974b, and Cozby, 1973, for reviews). When one person in a pair discloses, the other tends to return a disclosure of approximately the same intimacy. This tendency for people to match each other in intimacy tit-for-tat cuts across individual differences. Even people who are characteristically low disclosers reveal more when someone else does (Jourard & Resnick, 1970). The best explanation for the reciprocity effect so far is that people feel an *obligation* to disclose themselves when they receive a disclosure from another, whether they want to disclose or not. Chaikin and Derlega (1974b) trace this obligation to social norms of reciprocity based upon the principles of equity theory (Walster, Walster, & Berscheid, 1978). According to this theory (see Chapter 7), people experience distress when one person in a relationship is giving or getting more than he or she deserves. Disclosure from another is a thing of value that must be paid back.

Returning to our victimized customer in the bar, it is easy to see why he or she might experience a conflict. On the one hand, by listening to the troubles of the next person, he or she incurs an obligation to reciprocate. On the other hand, if the listener returns a disclosure, then he or she gives up privacy. Archer and Berg (1978) found that subjects in public places of a Southwestern city, when faced with this dilemma, attempted to restore their threatened freedom by reducing their written return disclosure. Again, it was primarily male subjects who reacted this way. But when the intimate stranger assured subjects that whatever they wrote about themselves was all right, the feeling of threat was eliminated, leaving the reciprocity effect. Subjects matched the intimacy of the stranger who gave the assurance. Interestingly enough, female strangers were more successful in restoring freedom through this kind of assurance.

The potential threat to privacy implied by intimate disclosure can also be defused by *timing* the revelation correctly. Hitting someone with an account of your sex life too soon in the relationship is a sure way to end it prematurely. Archer and Burleson (1979) did an experiment in which male subjects heard a confederate disclose about either his sister's or his girl friend's unwanted pregnancy either early or late in the half-hour get-acquainted session. Despite the small time difference involved, subjects in the early condition liked the confederate less. They were also less intimate in their own disclosures across the session than subjects in the late condition.

DISCLOSURE IN CLOSE RELATIONSHIPS

For the most part, this chapter has taken an individual perspective on self-disclosure. The feelings of the revealer and the functions of disclosure for him or her have occupied center stage. When viewed from this perspective, disclosure appears to hold as many risks as it does rewards. By trying to be open with others, we may be labeled as deviants or violate another's sense of privacy. But consider the alternative. To avoid intimate self-disclosure is to chart a lonely course in life. According to Peplau and Perlman (1977), "loneliness exists to the extent that a person's network of social relationships is smaller or less satisfying than the person desires" (p. 1). It is an emotionally unpleasant experience associated with feelings of general dissatisfaction, unhappiness, depression, anxiety, emptiness, boredom, restlessness, and marginality. These feelings become a way of life for the chronically shy (Zimbardo, 1977). In spite of its perils, then, disclosure plays its most vital positive role in forming and sustaining close relationships.

Levinger (1977) echoes the opinions of many social psychologists by including the exchange of personal self-disclosures in his *definition* of a close relationship. The study by Rubin and Schenker (1978) of disclosure between roommates and hallmates in freshman dormitories bears out this definition; the closeness of the friendship was more highly related to intimate than to superficial disclosure. But beyond its value in identifying close relationships, disclosure is also a predictor of emotional attachment and satisfaction within the relationship. For example, Levinger and Senn (1967) found that among married couples in Cleveland, Ohio, disclosure of feelings, especially pleasant feelings, was positively related to satisfaction with the marriage.

DEVELOPING RELATIONSHIPS

Spurred by results linking disclosure and relationships, Altman and Taylor (1973) have proposed a theory of how relationships develop called *social penetration* theory. Needless to say, people are aware of the *costs* of intimacy, but according to the theory, people are prone to seek close relationships because of the attractive *rewards* they promise. Altman and Taylor emphasize the tendency toward gradual increases in depth and breadth of disclosure in budding relationships. They consider this the safest strategy to assure high rewards. Figure 8.3 depicts this process of revealing self-information as an ever-widening wedge. Sudden plunges of extreme intimacy, like the proverbial summer romance, flourish only briefly. They usually run into difficulties when the couple discovers unanticipated costs (e.g., fundamental differences in their beliefs) without a history of rewarding interactions to fall back on. So, the policy for disclosure in developing relationships, according to social penetration theory, is "Slow and easy does it (nearly) every time."

The obligation to reciprocate disclosure seems to play an important part in maintaining a new relationship. Altman and Taylor (1973) pinpoint the acquaintance stage as the period in a relationship when the pull of reciprocity will be strongest. As the relationship matures, immediate reciprocation is no longer so important. After all, the very permanence of an older relationship makes exchanging self-disclosure more a question of "now or later" than "now or never" (Walster et al., 1978). This increasing flexibility in disclosure exchange between intimates has been demonstrated with both friends (Derlega, Wilson, & Chaikin, 1976) and married couples (Morton, 1978).

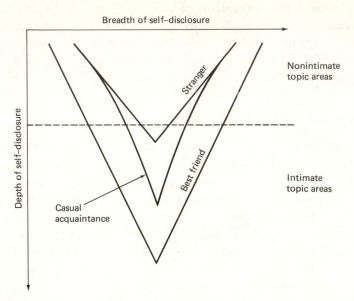

FIGURE 8.3. The relationship between depth and breadth of self-disclosure in the social penetration process. (Adapted from Altman and Taylor, 1973. Copyright © 1973 by Holt, Rinehart, & Winston, Inc. Reprinted by permission of Holt, Rinehart, & Winston.)

SUMMARY

The study of self-disclosure is a longstanding tradition in social psychology that cuts across many of its subareas. In this chapter, our discussion of self-disclosure has taken us from perceptions of intimacy (the *dimensions* of disclosure) to experiences and motives connected with the act of revealing (*feelings* and *functions*). It seems fitting that in the end the individual perspective was exchanged for a social one based upon the couple (*close relationships*). By now it should be obvious to the reader that, despite all the interest, social psychologists studying self-disclosure have only scratched the surface. In the first place, although it has been possible to point to various dimensions of disclosure—depth, breadth, uniqueness, and visibility—we still have not properly investigated how people react to them. Do people substitute breadth of disclosure for intimacy, and vice versa? And which properties of depth are most important in determining intimacy?

The feelings and functions of disclosure have occupied center stage in self-disclosure research from the very beginning. Nevertheless, from the standpoint of scientific data, little has been done to capture the feelings of the revealer. The focus upon the connection between self-disclosure and psychological adjustment may have outlived its usefulness, but few researchers have redirected their efforts toward determining what motives and goals encourage and inhibit verbal intimacy. Is it really a feeling of obligation that drives reciprocity of disclosure?

Perhaps the most important aspect of disclosure, and the one that is virtually uncharted by researchers, is its role in relationships. Is intimate self-disclosure a cause of successful relationships, or is it primarily an effect? Perhaps it is both. Should people in relationships have secrets from each other or not?

It is a little frustrating to have to end with so many questions. On the other hand, the questions emphasize how necessary research on self-disclosure has become. The evidence presented in this chapter shows that disclosure is neither simply all good nor all bad. Intimacy cannot be praised as ideal for all persons at all times, nor can it be dismissed as an embarrassing error or an invasion of privacy. Self-disclosure is a complex process; and because it forms the raw material for social interaction, it will command the attention of social psychologists for a long time to come.

9

Self-reports and Behavior

JOHN B. PRYOR
OHIO STATE UNIVERSITY

> *If we want to know how people feel: what they experience and what they remember, what their emotions and motives are like, and the reasons for acting as they do—why not ask them?*
> G. W. ALLPORT,
> (1942, p. 37)

Historically, social psychologists have relied heavily on subjects' self-reports as indices of underlying psychological processes (Boring, 1950). A *self-report*, in the sense that it is used here, is any verbal or written response that a person makes when asked some personal question. The questions may concern such things as the expression of attitudes or preferences, recollections of past behaviors or experiences, and the individual's reactions to social situations. The responses that the individual makes can range from a mark on a rating scale to lengthy verbal self-descriptions.

In a general sense, self-reports are used primarily to make inferences about an individual's *behavorial dispositions*. A personality trait such as "sociability" is an example of a behavioral disposition. A person possessing this trait is *disposed* to *behave* in a sociable manner. Attitudes may also be considered behavorial dispositions in that certain attitudes are usually thought to dispose people to behave in certain ways. For example, a person who has a positive attitude toward a political candidate might be expected to vote for

206

that candidate in the next election. An understanding of a person's behavioral dispositions, in conjunction with an understanding of the environmental forces which influence the person's behavior, ideally allows for prediction of the person's behavior. Behavioral prediction is one of the goals of psychological inquiry.

Self-report is not the only technique employed by psychologists in attempting to understand behavioral dispositions. Other common assessment strategies include the systematic observation of naturalistic behaviors (Weick, 1968), the use of projective techniques, or the measurement of response latencies when people are asked to endorse trait adjectives as either self-descriptive or not (see Chapter 5). Historically, however, self-reports of people's attitudes, beliefs, feelings, past experiences, and future intentions have provided much of the empirical foundation of social psychology. In everyday life, many self-reports are routinely accepted as valid. For example, when we ask a friend how he or she feels about Marx Brothers movies and the person says, "I think they are wretched and nauseating," we generally accept that this statement of an attitude or a feeling is correct. Furthermore, we can use this information to predict what our friend would probably say if asked to go to a Marx Brothers film festival.

However, the limitations of relying on self-reports as an accurate source of information are recognized both in everyday social interaction and in systematic social psychological investigations. As lay observers, we often discount someone's glowing self-report if we have reason to believe that a candid self-report would cast the person in an unfavorable light. In this same vein, social psychologists are sensitive to the difficulties in interpreting self-reports in which a subject depicts the self in a *socially desirable* way (Edwards, 1957). For this reason, self-report inventories aimed at exploring attitudes or personal characteristics are typically designed to avoid questions with obvious social desirability implications.

While the tendency toward social desirability is generally recognized as a factor in analyzing self-reports, other more complex factors also seem to add to the difficulty of self-report interpretation. The importance of these factors has become apparent from the vast number of studies which have found inconsistencies between self-reports and overt behaviors. These inconsistencies do not seem to be solely related to problems concerning social desirability biases.

Self-report/behavior inconsistency is a longstanding problem in social psychology (Liska, 1975). For example, in an extensive series of studies on childhood morality, Hartshorne and May (1930) found no significant correlation between stated belief in the wrongness of cheating and actual resistance to an opportunity to cheat. Recent reviews by Mischel (1969) and Wicker (1969) have indicated that the problem still exists today, even with modern advances in questionnaire construction and measurement theory. Personality inventories and attitude questionnaires typically bear only a weak predictive relationship (if any) to overt behaviors. For example, Wicker (1971) found that general attitudes toward church were not very predictive of the actual frequency of church attendance. These findings present a substantial problem for psychologists who are interested in predicting human behavior.

In attempting to understand the nature of self-report/behavior inconsistency, several basic problem areas may be defined. First, we must address the question of self-knowledge—that is, what kinds of things can a person know about the self? And how is this understanding obtained? Second, how does a person answer questions about the self relative to what the person potentially knows? Third, how do the person's answers relate to future behaviors? These questions are taken up successively in the next three sections of this chapter. Then, we will look at some of the ways in which the relationship between self-report and overt behavior may be influenced by self-focused attention.

SELF-KNOWLEDGE

Trying to understand the relationship between self-reports and behavior is like trying to trace the route of a long trip using a map which only indicates major landmarks; there are many places where the route may be lost. Perhaps the most logical starting point in tracing this process is to explore what sort of knowledge an individual might be expected to have about his or her own characteristics and how this knowledge is acquired. At first, you might think that any inquiry concerning the nature of self-knowledge is a pointless exercise. If there is anything one knows about, it is oneself. But you may have never really seriously considered *how* you know yourself.

One of the most forceful arguments concerning the nature of self-knowledge is found in the work of the British philosopher Ryle (1949). In his book *The Concept of Mind,* Ryle argues that knowledge concerning one's own psychological characteristics is derived in much the same way that one derives knowledge concerning another person's psychological characteristics. Self-knowledge, in this view, is not something that one has through a direct and intimate understanding of one's own thought processes; rather, it is derived through self-observation (or personal reflection) and inference. For example, a person may come to believe that she is *asocial* because she recalls many instances in which she has shunned the company of others and recalls having actively thought about ways in which she could maintain a solitary life style.

In social psychology, experimental investigations have indicated that at least part of one's self-knowledge is derived from inferences based upon one's behavior. Experiments have shown that if a person is induced to write an essay advocating a position counter to his or her own attitude under conditions where there are no obvious or compelling external reasons for writing the essay, the person's attitude will subsequently change in the direction of the advocated position (see Chapter 3). For example, inducing a person who initially opposes the legalization of marijuana to write a pro-legalization essay is likely to change that person's attitude in the direction of the pro-legalization position when there are no obvious external incentives (such as a monetary payment) for writing the essay. In this type of experiment, subjects seem to respond *as if* they are basing their final attitude statements on inferences made from the self-observation of their own behaviors. This inferential process is certainly consistent with Ryle's (1949) analysis of how people come to "know" their own attitudes.

SELF-PERCEPTION THEORY

As a synthesis of Ryle's (1949) ideas and numerous experimental investigations, Bem (1972) has proposed a self-perception theory concerning the informational basis of self-knowledge. While Bem's theory has been previously described (Chapter 3), some of the highlights will be recounted here. The primary postulate of self-perception theory states: "Individuals come to 'know' their own attitudes, emotions and other internal states partially by inferring them from observations of their own overt behavior and/or the circumstances in which this behavior occurs" (1972, p. 5). It should be noted that Bem includes general personal dispositions such as personality characteristics under the rubic of "other internal states" (1972, p. 37). In his analysis of the possible role of "circumstances" in the interpretation of behavior, Bem follows Ryle in casting self-knowledge into the same mold as knowledge of others. As Ryle put it: "John Doe's ways of finding out about John Doe are the same as John Doe's ways of finding out about Richard Roe" (1970, p. 208). One of the primary decision rules which people seem to use in interpreting their own and others' behavior is whether or not the circumstances surrounding a behavior are a plausible *cause* of the behavior. If the circumstances are judged to have caused the behavior, then the behavior is seen as implying little about the person's characteristics. If not, then the behavior may indeed imply a great deal about the person's characteristics.

While *in principle* Bem's theory suggests that there are no differences between self and other knowledge, *in practice* it allows for vast differences. This is principally because a person has far more information available about the self than about other people—not only more information about overt behaviors but also (at least, according to Ryle, 1949) knowledge of previous thoughts. Often these latter objects of reflection (the person's thoughts) are never made available to others for consideration.

By including the word "partially" in the aforementioned postulate of self-perception theory, Bem (1972) allows for other *unspecified* forms of self-knowledge. However, Ryle (1949) included other forms of self-knowledge in the same conceptual mold. He contended that direct awareness of ongoing mental processes is not possible and that an introspective awareness of one's thought processes is just a reflection on past thoughts. You can easily detect this problem of introspection by trying to reflect upon your own thought processes. While it is easy enough to reflect on thoughts that have passed, thinking about your thoughts *while* they are occurring is like chasing your own shadow.

William James (1890) had a similar idea in mind when he postulated two general aspects of the self: "I" (or self-as-process) and "Me" (or self-as-content). According to James, the I "is that which at any given moment *is* conscious, whereas the *Me* is only one of the things which it is conscious *of*" (1890/1968, p. 46). The Me includes such things as one's material possessions, social roles, and past thoughts. For James, the Me represents the *content* of one's personal experience. In contrast, the I is a transcendent stream of consciousness—the experience or the *process* of presently occurring thought. Any personal understanding of the process of thought (the I) must necessarily be based on inferences derived from the content of thought (the Me), for the I cannot, by definition, be an object of its own contemplation.

To summarize these ideas, it is argued that people do not have a direct and intimate understanding of their own thought process. Whatever understanding they do have of their own thought processes is based on inferences derived from recollections of past thoughts and behaviors. Furthermore, these *self-inferences* seem to follow general rules of causal analysis that are used in trying to understand the psychological characteristics of *other* people.

INDIRECTNESS VERSUS INACCURACY

Recently some social psychological theorists have examined the implications that indirect awareness of mental processes may have for the accuracy of self-reports concerning these mental processes. Nisbett and Wilson (1977a) reviewed many studies which indicated that subjects in psychological experiments often have difficulties in accurately reporting the actual causes of their own behaviors. An extreme example would be subjects' inability to report that they had been influenced by certain stimuli in a subliminal perception experiment. On the basis of these studies, Nisbett and Wilson postulated that the "accuracy of subjective reports [of mental processes] is so poor as to suggest that any introspective access that may exist is not sufficient to produce generally reliable reports. . . . Subjective reports are sometimes correct, but even the instances of correct report are not due to direct introspective awareness. Instead they are due to the incidentally correct employment of a priori causal theories" (p. 233). By "a priori causal theories," Nisbett and Wilson refer to popular ideas which people hold concerning the dynamics of mental process. For example, most people may believe that getting older causes a slowing down in one's thought process. Even for older people, this idea would not be based upon a direct experience of slower thinking but rather the application of the commonly held belief to oneself.

The arguments made by Ryle and by Bem, presented above, concur with Nisbett and Wilson's basic tenet that direct conscious access to the dynamics of mental processes does not seem possible. However, indirect access should not necessarily be equated with inaccuracy. There are two primary differences between the inferences made by a person concerning his or her own characteristics and the inferences made by an expert outside observer such as a psychologist (the ostensible standard of comparison by which Nisbett and Wilson propose to measure "accuracy"). First, self-observers have a vast quantity of personal information potentially available to them that outside observers could never practically obtain; this difference favors the accuracy of self-inference. Second, expert observers, through their training, have more advanced conceptual models that can be used to analyze personal characteristics; this difference favors the accuracy of psychologists. Therefore, indirect access to mental processes by itself constitutes no basis for arguing that self-inference is always inaccurate. Indeed, self-knowledge and knowledge of others' mental processes may both be thought of as involving indirect access. Ideally, psychologists strive to tap some of the vast wealth of self-information that people have stored in memory in ways which allow for the application of sophisticated models of thought. However, a person's memory of his or her past behaviors and the person's interpretations of what is remembered are subject to variation. It is also possible that self-reports do not represent one's self-knowledge at all. The determinants of self-report are taken up in the next section.

INFORMATIONAL AND HABITUAL DETERMINANTS OF SELF-REPORT

When someone is asked to report on his or her attitudes or personal characteristics, a wealth of information might be recollected and assessed. For example, if someone were to ask you, "How sociable are you with strangers?" on what particular recollections would you base your answer? Would you recount your behaviors toward strangers you have encountered in the last week? In the last month? In the last year? As you can readily see, the answer to this seemingly simple question could involve a great deal of thought and effort. When people do answer this sort of question by thinking about their own past behaviors, such extensive recollection does not usually take place; instead considerable selectivity is used. A self-report may thus be derived from only a limited sample of the person's recollections of past behaviors. In other instances, the self-report might reflect no process of behavioral recollection and assessment at all, but rather a preconceived self-description which comes to mind because of situational cues or because it has been frequently used. These various determinants of self-reports will be discussed in some detail below.

MEMORY FOR PAST BEHAVIOR

One general principle which seems true for most of the information stored in memory is that the information we have thought about most recently is easiest to recall. From the perspective of a person thinking about his or her past behaviors, this principle implies that *behaviors* which have been thought of most recently should be easiest to recall. Considering that a self-reporting individual typically bases his or her report on a relatively small sample of the behavioral information stored in memory, it seems likely that the relevant information which comes to mind first should play a strong part in that report. Experimental studies have typically borne out this idea. For example, recent behaviors have been shown to be more related to current self-reports of attitudes than even previous self-reports of the same attitude (Bem & McConnell, 1970).

In other experimental investigations, Salancik and Conway (1975) have shown that it is even possible to *manipulate* what people readily remember about themselves and, thereby, manipulate their self-reported attitudes. In one clever experiment, a series of questions induced subjects to recall past behaviors which implied either a positive attitude toward religion or past behaviors which implied a negative attitude. Various statements were selected which implied either a positive (e.g., "I donate money to a religious organization") or a negative (e.g., "I refuse to go to church or synagogue") attitude toward religion. Subjects were asked to indicate which statements were true for them. For some subjects, the adverb "on occasion" was inserted in the pro-religion statements (e.g., "I donate money to a religious organization on occasion") and the adverb "frequently" was inserted in the anti-religion statements (e.g., "I frequently refuse to go to church or synagogue"). For other subjects, these adverbs were paired with the statements in the opposite manner—"frequently" with the pro-religion and "on occasion" with the anti-religion statements.

Salancik and Conway hypothesized that subjects would be more likely to endorse a statement which included "on occasion" rather than "frequently." Furthermore, they proposed that subjects who endorse the statement, "I donate money to religious organizations," should recall instances in which they have done this, whereas subjects who do not endorse the statement may recall instances in which they failed or refused to do so. The recalled instances would then be available for use as behavioral information in formulating an attitude about religion.

The insertion of "on occasion" did indeed result in more endorsements than the insertion of "frequently." And as predicted, subjects who received the questionnaire which paired pro-religious statements with "on occasion" and anti-religious statements with "frequently" tended to rate their attitudes subsequently as more pro-religious than did subjects who received questionnaires with the opposite adverb pairings. Thus, subtle environmental stimuli which induced subjects to recall different information about themselves resulted in significant differences in self-reports. In generalizing from these findings, we might assume that many different kinds of environmental stimuli may bring various instances of our own past behaviors to mind by association. For example, if we see someone else enjoying a cold beer on a hot day, we might remember instances of having done the same. Our self-reported attitudes toward beer drinking would likely be more positive under these circumstances than if we had observed someone recovering from a bad hangover.

BEHAVIOR INTERPRETATION

The results of the Salancik and Conway study and the others mentioned above suggest that self-reports may only reflect what an individual is currently thinking about or can recall with relative ease. But in all of these studies, self-reports were based upon a sample of the subject's behavior, and it was assumed that the behavior which was brought to mind had direct implications for self-reported behavioral dispositions. However, in most everyday situations behavior may not be so clearly interpreted. We can all think of instances in which two people interpreted a third person's behavior in different ways. In an analogous fashion, one person may interpret his or her own behavior differently in different situations. While cultural norms and personal learning histories account for some of our varying interpretations of behaviors, interpretation may also be influenced by subtle situational cues which bring a particular interpretation to mind. One example of this process was shown in Schachter and Singer's (1962) research on emotions, discussed in Chapter 4.

An experiment by Kiesler, Nisbett, and Zanna (1969) serves to illustrate this process in the area of attitude research. These researchers induced subjects to agree to oppose a position with which they initially agreed. A confederate simultaneously agreed to argue a different issue. The confederate openly stated that his willingness to argue his assigned position was related to either (1) his strong belief in the issue (belief-relevant condition) or (2) the scientific value of the present experiment (belief-irrelevant condition). Subjects in the belief-relevant condition were found to be more favorable to the position they were to argue than either belief-irrelevant subjects or control subjects who were not committed to the behavior. Thus, the subjects in the belief-relevant condition were provided with a situational cue which influenced their interpretations of their behaviors. The relationships between specific behaviors and self-reported dispositions are always subject to interpretation. Specific interpretations often relate to an individual's most recent information inputs.

HABITUAL SELF-REPORTS

It is also possible that self-reports involve some sort of habitual or learned set of responses which are independent of one's behaviors. From this perspective, self-reports can be viewed merely as a behavior—and as with other behaviors, variations in self-reports are related to the learning history of the individual (Skinner, 1957). An individual may thus self-report in a manner which has proven in the past to be rewarding or which has been modeled on others' observed behaviors. Habitual self-reports may be classified into two broad categories: habits which are related to the specific content of the self-report question and habits which seem to influence self-reports across a variety of content areas.

With regard to content areas, habitual self-reports can reflect specific answers which one has learned in response to specific questions. This sort of self-report might be particularly true of children who have not refined the capacity for self-reflection. However, such habitual responses may characterize many adult self-reports as well. For example, it is well known that children's reports of their attitudes tend to correlate highly with those of their parents (Hess

& Torney, 1967) and that these high correlations, though somewhat attenuated, persist into the college years (Goldsen, Rosenberg, Williams, & Suchman, 1960). These findings may be viewed
as evidence for the transmission of specific self-report habits from
parents to children. Children may model the attitude statements
or self-descriptions they witness by their parents. Because such
self-statements tend to be unrelated to overt behaviors in the parents, they are also unrelated to overt behaviors in children. The
influence of peer models upon self-reports may be viewed from the
same perspective.

Habitual biases in self-report which exist across different content
areas are known to personality assessment theorists as *response
styles* (Wiggins, 1973). Though response styles often simply reflect the content of the specific question being asked (Goldberg &
Slovic, 1967; Rorer, 1965), they can have an influence across a
wide variety of self-reports. One of the most commonly recognized
response styles is the tendency to answer self-related questions in
a socially desirable fashion (Edwards, 1957). As indicated earlier,
this tendency is characteristic of most people's self-reports; however, some people tend to manifest it more strongly than others
(Crowne & Marlowe, 1964). In attempting to compensate for social desirability biases in self-reports, psychologists typically take
several precautions: (1) self-report questions are worded so as to
avoid obvious socially desirable answers; (2) if that is not feasible,
both questions with socially desirable answers and questions with
socially undesirable answers aimed at the same information are used;
and (3) subjects are informed that their answers will remain
anonymous. None of these solutions to social desirability biases is
foolproof; however, collectively they provide a tolerable level of
control for this bias.

Some other well-studied response styles which seem to vary
in their influence from person to person are: *acquiescence,* the
tendency to agree to questionnaire items as self-descriptive (Messick, 1967); the tendency to be *critical* (Frederiksen & Messick,
1959); and *response deviation,* tendencies toward extreme answers (Berg, 1967). While response styles may be seen in terms of
habitual modes of answering self-related questions which interfere

with the accuracy of self-report inventories, they may also be viewed as indicative of personality characteristics. Although this idea seems reasonable, the research concerning response styles as independent personality characteristics is sketchy at present (Wiggins, 1973).

In comparing this section with the previous section on self-knowledge, we can readily see that a number of factors besides self-knowledge can potentially influence a self-report. In terms of trying to predict future behavior, self-reports based upon some sample of past behavior would appear to be more useful than those which reflect habitual responses. The reason for obtaining a self-report is to tap the vast reservoir of self-related information that a person has in memory. Habitual forms of self-report fall short of this goal because they do not involve any process of reflecting on past behaviors. However, even when self-reports are based on a recalled sample of past behaviors, the sample may not necessarily be representative of the individual's *typical* past behaviors. Therefore, the report may not be useful in inferring the person's behavioral dispositions.

So far, we have looked at problems in assessing what an individual potentially knows about his or her own characteristics. In the next section, we will examine the problems encountered in relating self-reports to overt behaviors.

PREDICTING BEHAVIOR
FROM SELF-REPORTS

As stated earlier, the relationship between self-reports and overt behavior is often inconsistent. Many points at which a *potential* relationship between the two may break down were indicated in the last section. Self-reports are sometimes not based upon past behaviors at all and, under these conditions, are not likely to reflect behavioral dispositions. In this section, we will explore the role of behavioral dispositions in causing overt behavior. Subsequently, we will consider the utility of a narrowed view of behavioral dispositions in trying to predict behavior.

THE CAUSES OF BEHAVIOR

Many theorists (e.g., Wicker, 1971), particularly in the realm of attitude self-reports, believe that the weak relationship between self-reports and behavior is due in part to the multiple determinants of behavior. People have many attitudes or personality characteristics which are potentially relevant to a particular behavior. Also, overt behavior is often facilitated or inhibited by situational constraints, such as rewards or punishments inherent in specific social contexts. Given the multiple causes which may influence the expression of a behavior, it is not surprising that a single attitude or personality characteristic may be only weakly correlated with actual behaviors. In support of this notion, studies which have attempted to take into consideration the variables which *moderate* the expression of a self-reported attitude have found significant increases in the predictability of attitude-relevant behaviors. For example, Wicker (1971) found a relatively low correlation between stated attitudes toward church and the actual frequency of church attendance. However, Wicker also asked subjects in his study about: (1) the perceived influence of extraneous events (such as weather conditions) upon church attendance, (2) their evaluations of going to church (whether or not they actually enjoyed it), and (3) their perceptions of any actual consequences of going to church. When Wicker included all of these variables in a *multiple correlation* analysis (where the effects of all of the variables were considered simultaneously), he found a significantly higher correlation. Thus, knowing that behavior is likely to be *multiply determined* and trying to assess the multiple causes related to a particular behavior seems to increase the likelihood of behavioral prediction. Studies concerning the influence of "moderator variables" in personality research have produced comparable findings (Wiggins, 1973).

A different and perhaps much more extreme perspective on the self-report/behavior consistency problem has been suggested by Mischel (1969). Mischel did an extensive survey of research reports concerning the relationship between personality characteristics and overt behaviors and found that the average correlation between personality inventories and behavior was only about .30. This means that, on the average, 90 percent of the variance in overt behavior is left unexplained by personality measures. Wicker (1969) found a similar average correlation in his own survey of attitude/behavior studies. While these findings might be explained by the possible inadequacy of the testing instruments used, Mischel suggests another interpretation: that behavior is by nature situationally specific. The principle determinants of behavior lie in the social forces and demands inherent in situations and not in the self-described characteristics of the persons involved in those situations. The plethora of studies which demonstrate the impact of social situations on behavior seem to add some credence to this analysis. However, other theorists have been reluctant to discard the idea that individual differences in attitudes and personality characteristics can contribute to variations in behavior.

THE NATURE OF BEHAVIORAL DISPOSITIONS

Bem and Allen (1974) have suggested that self-reports *are* related to the behavioral dispositions they reflect when they are interpreted from an *idiographic* perspective. This is an attempt (first described by Allport, 1937) to view personal characteristics from the vantage point of the individual who possesses them. Some personal characteristics may be particularly relevant for an individual and others may not. Also, the behaviors that one person perceives as related to a characteristic may be different from the behaviors that another person perceives as related to the same characteristic.

Following the analysis of Allport (1937), Bem and Allen have pointed out that psychologists typically assess personal characteristics in a *nomothetic* way; that is, they assume that one can measure the *relative* presence of a particular characteristic across all persons. For example, a large sample of people may be characterized from their self-reports as being more or less dominant, authoritarian, friendly, timid, and so on. However, it is possible that all characteristics do not apply to all persons. Certain characteristics may apply to some people but not to others. This is the essence of an idiographic approach. For example, some people may be friendly (or unfriendly) across a variety of situations. For these persons, friendliness is a relevant characteristic. Other people may be more or less friendly according to the situation. For them, friendliness is *not* a relevant characteristic. Thus, an idiographic approach analyzes traits in an individualistic fashion. (See Chapter 5 for a related discussion.)

Bem and Allen argue that the particular behaviors which are related to a self-reported characteristic may be different for different persons. One person might describe himself as "very aggressive" and think of his style of card playing and his behavior when driving his car on the freeway, while another person may describe himself as "very aggressive" and think of his behavior in a knife fight and his style in boxing. Thus, the behaviors which these two individuals equate with the self-description "very aggressive" are quite different. Following Allport's analysis, Bem and Allen suggest that the interpretations of self-descriptions must allow for such differences in *equivalence classes*, or the categories of characteristics into which various behaviors are organized.

In support of the idiographic approach, Bem and Allen (1974) assessed the degree to which subjects rated themselves as friendly. Subjects were also asked to rate the *variation* in their friendliness across different situations. For those subjects who remained relatively constant, friendliness was judged to be a personally relevant characteristic. For those who varied highly, friendliness was judged *not* to be a personally relevant characteristic.

Bem and Allen also asked subjects the likelihood of their behaving in typically friendly ways (e.g., "When in a store, how likely are you to strike up a conversation with a sales clerk?"). By correlating the answers to these behavioral questions with the subjects' self-reports of how friendly they were, Bem and Allen were able to assess the subjects' perception of the various behaviors as relevant to friendliness This correlation was very high (.92).

Subsequently the friendliness of subjects' actual behavior was assessed in various situations for which friendly behaviors were judged to be relevant. For those subjects for whom friendliness was a relevant characteristic, the average correlation between self-reported friendliness and behavior was relatively high (.57). For

those subjects for whom friendliness was not a relevant characteristic, this correlation was much lower (.27). Thus the Bem and
Allen experiment shows that we can significantly improve the predictive validity of self-reported characteristics if we take into consideration whether the characteristics are personally relevant for
the individual and whether the behaviors measured are seen by
the individual as related to the characteristics.

A general conclusion which can be drawn from the Bem and
Allen (1974) study is that abstract characteristics mean different
things to different people. In order for a self-report of personal
characteristics to be interpretable, it must refer directly to specific
behaviors. The importance of specificity in ascertaining *attitude*
self-reports has also been pointed out recently by Ajzen and Fishbein (1977). They have shown that self-reported attitudes which
specify actions, attitude targets, social contexts, and the time at
which the action is performed are more predictive of behavior than
are general or global self-reported attitudes. For instance, you may
ask a person his attitude toward "helping Muhammed Ali raise
funds for the United Negro College Fund by answering phone calls
at a telethon on October 28 from 5 to 11 P.M." This attitude might
be more closely related to the person's behavior in this setting
than his or her general attitude toward blacks.

All these findings seem to be conceptually congruent with
Bem's notion that people know their personal characteristics
through inferences based on their own observed behaviors. By asking questions which are directly related to behaviors, we can obtain self-reports which directly tap an individual's self-knowledge.

PERSPECTIVES ON SELF-OBSERVATION

Up to this point, we have considered what an individual can know
about the self, how this knowledge gets translated into self-reports,
and how these self-reports are related to overt behaviors. In this
final section, we will examine some of the limitations of self-observation, the basis of self-knowledge. We will also look at how the

process of self-observation may be enhanced, and how this affects self-report/behavior consistency.

LOOKING INWARD VERSUS LOOKING OUTWARD

In Chapter 2, Wicklund and Frey discussed the theory of self-awareness. This theory describes some of the cognitive and behavioral consequences of self-focused versus environmentally focused attention. It postulates that most people focus on the environment. There are two basic reasons for this. One is that the environment typically provides a high degree of perceptual stimulation; it naturally attracts your attention. The second reason is that self-focused attention (thinking about yourself) is sometimes aversive; self-doubts and inadequacies may come to mind. Other theorists have noted other reasons for a characteristic environmental focus. Jones and Nisbett (1971) contend that it is partially the result of the simple fact that our sensory receptors are poorly located for observing nuances in our own behavior.

This characteristic outward orientation apparently greatly limits the capacity of most individuals to become self-observers as described by Bem. Consistent with this analysis, the explanations that most people offer about their own behaviors typically emphasize the situations they are in rather than their own personal characteristics (Jones & Nisbett, 1971). It follows, then, that one of the reasons self-reported characteristics often fail to relate to overt behaviors is that people see their own behaviors as related primarily to their environments and *not* their personal characteristics. Therefore, it is difficult for people to report on the role of their own characteristics in producing their behaviors.

CHANGING THE FOCUS

One possible means by which people may be sensitized to the role of their own characteristics is provided by self-awareness theory. Experiments have shown that such stimuli as mirrors may be used to focus a person's attention upon the self. Putting people in front of a mirror seems to sensitize them to the impact of their personal characteristics upon their own behaviors. For example, Pryor, Comer, & Banks (1976) asked subjects to rate the humor content of various magazine cartoons. Some subjects made the ratings while facing a large mirror; others had no mirror. Those subjects who faced the mirror subsequently indicated that their ratings were more closely related to their own characteristics than did subjects in the no-mirror condition. Several other experiments show basically the same findings. Furthermore, research by Gibbons (1976) indicates that a person's self-reports concerning the causes of his or her behavior may be more accurate when the person is made self-aware.

Conceptually, there are three ways in which self-observation may be enhanced by self-awareness procedures: (1) sensitizing a person to nuances in his or her past behavior; (2) sensitizing a person to variations in his or her behaviors as they occur; and (3) sensitizing a person to his or her personal characteristics during the process of self-report. Studies relating to these concepts are discussed below.

LOOKING BACK

An inaccurate understanding of one's own behavioral dispositions can be troublesome from several perspectives. In terms of social interaction, misunderstanding the role of your own characteristics in interpersonal relationships can lead to friction and difficulties in relating to others. In terms of learning new skills, an inaccurate appraisal of your own abilities and behavioral variations can make learning difficult. For these reasons, the distortion of personal inputs into behavior has traditionally concerned counseling and clinical psychologists. One technique that encourages self-observation is the use of videotape feedback. In this procedure, patients or subjects are videotaped while performing a problem-related behavior. Subsequently, they are shown these videotapes, often with a counselor or therapist pointing out nuances in the person's behavior. This procedure induces a *retrospective self-awareness*.

While the results of studies using videotape feedback procedures are not conclusive (Bailey & Sowder, 1970), some have found such procedures useful in promoting a realistic understanding of a subject's own behavior in therapy sessions (Boyd & Sisney, 1967), counselor training sessions (Walz & Johnston, 1963), and classroom settings (Alderfer & Lodahl, 1971). For example, Walz and Johnston (1963) found that after viewing videotapes of their own counselor training sessions, counselor candidates' self-evaluations of their performances were more in line with their supervisors' ratings, thus indicating a more accurate self-report of their actual past behaviors.

SELF-AWARENESS DURING BEHAVIOR

Many experiments indicate that self-awareness during the performance of behavior leads to a more consistent correspondence between the behavior and a person's self-reported characteristics. For example, Carver (1975) assessed subjects' attitudes toward the use of physical punishment in teaching situations. Subsequently he gave subjects an opportunity to use physical punishment (in the form of electric shock) as a means of teaching someone to perform a simple discrimination task. In this assignment, some subjects were positioned in front of a mirror, while others were not. Those subjects who observed their own behaviors in the mirror tended to behave more consistently with their previously stated attitudes than those who did not. If subjects had stated that they favored the use of punishment, they punished more under mirror conditions; if they had opposed punishment, they punished less. Recently Gibbons (1978) found similar results in a study of the relationship between subjects' attitudes toward pornography and their reactions to being shown pornography.

The theoretical explanation for such findings is that self-awareness motivates people to resolve cognitive inconsistencies, including attitude-behavior inconsistencies. Disparities between previously stated attitudes and overt behaviors are reduced or eliminated when the individual is self-focused.

SELF-AWARENESS DURING SELF-REPORT

Self-focused attention has also been found to be an important variable *during* self-report (Pryor, Gibbons, Wicklund, Fazio, &

Hood, 1977). Pryor and his colleagues found that the presence of self-focusing stimuli (such as mirrors) while subjects are self-reporting can lead to an enhanced predictive validity of such reports. In one experiment, Pryor et al. asked male subjects to indicate whether several statements concerning sociability with female strangers were true for them. Some examples of the statements used are: "I feel that I can usually communicate well with members of the opposite sex" and "I usually have difficulty in starting conversations with strangers." Some subjects were asked to respond to these statements while facing their own reflections in a large mirror, whereas others had no mirror. Several days later, each subject returned to the psychology laboratory for what he expected to be another, unrelated experiment. Upon arriving, he was asked to wait in a small cubicle with another subject while the experiment was being set up. The "other subject" was actually an attractive female confederate. The confederate did not speak until addressed by the subject, and even then her responses were minimal. During this waiting period, two measures of the sociability of the subject's behavior were assessed: (1) the number of words he spoke during the first two minutes; and (2) the confederate's overall impression of his sociability. These two measures were statistically combined into a single measure of sociability. When subjects were made self-aware during their self-report, the correlation between self-reports of sociability and measures of behavioral sociability was quite high, ranging from .55 to .73 across two separate replications of the study. However, in the no-mirror condition this correlation was low, ranging from .03 to .28. Thus, the predictive validity of subjects' self-reports was significantly enhanced if they reported under self-focused conditions.

In another experiment, Pryor et al. (1977) found that the relationship between subjects' self-reports and their *past* behaviors could also be enhanced with the same sort of manipulation during self-report. In other studies, Scheier, Buss, and Buss (1978) have shown that people who are chronically self-conscious (see Chapter 10) tend to give self-reports more consistent with their behaviors. The explanation for self-awareness *during* behavior is also applicable here. Close monitoring of their responses to the self-report inventories may help self-aware subjects bring those responses into close alignment with their actual behavioral dispositions or with recollections of their past behaviors.

Another recent study by Ickes, Layden, and Barnes (1978) also indicates that self-aware persons self-report in a manner strongly related to their personal behavioral dispositions. Subjects were asked to provide fifteen answers to the question, "Who am I?" under either self-focused (mirror) or control (no-mirror) conditions. Subjects in the self-focused condition were more likely to mention their personal interests and activities (i.e., their judgments, tastes, likes, intellectual concerns, hobbies and pastimes) and less likely to describe themselves in terms of abstract identifications (e.g., liberal, Christian, Marxist) or broad categories (e.g., a man, a black) than were subjects in the control group. Thus, self-aware persons seemed to base their self-descriptions more on their actual behaviors. Abstract indentifications and categorical self-descriptions are the types of self-reports one might expect if an individual responded in some *habitual* fashion. This study implies that with self-focused attention, a self-reporting individual breaks away from habitual or automatic forms of self-report and consciously considers the implications of his or her actual past behaviors. Self-focusing stimuli may well encourage an individual to become Bem's self-observer and thus to render more behaviorally relevant self-reports.

The experimental findings discussed in this section imply that the tendencies of most people to attend systematically to the nuances of their own behaviors may be minimal. However, the propensity to act as a self-observer may be encouraged by manipulations which focus attention on the self. Through the use of self-awareness manipulations, an individual may be sensitized to his or her personal behavioral dispositions and report on them more accurately.

SUMMARY

Throughout this chapter, the thorny path from self-report to behavior was traced. In the first section, the question of what a person can know about his or her own characteristics was addressed.

It was argued that self-knowledge is indirect and involves an inference process akin to the one we apply to other people. It was also pointed out that indirect self-knowledge does not necessarily lead to inaccurate self-reports. In the second section, the relationship between self-knowledge and self-report was examined. It was argued that self-reports often reflect a biased sample of the information which one has stored about the self in memory. Self-reports can also be habitual responses, reflecting nothing of one's potential self-understanding. The third section concerned the use of self-reports to predict behavior. The idea that behavior is multiply determined and often the response to overpowering situational factors provides a plausible explanation for self-report/behavior inconsistency. The importance of considering the personal relevance and specificity of self-reports was also discussed. In the final section, the influence of self-focused attention upon the behavioral validity of self-reports was considered.

10

Individual Differences in Self-concept and Self-process

MICHAEL F. SCHEIER
CARNEGIE-MELLON UNIVERSITY

CHARLES S. CARVER
UNIVERSITY OF MIAMI

Much of the material in the preceding chapters has dealt with broad principles that are believed to apply to everyone. This, of course, is the main current of thought and research in social psychology: an emphasis on the commonalities among people, in the ways that we think, feel, and behave. What this viewpoint tends to ignore—a point we are often reminded of by students of social psychology—is that people aren't all the same. Although on almost any dimension there are more people in the middle than at the extremes, there are innumerable differences between individuals. Some of the most important differences are intimately related to the person's self-concept and to recurring self-processes. This chapter discusses such differences.

There are two perspectives from which we may examine differences between people, two ways of conceptualizing their importance. One perspective is experiential. That is, we could "get inside" the experiences of people who have some particular characteristic and think about how these people perceive their moment-to-moment reality. We could then do the same for persons at the other extreme—those who have little of this characteristic. This perspective on individual differences helps us to see why that dimension is important, by highlighting the ways in which it influences one's subjective *experience*.

Another way to approach the individual-difference issue is to take the scientist's perspective. That is, we could consider two sets of people—those who do and those who do not have the characteristic—and study their behavior from the outside. This approach enables us to see what differences in people's *actions* are caused by the presence or absence of the characteristic. This scientific perspective is less concerned with how it feels to be a particular kind of person than with the possibility of predicting accurately what such a person will say or do when placed in a given situation.

We will try to include both of these perspectives on individual differences in this chapter. Before we begin, though, let us tell you briefly what we intend to do. Individual differences in the self have been studied off and on for a long time. One can think of such differences as falling into two general categories. The first is self-concept: aspects of the self that give it form and a recognizable uniqueness. The second category is self-process: dynamic aspects of the self in which reactions or processing of information are of central importance. Although this distinction is somewhat artificial, we will adopt it here. In the first section below, we will review briefly some of the ideas concerning self-concept that have commanded psychologists' attention over the last several decades. In the second section, we will do the same for some traditional approaches to self-process. In recent years, people have begun to develop different approaches to studying individual differences in self-process and have evolved new conceptual frameworks for talking about these differences. We will devote the final section of the chapter to these new approaches.

SELF-CONCEPT

An almost incredible array of constructs has proliferated around the term *self-concept* (see, e.g., Wylie, 1974). Most approaches to this area of the self, however, assume that the self-concept has both a "content" and a "structure." That is, our self-concept is, most basically, *what* we think we are, in various respects, and thus has content. But these component images of ourselves are integrated with each other in some way, thus implying structure. The latter point is subtle, but it is one that researchers in self-concept often emphasize. For example, one commonly used measure, the Tennessee Self Concept Scale (Fitts, 1964), has separate subscales for the physical self, moral-ethical self, personal self, family-related self, and social self. All these aspects of one's self-concept are logically distinguishable from each other. Yet it would be hard to imagine each of them existing in total isolation from the others. For example, people's images of their social selves often have important connections with their images of what they are like physically.

FOUNDATIONS OF IDENTITY

Our self-concept or sense of identity (we will use the two terms interchangeably) no doubt derives from a variety of sources. One important prerequisite would seem to be the human capacity for self-consciousness. Each person is aware of being an individual self and can reflect and react to himself or herself as an object. True, the capacity for self-consciousness has recently been demonstrated in a variety of higher primates other than humans (see Chapter 1), but the capacity for self-awareness exhibited by human beings is so far superior to that of lower animals that it appears qualitatively different. Without the advanced ability to be self-conscious, one could never develop a self-concept or have an identity. We will discuss the notion of self-consciousness in more depth later on in this chapter. For now, let us note that the capacity for self-consciousness is an important precursor to a sense of identity.

A second factor which enables us to achieve a self-identity is a sense of continuity over time. Each person, from the moment of birth, passes through a unique sequence of life events, and each person can recognize that these events have happened to no one else. Thus, a woman in her mid-thirties can reflect upon early childhood experiences and recognize them as having happened to her. Her body, attitudes, and behavior may be different now than

they were then, but she is aware that all of the events were experienced by the same person. It is this sense of continuity and
stability in the face of development and change which provides
a theme for our identity.

No two persons ever experience exactly the same set of life
circumstances. One person is a sickly child and another is healthy.
One person goes to college and another does not. Although each
of us may experience a continuity of self over time, the specific
sequence of events which gets integrated is different for each person, and there are as many different life histories as there are persons. Thus the various life events which befall us not only help
us to develop and maintain a sense of self, but to the extent that
life experiences differ among persons, they also provide a partial
basis by which each person comes to view himself or herself as
being unique and distinct from all other persons.

ROLES

There is another determinant of our individual identities: the various social roles we play in our daily interactions. A *role* may be
defined as a pattern of responses exhibited in particular social contexts which is directed toward another person playing a reciprocal
role. Several aspects of this definition merit further discussion.
First, social roles are rarely, if ever, played in isolation; rather, they
are played in conjunction with related roles. Roles are intertwined
and generally come in pairs. Thus, in order to play the role of
doctor, a person needs someone else to play a reciprocal role—the
role of patient. Second, we are talking about a *pattern* of responses rather than a single response. This means that role prescriptions are generally quite diffuse and encompass a wide range of
specific responses. Consider, for example, the masculine role; it
includes a variety of specific behaviors, such as aggressiveness, competitiveness, and achievement striving.

A third point to consider about our definition of role is that the
behaviors occur in specific social settings. Thus, it is possible to
enact a variety of roles as we encounter different social settings in
our daily interactions. Of course, the ability to play multiple roles
throughout the day raises the possibility that sometimes we may

be asked to play two roles simultaneously. If the two roles require different types of behaviors, we experience role conflict and are uncertain about how to act. Most of us have at some time been acutely aware of the conflict created by the opposing demands of contradictory roles, and role conflict has provided the basis for more than a few television soap operas. The theme is clear. A doctor in the middle of an emotionally draining episode with her husband is suddenly called back to the hospital for an emergency. What does she do? Does she adhere to her role of wife and stay to smooth things over with her husband, or does she act as a doctor and speed away to the operating room? The feelings aroused by role conflict can be intense and real. Presumably it is by resolving such conflicts that a person derives a better understanding of his or her own values and thereby a better understanding of self and identity. (See Chapter 3 for a more complete discussion of the way in which persons attribute attitudes and values to themselves on the basis of their overt behavior and choices.)

We play a wide variety of roles throughout our lives, roles that may be categorized in many different ways. One important distinction is that between assigned and achieved roles (Biddle & Thomas, 1966). Each person is assigned a particular niche in society. Such placement occurs regardless of special talents or skills that a person may have and occurs largely on the basis of age, family background, and gender. Different behaviors are expected of a child than of an adolescent, who in turn is expected to behave differently from an adult. There are also certain patterns of behavior asssociated with being from a particular family or with being a man or a woman. Imagine, for example, the role prescriptions thrust upon a new member of the Kennedy clan. Because a person playing an assigned role is never selected for any unique skills that he or she may have, there is always the danger that the person may be unable to fill the role. A considerable amount of discomfort is likely to result in such circumstances. No matter how hard the person tries, his or her role performance always falls short of the expectations of others. It may not always pay to be born blue-blooded.

In contrast to assigned roles, achieved roles must be learned. Role assignment is based not on placement in a particular category of persons (e.g., male-female, young-old) but rather on merit or self-selection. The person must actively choose to pursue the role and have the necessary skills and abilities to play it successfully. Of course, a person may always strive for and attempt to play a role for which the needed capabilities are lacking. Sometimes we feel sympathy for a person who strives for an unattainable role— for example, the lanky, uncoordinated kid who strives for the role of star athlete in high school or college. Occasionally we react to such persons with mirth—for example, witness our laughter when watching Peter Sellers portray the bumbling Inspector Clouseau in the *Pink Panther* movies.

Of the various roles that we may play throughout our lives, two of the most important are the masculine and feminine roles. Buss (1973) has discussed the various differences between them. He suggests that the overriding theme of the traditional masculine role is instrumentality—getting the job done. Normative behavior for men includes self-reliance, aggressiveness, competitiveness, toughness, and an orientation toward achievement. The major theme of the traditional feminine role, on the other hand, is expressiveness. The traditional woman is affectionate, nurturant, compassionate, and concerned about others.

Obviously we have described the sex roles as they have been defined in the past. Further, the sex roles are changing. It is now more acceptable for men to be sensitive and to show concern for the feelings of others. Too, women are seeking careers more today and becoming much more instrumental. We are less startled today to hear that a 240-pound interior lineman from the Pittsburgh Steelers relaxes by doing needlepoint or that a mother of four unwinds by racing the family sports car on weekends. In short, the sharp differences which once separated the two sex roles are eroding; there is a general movement toward androgyny (Bem, 1974) —a blending of the characteristics of the two sex roles into a single composite. At present, we can only speculate about the degree to which this mixing will occur. Two conclusions do seem warranted, however: (1) the sex roles are changing, and (2) in spite of this change, many persons still adhere to the traditional sex roles.

Regardless of how sex roles ultimately evolve, they provide the basis for a large part of the person's identity. When asked, "Who are you?" most persons will respond in part with, "I am a man" or "I am a woman." Clearly this answer represents more than a simple biological description. It is also a summary of all the behavioral tendencies which are attached to it. Thus, a more complete answer is, "I am a man, and because of this I am competitive, self-reliant, and achievement oriented" or "I am a woman, and because of this I am nurturant, sensitive to others, and socially oriented." Because we infer what kind of person we are partly from our behavior, it is easy to see why roles have such a profound effect on our identity, and why there are such important differences between the types of identities formed by men and women.

The profound effects that role-taking can have on a person's self-concept have been neatly demonstrated in a study by Haney, Banks, and Zimbardo (1973). Participants in the research were normal college men residing in a western university community. The study was straightforward. Half the participants were asked to play the role of prisoner in a mock prison that had been constructed in the basement of a psychology building, and half were asked to play the role of guard. Thus, all participants were thrust into new roles for the first time. Yet, the role demands were relatively clear. The prisoner role called for submissive, docile behavior and proper deference to the captors. The role of guard, on the other hand, called for a different set of behaviors—aggressiveness, sternness, and dominance.

What happened? The effect of the role assignment was profound. Within only six days, each group had adopted so totally the behaviors of their assigned role that the experiment had to be terminated. The guards became completely domineering, aggressive, and brutal. The prisoners reacted with complete submission and passivity to the guard's aggressiveness. This was the case despite the fact that there were no differences between the two groups on any important demographic or psychological characteristic at the outset of the study.

When the study was over, the guards and the prisoners were brought together and encouraged to talk about their experiences. Many expressed the feeling that during the experiment, they were becoming something that they had thought they were not. Guards who may have previously loathed aggression found themselves constantly abusing other persons and punishing them for no apparent reasons. Prisoners who may have thought of themselves as independent and individualistic became docile and passive. And these inconsistencies were being integrated into their self-concept. The participants started to define themselves more and more in terms of the behaviors they exhibited. The prisoners began perceiving themselves as passive and submissive, and the guards began perceiving themselves as aggressive, brutal, and sadistic. Fortunately, the study was stopped soon enough to avoid any long-term adverse consequences.

In many ways, this study raised more questions than it answered (as is so often the case with provocative research). Why, for example, did some participants adopt their roles more readily than others, and why were some guards more aggressive and some prisoners more submissive than others? What is the relationship between the effect of role playing in mock prison and the effect of role playing in the real world? Clearly there are many unanswered questions. One fact emerges, however. Roles provide an important part of one's identity. And to the extent that a person plays roles that are different from others, his or her identity and self-concept must also be different.

SELF PROCESS:
TRADITIONAL APPROACHES

We have been talking about differences in the way persons define themselves—that is, differences in their identities or self-concepts. The primary concern was with the specific content of the self-concept, the sources from which this content is derived, and the way it is structured and organized. This is only part of the story, however. In addition to examining the content of the self-concept, social psychologists are also interested in understanding self-processes—in particular, how people evaluate or react to themselves and how they process self-relevant information. In this section, we consider some of the traditional approaches to self-reactions and self-processes, and the ways in which people differ on these dimensions.

SELF-ESTEEM

If there is one apparent truism about people, it is that they have a seemingly irresistable urge to make evaluations. Movies are good or bad, a particular movie star is attractive or not, the government is being run efficiently or wastefully, students attending a certain college are smart or stupid. Given people's propensity to make evaluations, we should not be surprised to find that they also make *self*-evaluations, and that their self-evaluations differ. Some people consider themselves to be bright, competent, and well-adjusted; their self-esteem is high. Others consider themselves to be dull, incompetent, and poorly adjusted; their self-esteem is low. What are the variables that affect a person's self-esteem, and how does self-esteem, in turn, affect the person's subsequent behavior? These are the questions to which we turn next.

The most widely cited study of the development of self-esteem was conducted by Coopersmith (1967) on fifth- and sixth-grade boys and girls. Self-esteem was assessed by means of a self-report inventory, as well as by teacher ratings. High self-esteem children tended to do better scholastically and obtained higher scores on intelligence tests than low self-esteem children. In addition, high self-esteem children set higher aspirations for themselves than did their low self-esteem counterparts. Although all the children came from the same social background (middle class), Coopersmith found that high self-esteem children were more likely to come from the upper portion of that range. They also tended to be first-born or only children, an effect that was much stronger for boys than girls.

A number of interesting relationships were found between the child's level of self-esteem and parental personality characteristics and child-rearing techniques. For example, the parents of high-esteem children tended to be more stable and to have a higher level of self-esteem than did the parents of low self-esteem children. In addition, the fathers of low self-esteem children tended to be absent from the home more frequently than the fathers of high self-esteem children. With regard to child-rearing practices, mothers of high self-esteem children tended to be closer and more loving toward their children. Somewhat surprisingly, parents of high self-esteem children were found to be firmer and more demanding of their children than parents of low self-esteem children, but they also tended to be fairer in punishing transgressions.

What are the implications of self-esteem for people's behavior? There are at least two ways for self-esteem differences to result in behavioral differences, and researchers are still uncertain about which is more likely (see, e.g., S. C. Jones, 1973; Shrauger, 1975). One possibility is that people with high self-esteem have a personal investment in maintaining this good reaction to themselves, whereas people with lower self-esteem do not. Following this reasoning, the highs might be especially sensitive to threats to their self-esteem—which often occur in interpersonal situations—and might work especially hard to counter the threats. The lows, less concerned about maintaining positive self-images, would be less responsive to such threats. The other possibility, which seems just as reasonable, is that persons with high self-esteem are sure enough of themselves not to worry about outside threats. Those with low self-esteem, on the other hand, have less to feel proud of and are more likely to feel threatened when things begin to go wrong.

THE APPROVAL MOTIVE

We are often evaluated by others as well as by ourselves. The anticipation of such evaluations give rise to different reactions in different people. How much does it matter to you what others think of you? How much do you take their possible reactions into account when you decide how to act or what to think? How frequently or how hard do you try to portray yourself in the best light? How sensitive are you to social reward or to rebukes from others? These are among the questions dealt with by research on the *approval motive*. (The approval motive was discussed in a slightly different context in Chapter 7.)

The discovery by Edwards (1957) that people tend to agree with self-descriptive statements that say socially approved things and disagree with those that say disapproved things (regardless of what the "things" are) was the beginning of this area of inquiry. It was quickly discovered that people's reactions differ drastically. Why are people differentially sensitive to the social desirability of such self-reference statements? Crowne and Marlowe (1964) argued for a simple answer: that each person is motivated differently in the desire for approval from others. Thus, their conceptualization emphasizes that persons high in the need for approval rely heavily on the *evaluative* judgments of others. People look to others not just for social stimulation or information but also because they need the social rewards that others can provide.

The effects of need for approval on behavior have been assessed in many ways (see Millham & Jacobson, 1978). Many of these involve the differential sensitivity that people show to social rewards and punishments. For example, people high in social desirability show improved performance on difficult tasks after receiving positive evaluations, whereas no such improvement occurs among people lower in this characteristic. Several studies have tested the "conditioning" effect of social reinforcement (verbalizations of "mm-hmm" from the experimenter) on the emission of specific categories of words. Persons high in social desirability, who are presumably most sensitive to social reward, have typically been the ones who are most affected by the experimenter's murmurs of approval.

Because these people are so sensitive to social reward contingencies, it should come as no surprise that they are more likely than others to conform to other people's opinions. This has been shown even in contexts that make it clear that it's a matter of conformity rather than unsureness about the accuracy of one's own judgments. High scorers also inhibit their aggressiveness when they have been provoked. Presumably this reflects their desire to behave in such a way that others won't disapprove of them.

Interestingly, there are occasions when people high in the desire for approval are especially likely to do socially *un*desirable acts. In studies of cheating, these persons were found to cheat more than those with less need for approval when it helped them to avoid a dismal failure. They did not cheat more, however, when to do so only increased an already substantial success. This and other evidence suggests that persons high in need for approval are more motivated to avoid being thought of in a bad light than to gain ever-increasing approval. In effect, they seem obsessed by the need to "play it safe," but always with *other* people's reactions in mind rather than their own.

How important is this self-aspect? Early studies found that social desirability correlated highly with many other personality dimensions. This led Crowne and Marlowe (1964) to remark that "from the magnitude of these correlations, it is apparent that the systematic variance remaining after the correlations with the [social desirability] scale have been accounted for is small indeed. Evidently, then, there is little left in personality testing but social desirability" (p. 15). That statement may be a bit strong. However, there is no denying that our need for social approval is an important aspect of ourselves.

The concepts of self-esteem and the approval motive deal with our reactions to ourselves and our concern over other people's reactions to us. Let us now turn to a fundamentally different kind of self-process—a difference between people in the way they learn.

LOCUS OF CONTROL

Probably the assumptions about human behavior that have been most widely accepted over the last three decades hinge on the concept of reinforcement. Most of us take it for granted that rewards and punishments have a powerful impact on people's future actions. After all, that's what learning is all about, isn't it? Doesn't reinforcement shape the way we respond the next time?

Well, yes and no. An important aspect of self-process has to do with the way we *understand* the occurrence of reinforcers. We are not talking about the simple awareness that the reinforcement did happen but rather the meaning that we attach to that event. The way we process this information can have a major impact on what we learn or even whether we learn at all.

Imagine a man who comes to a psychologist for therapy. His problem is not a deep-seated neurosis but simply the fact that he does not understand certain important aspects of interpersonal relations. The psychologist spends hours working with the man to develop techniques through which he can alter his behavior, find a job, feel more comfortable with women, and so on. As the patient returns to the broader context of his day-to-day life, he finds that he is sometimes quite successful in these efforts. The curious point is this: the man seems completely unaffected by his successes! He acts as if the good outcomes were unrelated to his efforts. The reinforcement that he got has not caused him to change his behavior at all. In effect, he does not learn.

This "hypothetical" example actually occurred (Phares, 1978). Attempts to understand cases of this kind led to the development of a rather "cognitive" theory of the learning process and to an expanding research area concerning individual differences in learning. At its core, the idea is quite simple. Perhaps rewards do not automatically reinforce the behaviors that they follow. Perhaps, if reward is to have an effect, the person must perceive that his or her own actions *caused* the reward to happen. Logically, if the good outcome is seen as a direct consequence of one's behavior, one will tend to do the behavior more often. On the other hand, if the outcome is seen as unrelated to the behavior, the frequency of the behavior will not tend to change.

In putting forth this idea, Rotter (1966) also suggested that people differ in their *expectancies* for controlling outcomes. He gave the term *locus of control* to the place (or locus) where the person sees control as residing. *Internals* perceive that events or outcomes are contingent on their own actions ("When I make plans, I am almost certain that I can make them work"). *Externals*, on the other hand, perceive reinforcements as caused by luck, chance, fate, or powerful others ("It is not always wise to plan too far ahead, because many things turn out to be a matter of good or bad fortune anyway"). These orientations to one's outcomes are theoretically applicable to both good outcomes and bad. That is, an internal orientation sometimes implies self-congratulation, but sometimes it implies self-blame. An external orientation means not only lack of credit for successes but lack of fault for failures. Rotter believed that these orientations are very general; they apply to many different kinds of experiences. Because it affects the way we learn in a variety of situations, locus of control is assumed to be a fundamental aspect of self-process rather than limited to one small behavioral content area.

Since this idea was set forth, many studies have investigated the differences between internals and externals in terms of how and what they learn, and how they behave under a variety of different conditions (see Lefcourt, 1976, or Phares, 1978, for comprehensive summaries). Internality in people seems, for example, to be related to active tendencies to control or change their own lives. Internals, especially those who find the Surgeon General's report on smoking to be convincing, are less likely to be smokers than are externals. Internal women are more likely than externals to practice effective birth control. Internality has also been shown to be a predictor of success in weight reduction programs. Finally, hospitalized internals seek out and obtain more information about their own condition from the hospital staff than do externals and are less satisfied with the (still restricted) amount of information they get.

Seeking out information can be thought of as preparation for action, and thus is consistent with internals' beliefs that they can exert control over outcomes. In other research, when subjects believed that they were going to attempt to change another person's attitudes, it was the internals who most actively sought out information about that other person, in order to be more effective in influencing him later on. Indeed, in working at a variety of tasks, internals seem to focus on task-relevant information and avoid task-irrelevant thoughts.

Does this mean that internals are more competent or better adjusted than externals? Not necessarily. Remember that along with credit for successes may go self-blame for failures. Thus an extremely internal person who is failing may be more upset than a person who is extremely external. This view is complicated by two additional considerations. First, internals should be more likely to try to help themselves when they are down than should externals. Second, helping oneself isn't always easy. This holds out the potential for further self-blame on the part of internals if they are unsuccessful in changing things.

The fact that internals perceive outcomes as dependent on their own efforts suggests that they should be more resistant to interpersonal influence than externals. This has proved to be the case in both conformity research and persuasion research. Internals seem to prefer to make up their own minds rather than being manipulated, even subtly, by others. This is consistent with their preference for skill-based activities, as opposed to activities whose outcome is dictated by chance.

SELF-PROCESS:
RECENT APPROACHES

The traditional approaches to self-process examined in the preceding section have emphasized differences in people's affective reactions to themselves, in their concerns over other people's reactions to them, and in their orientations to the learning process. These topics reflect the assumptions that were made by early motivational theorists concerning the central determinants of human behavior—that is, that people's actions are caused by a need to defend their self-images, by a need for social approval, or by the fundamental laws of reinforcement-based learning.

More recently, however, some different approaches to self-process have begun to evolve. These newer approaches tend to place more emphasis on the cognitive and attentional aspects of self-process. Thus, self-regulation is seen as being more dependent on the specific kind of information and cues used to guide moment-to-moment actions, on the type and extent of social knowledge that is stored from previous social interactions, and on a variety of attentional processes. It is to these newer approaches that we turn next.

SELF-MONITORING

Much of current social psychological theorizing focuses on the making of decisions, explicitly or implicitly, about how to behave in a given social setting. Both the variables that influence the specific outcome of a decision and the nature of the decision-making process itself have been the objects of closer and closer scrutiny over the years. One recent conceptualization of differences between people focuses on the use of two different strategies for making these decisions. Differences in people's predominant strategy result in differences in their portrayal of themselves to others.

Consider the contrast between two people you know well. One of them seems solid as a rock. She's completely true to herself. When in doubt, her strategy in interpersonal relations is to examine her own beliefs and attitudes and depend on them for guidance. The behavior of others often seems to her to be irrelevant to her own decisions. You probably view this person as being either independent or bullheaded, depending on whether or not you agree with her at the time.

Your other friend changes with the situation. Her strategy, when in doubt, is to "read" the context, to decide what kind of response the situation calls for. In fact, it sometimes seems hard to know who this person really is. She's an expert in reflecting back the expressive aspects of whatever group she's in, and always seems to know just which way the group is headed.

The difference between these two characters is at the heart of a dimension of self called *self-monitoring* (Snyder, 1979). This concept has grown out of an examination of the way social comparison processes occur in various people. *Social comparison* (Festinger, 1954) is the tendency, especially in highly ambiguous circumstances, to "define reality" by social consensus. That is, since we don't always have objective evidence about what is going on or what is the most appropriate way to react in a situation, we look to others to help us make up our minds. We use the cues that others are constantly emitting to guide our own reactions. We all do this to some degree, but the essence of self-monitoring as a self dimension is that some of us do it a great deal more than others. The person who is high in the self-monitoring tendency is your chameleonlike friend who is so flexible in her behavior. The person who is low in self-monitoring is your friend who disregards the actions of others and relies instead on her own standards. (Note: this term can be slightly confusing. High *self*-monitoring means determining what standards of behavior are suggested by the *environmental* context.)

Self-monitoring as an individual difference has been studied in a variety of behavioral settings. Many of these studies concern the correspondence between people's actual behavior and their previously expressed attitudes. This question (which is addressed in detail in Chapter 9) is one that has plagued social and personality psychologists for decades. The question was once framed as, "Why don't people act like their attitudes indicate they should act?" Today, though, this single question has become several interrelated ones, such as, "Whose behavior will fit well with their attitudes, and whose won't?" and "What are the reasons for this difference between people?" The self-monitoring dimension suggests one answer to each of these questions and backs up the answer with data. The behavior of people high in self-monitoring shouldn't be expected to fit well with their attitudes, and in fact it doesn't. These people tailor their actions to fit their social context. They perceive their attitudes as less relevant to their actions than are cues from their behavioral setting. But those low in self-monitoring—a dream come true to the psychologist who is trying to find a way to predict behavior from attitudes—fit their actions to their opinions. Why the difference? Perhaps because these two sets of people have fundamentally different orientations to how best to go about regulating their behavior.

This same reasoning suggests some other behavioral differences between the two groups. High self-monitoring people should be, and are, especially likely to seek out social comparison information when preparing to undertake self-presentation tasks (see Chapter 7 for more information on self-presentation). When they anticipate interacting with another, they are especially likely to notice and accurately remember information about that person. They spend a good deal of time and effort "reading" others. This is reflected, for example, by their thorough inferences about others' intentions. These inferences presumably are gained from attending to the interplay between those others' behavior and its context. With this kind of orientation to others, you'd expect persons high in self-monitoring to be good at reading others' feelings and emotions, as well. This has also been supported by research findings.

The fact that people who are high and low in this tendency spend such different amounts of time and effort in examining their social contexts suggests that they also might differ cognitively. That is, high self-monitoring people—who have looked long and hard at social exchange—should have much knowledge about other peoples' typical behavior in various contexts. Presuming that they are able to categorize other people into different "types" (which is certainly a reasonable assumption), they may thus develop a particularly complex and rich set of social stereotypes. These stereotypes, which would be stored in memory as cognitive schemas (see Chapter 5), serve two functions. First, they provide a firm basis for categorizing people in new social contexts (as well as the nature of the context itself) on the basis of very few behavioral and expressive cues. Second, they provide a wealth of information to use in designing one's own self-presentation. That is, if you are going to act a role that seems appropriate (e.g., the "extrovert"), you must first know what the role is. The better you know what the role consists of, the easier it is to take it on. And high self-monitoring people do seem to have fuller images of such role prototypes than low self-monitoring people.

On the other hand, low self-monitoring people may spend more time than the highs in organizing the knowledge that they have about *themselves*. Their self-schemas may be more complex, and their images of who they are may be richer and more accurate. After all, it is presumably these self-schemas that they refer to repeatedly in choosing their behaviors in social exchange.

All of this raises certain interesting questions for which there are not yet answers. For example, what causes people to become either high or low in this tendency? Do people start out fascinated by social interaction (or not) and then develop huge storehouses of knowledge about how things work? Or do people drift into an absorption with social exchange because their schemas for categorizing others are well developed?

Perhaps more interesting is the question of the motivations behind the two tendencies. Why does the low self-monitoring person ignore the cues that are presented? We don't know whether such people want to be true to themselves, whether they have doubts about others' ideas being better than their own, whether they haven't had much success at going along with the crowd, or whether it simply hasn't occurred to them to use others' opinions as a guidepost. To turn the question around, we don't know whether high self-monitoring persons are pragmatists who want to maximize outcomes in any social setting, whether they don't have confidence in their own judgments, or whether it hasn't occurred to them that all decisions need to be made by consensus. These are, however, interesting issues that will no doubt be explored in the future.

SELF-CONSCIOUSNESS

Another recent approach to self-process concerns the focus of a person's attention. Social commentators have been intrigued for centuries by the nature of the self. Undoubtedly this interest was derived in part from the self's unique property of reflexivity—that is, its capacity to think about itself. The notion of taking oneself as the object of attention has provided the cornerstone for the theory of self-awareness (Carver, 1979; Duval & Wicklund, 1972; Wicklund, 1975). Self-awareness theory, which was discussed in Chapter 2, primarily concerns a self-regulation process that controls the intensity and direction of ongoing behavior. Specifically, self-attention is presumed to evoke a matching-to-standard process, whereby the person conforms to whatever he or she takes as the standard of appropriate behavior. Hence, the major outcome of increased self-focus is a greater correspondence between behavior and behavioral standards. If no behavioral standard is salient, then self-focus simply increases the person's cognizance and awareness of the particular self-dimension on which his or her attention is centered.

Self-awareness is presumed to increase whenever one confronts a stimulus that reminds one of oneself. However, in addition to *situational* stimuli that increase or decrease self-awareness, there also appears to be a *disposition* to be self-reflective. The disposition to focus attention inward has been labeled *self-consciousness*, to distinguish it from situationally induced states of self-focus, and is measured by the Self-Consciousness Scale (Fenigstein, Scheier, & Buss, 1975). Statistical analyses of the scale have revealed that dispositional self-consciousness is composed of two separate components, private and public, that are only weakly correlated.

Private self-consciousness involves a focus on the more covert and personal aspects of oneself. Persons high in private self-consciousness are highly aware of their bodily sensations, beliefs, moods, and feelings. In everyday parlance, they are in better touch with themselves than persons low in private self-consciousness. They tend to be generally introspective and have a rich imagery life. The thoughts of such persons presumably center on themselves. Rather than reflect about an incident that happened to someone else, such a person thinks about things that happened to him or her. A person high in private self-consciousness would be inclined to agree with statements like "I'm always trying to figure myself out" and "I'm generally attentive to my inner feelings." If these items remind you of yourself, then the odds are good that you are high in private self-consciousness.

Public self-consciousness, on the other hand, involves an awareness of the self as a social object. Persons high in public self-consciousness are concerned about their social appearance and the kind of impression they make on others. They are constantly thinking about what others think of them and how they are coming across in social contexts. This kind of person would agree with statements such as "I'm usually aware of my appearance" and "I'm concerned about my style of doing things."

It might seem that public self-consciousness sounds similar to the need for approval or to self-monitoring, both of which have been discussed earlier in this chapter. Empirically and theoretically, however, the dimensions are different. Public self-consciousness has been found to be relatively independent of the need for approval and to be only moderately related (in a positive direction) to self-monitoring. Why is this so? Apparently public self-consciousness deals only with people's *awareness* of how they come across in social contexts. Persons high in public self-consciousness may be aware of the kind of impression they are making, but do little to use this knowledge either to gain the approval of others or to guide their self-presentation. Thus, although public self-consciousness may make people aware of the type of knowledge that would be required to seek the approval of others, or to engage in self-monitoring, this knowledge alone does not insure that they will automatically do so.

There is now a large body of research on the behavioral effects of dispositional self-consciousness. An implicit assumption of researchers working on this area has been that individual differences in self-consciousness will produce the same effects on behavior as will situational manipulations of self-focused attention. This assumption has tended to be borne out by the experimental findings. For example, as was discussed in Chapter 2, exposure to a mirror increases the amount of causality attributed to the self for hypothetical events. Private self-consciousness has a similar effect: persons high in private self-consciousness also attribute more causality to themselves than do persons low in private self-consciousness (Buss & Scheier, 1976). Other research has shown that situational self-awareness can increase the subjective experience of and responsivity to one's transient affective states, and so does private self-consciousness (Scheier, 1976; Scheier & Carver, 1977). Manipulated self-awareness increases the degree to which a person reacts when important freedoms are threatened, and so does private self-consciousness (Carver & Scheier, 1979). Exposure to a mirror increases a person's cognizance of his or her various bodily states, and so does private self-consciousness (Scheier, Carver, & Gibbons, 1979). Finally, as was noted in Chapter 9, induced self-awareness increases the validity of a person's self-report about his or her behavioral characteristics, and so does private self-consciousness (Scheier, Buss, & Buss, 1978).

Nor are the effects of dispositional self-consciousness limited to the private self-consciousness dimension. Individual differences in public self-consciousness have also been shown to be important determinants of behavior. For example, persons high in public self-consciousness are presumed to be especially sensitive to others' reactions to them—that is, how they are being received as social objects. One study has confirmed this, finding that women who were high in public self-consciousness were more sensitive to rejection by a peer group. Following exclusion from the group, they were found to be less attracted to the group and less willing to affiliate with the group in the future than were women low in public self-consciousness (Fenigstein, 1979). Although the public self-consciousness dimension has thus far received less research attention than the private dimension, it seems likely that future work will be aimed at further exploring the behavioral effects of public self-consciousness. Indeed, in light of the increasing interest in self-presentation and impression management (see Chapter 7), research on the consequences of attending to our public selves may ultimately prove to be as important as prior research on attending to our private selves.

SUMMARY

This chapter has been concerned with individual variations in self-concept and self-process. Each of us, through the course of our lives, develops a sense of who we are and what we are about. In the first section of the chapter, we suggested that a large part of people's identities is determined by the unique life circumstances that have confronted them and by the different roles that they play during their daily social interactions. Extended discussion was given to the sex roles, including the manner in which they have been traditionally defined and the way in which they help shape a person's self-concept. We also briefly mentioned the types of roles one might play (assigned versus achieved) and the problems created by role conflicts.

Given that each person has developed an individual identity, it follows that each person also has some specific self-conceptualization to react to. One who views the self as having a particular characteristic can evaluate and respond to that aspect of the self as one would to any other person who might also have that characteristic. Ideas and research concerning the development and consequences of self-evaluation tendencies were considered in the second section, on traditional approaches to self-process. Also discussed here were individual variations in the need for approval, as well as the experiential and behavioral differences between persons with internal versus external expectancies for control over reinforcement.

In the third section, we considered two new approaches to self-process. First, we discussed self-monitoring, an individual difference dimension regarding the strategies that people employ to determine how to behave in social interaction and how to portray themselves to others. High self-monitoring is the tendency to look to one's context for cues to guide one's actions; low self-monitoring is the tendency to look instead to one's own attitudes for such guidance. Then, we examined individual differences in the direction of attentional focus. Private self-consciousness refers to the person's awareness of his or her inner thoughts, motives, and feelings. Persons high in this characteristic are in close touch with the covert aspects of themselves. Public self-consciousness is awareness of oneself as a social object. Persons high in this characteristic are conscious of how they are viewed by others.

11

A Postscript on Application

·

ROBIN R. VALLACHER
ILLINOIS INSTITUTE OF TECHNOLOGY

DANIEL M. WEGNER
TRINITY UNIVERSITY

HASKEL HOINE
TRINITY UNIVERSITY

This book is in some ways like a mirror. True, putting on makeup or shaving while gazing at this book could be dangerous; the book is a mirror in the deeper sense that it speaks of your personal processes. Each chapter offers a reflection of you, a scientific view of what you are like and how you operate. The social psychological study of the self is relevant to you in a way that no other science can be; no other field of inquiry is so uniquely a study of the person who studies it. We hope to make this chapter unusually reflective by collecting and bringing into focus the *applications* of self theory you may have glimpsed in the other chapters, and mirroring in a personal way the aspects of this book that could be useful to you in considering personal problems and everyday life.

Self theories *should* have something to say about personal problems. After all, if self principles are implicated in much of our daily living, then surely the difficulties in living should be explainable with reference to those principles as well. But from another perspective, problems in adjustment would seem to present a paradox for self theories. An assumption common to many self theories is that people are sensitive to their own dispositions, attitudes, and behaviors, and can evaluate these features of the self. It would seem that this capacity should prevent maladjustment from developing in the first place, or at least allow for self-correction. If a person sees a bad feature of the self, why shouldn't he or she simply change that feature and make it good? Shouldn't self-understanding naturally lead to self-control?

To understand from a self theory perspective how maladjustment can develop and be maintained, it is important to distinguish between the self as a set of *rules* for processing personally relevant information and the self as a *product* of those rules. In our everyday experiences, we normally think of the self as a set of qualities—the roles we occupy, our attitudes and dispositions, our physical attributes, and so forth (Gordon, 1968). The rules by which we understand and evaluate these self-aspects are rarely the object of our attention; in a sense, we look "through" these rules, not "at" them. Yet, these rules are as central to most self theories as are the rules' products—the self-aspects we hold in conscious awareness (see Chapter 1). Within a self theory perspective, then, a person's maladaptive or ineffective functioning may represent flaws in the operation of the rules by which he or she understands and evaluates the self. In this view, change involves getting the person to focus on the ways in which he or she interprets self-relevant events. By understanding the rules by which the self operates, the person is in a better position to control the rules' products.

Maladjustment also seems possible within a self theory perspective when we consider that the self represents the distillation of social encounters experienced since childhood. Just as a theory is no better than its data base, the quality of one's experiences sets a limit on the potential "healthiness" of one's self. The rules by which we interpret self-information in adulthood can be adversely affected by a variety of childhood experiences—traumatic events, inconsistent or otherwise confusing social feedback, inadequate adult models, and so on. Betty, for example, may have learned to discount all positive feedback from Mom and Dad ("You're such a nice little girl") because it was invariably followed by a negative "punchline" ("What'd you say your name was again?"). In effect, she developed a rule for processing parental feedback that could cause problems later should she try to process all self-relevant information in this way. Marriage proposals might lead her to anticipate divorce proceedings.

At the same time, personal problems do not always reflect defects or peculiarities in the rules for understanding and evaluating the self. In fact, the very nature of certain rules tends to produce frequent errors; the misattribution of arousal (see Chapter 4) is an example. Beyond that, quite often there are quirks in the situations encountered by the person that promote adjustment problems. Such situations may be stacked against the person in that the information that is most salient, and is therefore most likely to be given the most weight, is also the least reliable or valid (see, e.g., Ross, 1978).

In the sections that follow, we attempt to demonstrate more precisely how normal rules for processing self-relevant information can result in personal adjustment difficulties. We consider first anxiety, then depression, and finally self-defeating behavior—common problems all—by reviewing a case of a person confronted by the problem and then by analyzing the case from the perspective of relevant self theories. There is much more than this in the literature on applied self theory (see, e.g., Brehm, 1976), but these applications represent some of the most compelling and current views.

ANXIETY

"Anxiety" is perhaps the most familiar catchword used in clinical psychology. It is an unpleasant internal sensation, much like fear, that is characterized by symptoms of physiological arousal such as a racing heart, sweaty palms, or constriction in the abdomen. When anxious, a person feels nervous, insecure, and unable to concentrate on an activity. Everyone, of course, experiences this state from time to time, but for some people it is experienced to an incapacitating degree in one or many situations.

THE CASE

Franklin, age twenty, came to the university psychological services center because of his intense fear of public speaking. He was a good student, having obtained a 3.5 grade average in his first three years of college. Up to the time of his clinic visit, however, he had managed to avoid all classes that required presentations or oral reports. Now he could no longer delay the required course in communication, so he sought help to relax when speaking in front of people.

Franklin's anxiety about public speaking began in his junior year in high school when he took a course that required a series of oral presentations to the class. His grade in the course depended a great deal on his performance, so he felt highly apprehensive not only about classmates' evaluations of him but about the teacher's as well. In the last of his presentations, he dropped his notes, became temporarily confused, and lost his train of thought. Unable to regain his composure, he gave up and sat down, feeling extremely embarrassed. Since that time, he has avoided similar circumstances for fear that he would "blow it" again. Presently, even thinking about public speaking causes him to experience symptoms of anxiety.

THE ANALYSIS

Several different self-processes—self-awareness, self-presentation, self-perception of emotion, and self-labeling—are relevant to Franklin's problem. It should be noted, first of all, that Franklin's reaction in front of his high school class was actually quite normal. When observed by an audience, it is natural to experience a certain amount of self-awareness. The self-evaluation inherent in self-awareness, coupled with the implied evaluation by an audience, produces a certain amount of apprehension, which is experienced as physiological arousal and perhaps poor concentration (Wine,

1971). Quite likely, Franklin's experience of arousal was no greater than that of his classmates. In attempting to understand his apprehension, Franklin—like every other kid in the class—looked at the reactions of others when they presented to the class. Of course, when he was presenting, Franklin did his best to cover up his arousal (forced yawns were his favorite ploy) so as not to appear nervous to his classmates. Because everyone else had the same concern and thus attempted to appear unruffled, Franklin probably became concerned that he was unduly anxious ("they all look so dry"). Not fully appreciating the self-presentational nature of his classmates' reactions, Franklin may have begun to doubt that his nervousness was simply a natural response to the situation; he may have begun to fear that he was an unnaturally anxious person, unable to control his behavior in this situation.

Although Franklin had some concern about being unduly anxious, his classmates probably had a similar concern. However, Franklin's parting performance in the high school class—dropping his notes and losing control of his presentation—served to confirm his fears. Of course, if he had dropped his notes somewhere else, he might have attributed the event to momentary clumsiness or perhaps the salad oil he forgot to wash from his hands. But his concern about being unduly anxious functioned as a hypothesis with which he assessed his behavior in front of the class. Dropping the notes confirmed the hypothesis. With his new self-label, Franklin felt he had good reason to avoid audience situations in the future. And in a sense, he was justified in that belief. Natural anxiety, augmented by self-label-induced anxiety, might impair his concentration to the point where he could not function effectively in front of an audience.

Franklin's problem is not uncomon, nor are the self-processes underlying the problem confined to audience anxiety. A number of anxiety-related disorders—insomnia, sexual impotence, and stuttering, for example—can be interpreted in this way (Storms & McCaul, 1976; Valins & Nisbett, 1971). The person first becomes aware of some undesirable aspect of his or her behavior, which is then attributed to some deep underlying problem or inadequacy.

The resultant self-label promotes self-deprecation and anxiety about one's ability to control that behavior in the future. The label-induced anxiety adds to the anxiety normally associated with the unwanted behavior and thus turns what may have been a natural response to the situation into a problem behavior. In short, worrying about a problem can often serve to make it worse.

Successful therapy in Franklin's case would involve convincing him to drop his self-label and to reattribute his nervousness to the nature of the situation. By renouncing the label, a good part of his anxiety in front of an audience would be reduced. One way of doing this has been investigated by Meichenbaum (1977). In several different kinds of research, Meichenbaum has arranged for people who are anxious about certain situations, behaviors, or objects, to think about those stimuli when the stimuli themselves are not present. Thinking "good thoughts" about what could happen in a class presentation, for example, might be the treatment prescribed for Franklin. Later, when people enter the settings that usually produce anxiety, they have newly expanded self-views that allow them to anticipate success in dealing with the anxiety. Another tactic, one which is highly successful in reducing *phobic* anxiety, is simply to expose the person to the anxiety-producing object or situation. By confronting a "mild" audience situation—a small group, perhaps, or a large one in which everyone wore blinders—Franklin might experience success and thereby regain a sense of subjective control over his behavior. Such an approach has been shown to be one of the most effective treatments for anxiety disorders of this type (Bandura, 1977).

DEPRESSION

The syndrome described as depression is marked by passivity, unusually strong self-criticism, an outlook of hopelessness, and quite often, changes in eating and sleeping habits. Although everyone feels depressed once in a while, the stronger forms of depression can be severely debilitating.

THE CASE

Ginger, age nineteen, arrived at the university clinic because her roommate had threatened to call her parents. She reported that she was having some difficulty with sleeping that made it hard to get up for class, and that she had missed all her morning and most afternoon classes for the last two weeks. She felt strongly that none of this was her roommate's business. When asked what else had been different these past weeks, she reported that she was constantly hungry, ate anything that wasn't nailed down, and had gained over ten pounds. This got her down and she started thinking about herself as a "fat slob" who couldn't stop eating because she was "too dumb to stop." For most of the interview, she spoke in a monotone that was tinged with sadness. But for a brief period, she broke down and cried. "There's no hope," she whispered, "nothing will ever change. I'm just a dumb fat slob."

Ginger's problem began about one month after she started her freshman year at the university. She had been a top student in high school, never working too hard but always getting good grades. The many extracurricular activities she enjoyed made her feel very much a part of things. When she arrived at the university, however, she felt somewhat awkward and very alone. This was her first time away from home, and everything was unfamiliar and somehow "empty." People looked like they were enjoying themselves, but she felt frightened. She was considered "charming" and "cute" in high school, but she kept thinking that she was not as smart as the others in her classes at college. Although she studied frequently during her first few weeks at school, she received only a C on her first exam. She felt she had failed. As a way of trying to "straighten out" her life, she spent a lot of time going over what was happening, what she was like, the reasons she had entered college in the first place, and even her justifications for being alive. Her thoughts would race as she searched for answers to these deep questions about herself. Eventually, all her waking hours were spent in self-contemplation, and it was at this point that she came to the clinic.

The depression experienced by Ginger, and by many people at some point in their lives, can be understood in terms of social psychological self theories. Abramson and Sackheim (1977) have pointed out that depression seems to consist of two major disturbances in a person's self-view. First, the person expresses an extraordinary amount of self-blame. This can be explained by suggesting that depressed people are more likely than others to focus attention on themselves and, hence, to experience strongly the discrepancies between what they are and what they would like to be (see Chapter 2). Second, the depressed person is likely to be concerned about the apparent uncontrollability of events in his or her life. This can be explained by noting that depression is often associated with experiences of helplessness (see Chapter 3).

The events that precipitated Ginger's depression can be traced to these two factors—self-awareness and helplessness. When she arrived as a new student at school, she was confronted with a new situation, and because of her status as a "new" student was also placed in a minority among her compatriots. Many of the familiar things that had helped her to keep her life full in high school were missing, so she had a great deal of time for self-contemplation. These factors—lack of structure, minority status, and a lack of familiar activity—all add up to an increased likelihood of self-awareness. Because the self-aware state brings about self-evaluation, Ginger was ripe for the onset of self-blame and self-criticism that are hallmarks of depression.

A different set of observations about Ginger suggests that she could well have experienced helplessness, too. Recall that she usually did well in high school without trying much, and that she felt she was a failure following her first college exam. It could be that Ginger had never really tested herself in the past—after all, she was "cute" and "charming" and got by without doing much. The failure on the exam led her to believe that her academic performance was something that could not be controlled; all her efforts produced what seemed like nothing. So, with little hope for future control over this one aspect of college life, she may have accepted a "helpless" approach to many other aspects.

What form of therapy would be helpful in changing Ginger's mood? Obviously, as a first step, we would suggest something to reduce her self-awareness. In fact, clinical studies have shown that introducing diversions and distractions from self-focus (Ellis, 1977) or introducing highly structured activity schedules (Rush, Khatami, & Beck, 1975) can help to relieve the depressive condition. The helplessness facet of this problem could be alleviated by yet other means. Both Beck (1976) and Meichenbaum (1977) have used simple persuasion—attacking the person's negative distortions of self-view that result from failure. For both of these clinical theorists, as well as for Seligman (1975), however, the best treatment for helplessness is to induce additional attempts at control. If Ginger could be coaxed back to class and back "into the fray," her helplessness could be reduced by demonstrations that she actually *does* have some control. Even small demonstrations of this type could pave the road to personal well-being.

SELF-DEFEATING BEHAVIOR

This final application of self theory represents a set of behavior problems that reach clinical psychologists only in severe cases. Most self-defeating behavior does not "win the war" against the self, so people who engage in such actions may feel the effects in only minor ways. But when people repeatedly act contrary to their own best interest, some extreme forms of self-defeat can occur; these are at the root of many chronic behavior problems.

THE CASE

Rudy is a twenty-three-year-old college senior who is just getting by. No one who knows him is quite sure how he has gotten this far. He is always ready to "party," has beer cans and liquor bottles stacked over five feet high in front of his apartment's picture window, and frequently passes out on dates, forcing the women to drive him home. He has slept through more exams than he can remember and has an impressive list of "incomplete" grades in classes. He jumps at any excuse to have a drink and often calls up his friends to start impromptu parties at odd hours. His driver's license was revoked recently (for the second time) because of a conviction for driving while intoxicated. His behavior while sober is usually mild-mannered and shy; his drunken actions are wild and sometimes destructive.

Rudy may not seek the aid of a clinical psychologist or psychiatrist, for the simple reason that he is "getting by." Though the drunken rowdiness puts off his friends at times, and though his comatose dating patterns keep him from having any close relationships with women, he keeps up a so-so (C+) average in school and has not done anything "crazy" enough to suggest that he needs attention. Rudy had a fine grade point average in high school and was the "model" son of an upper-middle-class family.

THE ANALYSIS

Rudy's problem is one form of a difficulty that may be manifest in everyone's life on occasion. There are probably many instances in which you—perhaps without even taking a drink—also engaged in a self-defeating behavior. Procrastinating until the very last minute on an important project, for example, can lead to poor performance; choosing tasks or projects that are simply too hard or too involved for the time you have available may also guarantee a less than sparkling performance. These and other self-defeating actions are easily interpreted within the context of social psychological self theories.

In an analysis of what they call *self-handicapping strategies*, Jones and Berglas (1978; also, Berglas & Jones, 1978) have argued that people will set themselves up for failure under certain conditions. Specifically, when a person is highly concerned with self-presentation in one area (like success at school or on dates), but has little invested in presenting a desirable self-image in another (like getting drunk or procrastinating), the person will engage in the less important activity to provide an excuse for anticipated failure in the more important activity. In a sense, a person throws up a smoke screen around the tasks in which a self-attribution of failure would be unthinkable by doing a variety of things that suggest he or she is not trying to succeed. Later, if success appears, the person looks good; if failure happens, the person has a "handicap" to blame. Rudy could say "I was drunk" or "I was hung over" as a response to any accusation of failure—from his parents about school or from his dates about his failure to win their admiration. Fearing the social disapproval we might obtain by testing ourselves and losing, we make sure we never test ourselves by stacking the deck from the start (see M. L. Snyder, 1979).

Self-defeating behavior can be quite costly to the individual. In providing an excuse for failure, the person probably increases the likelihood that failure will occur. According to self-perception principles (see Chapter 3), it would be expected that such costly yet freely chosen behaviors would be seen by the person as reflecting the self in a direct way. One who procrastinates and fails at a task, for instance, might later claim that procrastination is enjoyable. Rudy's failure following drinking has a similar impact on self-perception; he becomes more and more likely to believe that he enjoys drinking and wants to keep it up. Given this ever-increasing internalization of self-handicapping strategies, it seems that they should be highly resistant to change. In the case of alcoholism, this seems to be true; drinking is a very difficult behavior to modify.

Generally, the best track record for alcohol treatment has been established by Alcoholics Anonymous. Thinking about self theories again helps to see why this might be so. When a person joins AA, he or she is confronted with a new standard for self-evaluation— "Drinking is the worst thing I can do." This standard is supported by all group members, and so to gain the approval of this group, one must begin to present the self in a new way. Alcohol abstinence is now defined as the most important task related to gaining the approval of others, and other tasks (such as Rudy's school and interpersonal activities) that were previously the targets of the alcohol excuse become secondary. It is only through shifting standards of self-evaluation and social approval, then, that self-defeating behavior can itself be defeated. Hopefully, there will someday even be a "Procrastinators Anonymous" to aid those of us with this problem, but for now, the meeting has been postponed.

LIMITS OF SELF THEORY

In the process of applying a theory, the limitations of the theory come into focus. Looking back through this chapter, you might note that a number of human problems were left unsolved. We had nothing to say about severe mental disorders such as schizophrenia, no comment on the prevention of physical disease, another blank about drug addiction, and no recommendation for how to eliminate the human need for food. And sadly, even the applications that *were* explored might be seen as only limited answers to the problems that were addressed. Something that self theorists and researchers typically ignore, but realize deep down, is that there are certain boundaries to the operation of the self, and that these boundaries necessarily restrict the range of behaviors and problems to which self theories can be applied.

The limits of the self, and thus of self theory, are illustrated in the behavior of animals and babies. As noted in earlier chapters, most animals and most very young infants are without a reflective awareness; they do not have a self. Yet they learn things, behave in a wide variety of ways, and react to a range of information and stimulation. The fact that these activities can go on without self-understanding emphasizes the *biological foundations* of behavior and suggests that the self system should be seen as one that is superimposed on the biological, physiological, and genetic causes of behavior. The self is developed in human beings as an extension of these foundations, and hence must function within the limits of the human organism, operating along certain themes that are unchangeable through self-processes. Though self-processes could change a person's preferences for different kinds of beverage, for instance, and though they might even lead a person to believe that liquids could be foregone, no amount of self-image change could keep the abstaining person from turning into a prune.

At times, then, the self system seems like an ineffective and redundant appendix to the biological person—a moth hovering near the flame of physical reality. Changing the self system to influence pain perception (Meichenbaum, 1977), physical symptom reports (Pennebaker & Skelton, 1978), eating behavior in the obese (Rodin, 1977), and other biologically based phenomena produces measurable but hardly miraculous effects. Schachter (1978) reports, for example, that the explanations and self-perceptions people have about smoking (e.g., "I do it because it relaxes me") are just so much self-justification; there is good evidence that the real cause of smoking is physiological addiction to nicotine. Variations in smoking produced through the self system, then, are likely to be small and short-lived. In this light, the self system is only a weak tool for understanding and manipulating biological realities.

Turning to areas other than biological ones, however, we find that the self has a much more profound influence. In areas of human functioning that exhibit wide individual and cultural variation, the self can be an extraordinary force in changing the human condition. This is because the biological "givens" do not dictate exactly how behavior and experience are to be interpreted in these areas. When it comes to social interaction, then, or to social conventions, morals, interpretations of behavior, social attraction and rejection, intergroup relations, and the many other topics that comprise social psychology, the self takes center stage. Admittedly, social psychologists will probably keep on trying to extend self-theoretic explanations to biological functions, no doubt because this is one of the few ways that science at present can hope to control or understand them. But when all is said and done, self theory remains uniquely and specially qualified to explain the social psychology of human beings.

References

Abelson, R. P. A script theory of understanding, attitude, and behavior. In J. Carroll & T. Payne (Eds.), *Cognition and social behavior*. Hillsdale, N.J.: Erlbaum, 1976.

Abramson, L. Y., & Sackheim, H. A. A paradox in depression: Uncontrollability and self-blame. *Psychological Bulletin*, 1977, 84, 838–851.

Abramson, L. Y., Seligman, M.E.P., & Teasdale, J. D. Learned helplessness in humans: Critique and reformulation. *Journal of Abnormal Psychology*, 1978, 87, 49–74.

Adams, J. S., & Rosenbaum, W. E. The relationship of worker productivity to cognitive dissonance about wage inequities. *Journal of Applied Psychology*, 1962, 46, 161–164.

Aderman, D., Brehm, S. S., & Katz, L. B. Empathic observation of an innocent victim: The just world revisited. *Journal of Personality and Social Psychology*, 1974, 29, 342–347.

Ajzen, I., & Fishbein, M. Attitude-behavior relations: A theoretical analysis and review of empirical research. *Psychological Bulletin*, 1977, 84, 888–918.

Alderfer, C. P., & Lodahl, T. M. A quasi-experiment on the use of experimental methods in the classroom. *Journal of Applied Behavioral Science*, 1971, 7, 43–69.

Allport, G. W. *Personality: A psychological interpretation*. New York: Holt, 1937.

Allport, G. W. *The use of personal documents in psychological science* (Social Science Research Council, Bulletin 49). Ann Arbor: Edwards Brothers, 1942.

Altman, I. *The environment and social behavior*. Monterey, Calif.: Brooks/Cole, 1975.

Altman, I., & Taylor, D. A. *Social penetration: The development of interpersonal relationships*. New York: Holt, 1973.

Amabile, T. M., DeJong, W., & Lepper, M. R. Effects of externally imposed deadlines on subsequent intrinsic motivation. *Journal of Personality and Social Psychology*, 1976, *34*, 92–98.

Archer, R. L., & Berg, J. H. Disclosure reciprocity and its limits: A reactance analysis. *Journal of Experimental Social Psychology*, 1978, *14*, 527–540.

Archer, R. L., & Berg, J. H. *Self-perception and self-disclosure.* Unpublished manuscript, University of Texas at Austin, 1979.

Archer, R. L., & Burleson, J. A. *The effect of timing of self-disclosure on attraction and reciprocity.* Unpublished manuscript, University of Texas at Austin, 1979.

Archer, R. L., Hormuth, S. E., & Berg, J. H. Self-disclosure under conditions of self-awareness. In *The self in social psychology.* Symposium presented at the meeting of the American Psychological Association, New York, September, 1979.

Argyle, M., & Dean, J. Eye-contact, distance, and affiliation. *Sociometry*, 1965, *28*, 289–304.

Aronson, E., & Carlsmith, J. M. Effect of the severity of threat on the devaluation of forbidden behavior. *Journal of Abnormal and Social Psychology*, 1963, *66*, 584–588.

Bailey, K. G., & Sowder, W. T., Jr. Audiotape and videotape self-confrontation in psychotherapy. *Psychological Bulletin*, 1970, *74*, 127–137.

Bandura, A. Self-reinforcement: Theoretical and methodological considerations. *Behaviorism*, 1976, *4*, 135–155.

Bandura, A. Self-efficacy: Toward a unifying theory of behavioral change. *Psychological Review*, 1977, *84*, 191–215.

Baron, R. Aggression and heat: The "long, hot summer" revisited. In A. Baum, S. Valins, & J. Singer (Eds.), *Advances in environmental research*. Hillsdale, N.J.: Erlbaum, 1978.

Baron, R., & Ransberger, V. Ambient temperature and the occurrence of collective violence: The "long, hot summer" revisited. *Journal of Personality and Social Psychology*, 1978, *36*, 351–360.

Baron, R. S., & Roper, G. Reaffirmation of social comparison views of choice shifts: Averaging and extremity effects in an autokinetic situation. *Journal of Personality and Social Psychology*, 1976, *33*, 521–530.

Batson, C. D., Coke, J. S., Jasnoski, M. L., & Hanson, M. Buying kindness: Effect of an extrinsic incentive for helping on perceived altruism. *Personality and Social Psychology Bulletin*, 1978, *4*, 86–91.

Beaman, A. L., Klentz, B., Diener, E., & Svanum, S. Objective self awareness and transgression in children: A field study. *Journal of Personality and Social Psychology*, 1979, *37*, 1835–1846.

Beck, A. *Cognitive therapy and emotional disorders*. New York: International Universities Press, 1976.

Bem, D. An experimental analysis of self-persuasion. *Journal of Experimental Social Psychology*, 1965, *1*, 199–218.

Bem, D. Self-perception: An alternative interpretation of cognitive dissonance phenomena. *Psychological Review*, 1967, *74*, 183–200.

Bem, D. Self-perception theory. In L. Berkowitz (Ed.), *Advances in experimental social psychology* (Vol. 6). New York: Academic Press, 1972.

Bem, D., & Allen, A. On predicting some of the people some of the time: The search for cross-situational consistencies in behavior. *Psychological Review*, 1974, *81*, 506–519.

Bem, D., & McConnell, H. Testing the self-perception explanation of dissonance phenomena: On the salience of premanipulation attitudes. *Journal of Personality and Social Psychology*, 1970, *14*, 23–31.

Bem, S. L. The measurement of psychological androgyny. *Journal of Consulting and Clinical Psychology*, 1974, *42*, 155–162.

Berg, I. A. The deviation hypothesis: A broad statement of its assumptions and postulates. In I. A. Berg (Ed.), *Response set in personality assessment*. Chicago: Aldine, 1967.

Berg, J. H., & Archer, R. L. Disclosure or concern: A look at liking for norm-breakers. In *Self-disclosure and responsivity: An attributional analysis*. Symposium presented at the meeting of the American Psychological Association, Toronto, August, 1978.

Berglas, S., & Jones, E. E. Drug choice as a self-handicapping strategy in response to noncontingent success. *Journal of Personality and Social Psychology*, 1978, *36*, 405–417.

Berkowitz, L., & Walster, E. (Eds.). *Advances in experimental social psychology* (Vol. 9: Equity theory). New York: Academic Press, 1976.

Berlyne, D. E. *Conflict, arousal, and curiosity*. New York: McGraw-Hill, 1960.

Bertenthal, B. I., & Fischer, K. W. Development of self-recognition in the infant. *Developmental Psychology*, 1978, *14*, 44–50.

Biddle, B. S., & Thomas, E. J. (Eds.). *Role theory: Concepts and research*. New York: Wiley, 1966.

Boring, E. G. *A history of experimental psychology*. New York: Appleton, 1950.

Bower, G. An introduction to cognitive psychology. In W. Estes (Ed.), *Handbook of learning and cognition* (Vol. 1). Hillsdale, N.J.: Erlbaum, 1974.

Bower, G. Experiments on story comprehension and recall. *Discourse Processes*, 1978, *1*, 211–223.

Boyd, H., & Sisney, V. Immediate self-image confrontation and changes in self-concept. *Journal of Consulting Psychology*, 1967, *31*, 291–296.

Bradley, G. W. Self-serving biases in the attribution process: A re-examination of the fact or fiction question. *Journal of Personality and Social Psychology*, 1978, *36*, 56–71.

Bramel, D. A. A dissonance theory approach to defensive projection. *Journal of Abnormal and Social Psychology*, 1962, *69*, 121–129.

Braver, S. L., Linder, D. E., Corwin, T. T., & Cialdini, R. B. Some conditions that affect admissions of attitude change. *Journal of Experimental Social Psychology*, 1977, *13*, 565–576.

Brehm, J. W. *A theory of psychological reactance*. New York: Academic Press, 1966.

Brehm, S. S. *The application of social psychology to clinical practice*. Washington, D.C.: Hemisphere, 1976.

Brenner, M. The next-in-line effect. *Journal of Verbal Learning and Verbal Behavior*, 1973, *12*, 320–323.

Brundage, L. E., Derlega, V. J., & Cash, T. F. The effects of physical attractiveness and need for approval on self-disclosure. *Personality and Social Psychology Bulletin*, 1977, *3*, 63–66.

Bruner, J. S. *Beyond the information given*. New York: Norton, 1973.

Burhenne, D., & Mirels, H. L. Self-disclosure in self-descriptive essays. *Journal of Consulting and Clinical Psychology*, 1970, *35*, 409–413.

Burnam, M. A., & Pennebaker, J. W. *Social cues and interpretation of bodily state*. Unpublished manuscript, University of Virginia, 1979.

Buss, A. H. *Psychology: Man in perspective*. New York: Wiley, 1973.

Buss, D. M., & Scheier, M. F. Self-consciousness, self-awareness, and self-attribution. *Journal of Research in Personality*, 1976, *10*, 463–468.

Calder, B. J., Ross, M., & Insko, C. A. Attitude change and attitude attribution: effects of incentive, choice, and consequences. *Journal of Personality and Social Psychology*, 1973, *25*, 84–99.

Calder, B. J., & Staw, B. M. Self-perception of intrinsic and extrinsic motivation. *Journal of Personality and Social Psychology*, 1975, *31*, 599–605.

Cann, A., Sherman, S. J., & Elkes, R. Effects of initial request size and timing of a second request on compliance: The foot in the door and the door in the face. *Journal of Personality and Social Psychology*, 1975, *32*, 774–782.

Cannon, W. Again the James-Lange and the thalamic theories of emotion. *Psychological Review*, 1931, *38*, 281–295.

Cantor, N., & Mischel, W. Traits as prototypes: Effects on recognition memory. *Journal of Personality and Social Psychology*, 1977, *35*, 38–48.

Cartwright, D. Self-consistency as a factor affecting immediate recall. *Journal of Abnormal and Social Psychology*, 1956, *52*, 212–219.

Carver, C. S. Physical aggression as a function of objective self-awareness and attitudes toward punishment. *Journal of Experimental Social Psychology*, 1975, *11*, 510–519.

Carver, C. S. A cybernetic model of self-attention processes. *Journal of Personality and Social Psychology*, 1979, *37*, 1251–1281.

Carver, C. S., & Scheier, M. F. Self-consciousness and reactance. *Journal of Research in Personality*, 1979 (in press).

Chaikin, A. L., & Derlega, V. J. Liking for the norm-breaker in self-disclosure. *Journal of Personality*, 1974, *42*, 117–129. (a)

Chaikin, A. L., & Derlega, V. J. *Self-disclosure*. Morristown, N.J.: General Learning Press, 1974. (b)

Chaikin, A. L., & Derlega, V. J. Variables affecting the appropriateness of self-disclosure. *Journal of Consulting and Clinical Psychology*, 1974, *42*, 588–593. (c)

Chaikin, A. L., Derlega, V. J., Bayma, B., & Shaw, J. Neuroticism and disclosure reciprocity. *Journal of Consulting and Clinical Psychology*, 1975, *43*, 13–19.

Chaikin, A. L., Derlega, V. J., & Miller, S. J. Effects of room environment on self-disclosure in a counseling analogue. *Journal of Counseling Psychology*, 1976, *23*, 479–481.

Cialdini, R. B., Vincent, J. E., Lewis, S. K., Catalau, J., Wheeler, D., & Darby, B. L. Reciprocal concessions procedure for inducing compliance: The door in the face technique. *Journal of Personality and Social Psychology*, 1975, *31*, 206–215.

Coke, J. S., Batson, C. D., & McDavis, K. Empathic mediation of helping: A two-stage model. *Journal of Personality and Social Psychology*, 1978, *36*, 752–766.

Cooley, C. H. *Human nature and the social order*. New York: Scribner's, 1902.

Cooper, H. M. Statistically combining independent studies: A meta-analysis of sex differences in conformity research. *Journal of Personality and Social Psychology*, 1979, *37*, 131–146.

Coopersmith, F. *Self-concept: Its origin and its development in infancy*. Paper presented at the meeting of the American Psychological Association, San Francisco, August, 1977.

Coopersmith, S. *The antecedents of self-esteem*. San Francisco: Freeman, 1967.

Costrich, N., Feinstein, J., Kidder, L., Maracek, J., & Pascale, L. When stereotypes hurt: Three studies of penalties for sex-reversals. *Journal of Experimental Social Psychology*, 1975, *11*, 520–530.

Cozby, P. C. Self-disclosure: A literature review. *Psychological Bulletin*, 1973, 79, 73–91.

Crano, W. D., & Sivacek, J. General attribution theory versus self-perception. In *Perspectives on social attribution*. Symposium presented at the meeting of the Southwestern Psychological Association, New Orleans, April 1978.

Cravens, R. W. The need for approval and the private versus public disclosure of self. *Journal of Personality*, 1975, 43, 503–504.

Crowne, W. J., & Marlowe, D. *The approval motive: Studies in evaluative dependence.* New York: Wiley, 1964.

deCharms, R. *Personal causation.* New York: Academic Press, 1968.

Deci, E. L. *Intrinsic motivation.* New York: Plenum, 1975.

Derlega, V. J., & Chaikin, A. L. Norms affecting self-disclosure in men and women. *Journal of Consulting and Clinical Psychology*, 1976, 44, 376–380.

Derlega, V. J., & Chaikin, A. L. Privacy and self-disclosure in social relationships. *Journal of Social Issues*, 1977, 33, 102–115.

Derlega, V. J., Harris, M. S., & Chaikin, A. L. Self-disclosure reciprocity, liking and the deviant. *Journal of Experimental Social Psychology*, 1973, 9, 277–284.

Derlega, V. J., Wilson, M., & Chaikin, A. L. Friendship and disclosure reciprocity. *Journal of Personality and Social Psychology*, 1976, 34, 578–582.

Diener, E., Fraser, S. C., Beaman, A. L., & Kelem, R. T. Effects of deindividuation variables on stealing among Halloween trick-or-treaters. *Journal of Personality and Social Psychology*, 1976, 33, 178–183.

Diener, E., & Wallbom, M. Effects of self-awareness on antinormative behavior. *Journal of Research in Personality*, 1976, 10, 107–111.

Dutton, D., & Aron, A. Some evidence for heightened sexual attraction under conditions of high anxiety. *Journal of Personality and Social Psychology*, 1974, 30, 510–517.

Duval, S. Conformity on a visual task as a function of personal novelty on attitudinal dimensions and being reminded of the object status of self. *Journal of Experimental Social Psychology*, 1976, 12, 87–98.

Duval, S., Duval, V. H., & Neely, R. *Self-focus, felt responsibility, and helping behavior. Journal of Personality and Social Psychology*, 1979, 37, 1769–1778.

Duval, S., & Wicklund, R. A. *A theory of objective self-awareness.* New York: Academic Press, 1972.

Edison, N. G., & Fink, E. L. *Objective self-awareness as an interactional process.* Paper presented at the meeting of the American Psychological Association, Washington, D.C., August 1976.

Edwards, A. L. *The social desirability variable in personality assessment and research.* New York: Dryden, 1957.

Ellis, A. Research data supporting the clinical and personality hypotheses of RET and other cognitive-behavior therapies. In A. Ellis & R. Griegen (Eds.), *Handbook of rational emotive therapy.* New York: Springer, 1977.

Ellsworth, P., & Ross, L. Intimacy in response to direct gaze. *Journal of Experimental Social Psychology*, 1975, *11*, 592–613.

Enzle, M. E., & Harvey, M. D. Effects of a third-party requestor's surveillance and recipient awareness of request on helping. *Personality and Social Psychology Bulletin*, 1977, *3*, 421–424.

Enzle, M. E., & Look, S. Self vs. other delivery of extrinsic rewards and the overjustification effect. In *The self in social psychology.* Symposium presented at the meeting of the American Psychological Association, New York, August, 1979.

Enzle, M. E., & Ross, J. M. Increasing and decreasing intrinsic interest with contingent rewards: A test of cognitive evaluation theory. *Journal of Experimental Social Psychology*, 1978, *14*, 588–597.

Epstein, S. The self-concept revisited: Or a theory of a theory. *American Psychologist*, 1973, *28*, 404–416.

Farina, A., Gliha, D., Boudreau, L. A., Allen, J. G., & Sherman, M. Mental illness and the impact of believing others know about it. *Journal of Abnormal Psychology*, 1971, *77*, 1–5.

Farina, A., & Ring, K. The influence of mental illness on interpersonal relations. *Journal of Abnormal Psychology*, 1965, *70*, 47–51.

Fenigstein, A. Self-consciousness, self-attention, and social interaction. *Journal of Personality and Social Psychology*, 1979, *37*, 75–86.

Fenigstein, A., Scheier, M. F., & Buss, A. H. Public and private self-consciousness: Assessment and theory. *Journal of Consulting and Clinical Psychology*, 1975, *43*, 522–527.

Festinger, L. A theory of social comparison processes. *Human Relations*, 1954, *7*, 117–140.

Festinger, L. *A theory of cognitive dissonance.* Stanford, Calif.: Stanford University Press, 1957.

Festinger, L., & Carlsmith, J. M. Cognitive consequences of forced compliance. *Journal of Abnormal and Social Psychology*, 1959, *58*, 203–210.

Fitts, W. H. *Tennessee self concept scale.* Nashville: Counselor Recordings and Tests, 1964.

Flavell, J. H., Botkin, P., Fry, C., Wright, J., & Jarvis, P. *The development of role-taking and communication skills in children.* New York: Wiley, 1968.

Folger, R., Rosenfield, D., & Hays, R. Equity and intrinsic motivation: The role of choice. *Journal of Personality and Social Psychology*, 1978, *36*, 557–564.

Frederiksen, N., & Messick, S. Response set as a measure of personality. *Educational and Psychological Measurement*, 1959, *19*, 137–159.

Freedman, J. L. Long-term behavioral effects of cognitive dissonance. *Journal of Experimental Social Psychology*, 1965, *1*, 145–155.

Freedman, J. L., & Fraser, S. C. Compliance without pressure: The foot-in-the-door technique. *Journal of Personality and Social Psychology*, 1966, *4*, 195–202.

French, J.R.P., Jr., & Raven, B. The bases of social power. In D. Cartwright (Ed.), *Studies in social power*. Ann Arbor, Mich.: Institute for Social Research, 1959.

Freud, A. *The ego and the mechanisms of defense*. New York: International Universities Press, 1946.

Frey, D., Wicklund, R. A., & Scheier, M. F. Die Theorie der objectiven Selbstaufmerksamkeit. In D. Frey (Ed.), *Theorien der Sozialpsychologie*. Bern, Switzerland: Huber, 1978.

Frieze, I. H., Parsons, J. E., Johnson, P. B., Ruble, D. N., & Zellman, G. L. *Women and sex roles: A social psychological perspective*. New York: Norton, 1978.

Gaertner, S. L., & Dovidio, J. F. The subtlety of white racism, arousal, and helping behavior. *Journal of Personality and Social Psychology*, 1977, *35*, 691–707.

Gallup, G. G. Self-recognition in primates: A comparative approach to the bidirectional properties of consciousness. *American Psychologist*, 1977, *32*, 329–338.

Gardner, R. A. & Gardner, B. T. Teaching sign language to a chimpanzee. *Science*, 1969, *165*, 664-672.

Gergen, K. J. The effects of interaction goals and personalistic feedback on the presentation of self. *Journal of Personality and Social Psychology*, 1965, *1*, 413–424.

Gergen, K. J. *The concept of self*. New York: Holt, 1971.

Gibbons, F. X. *Self-focused attention and the enhancement of response awareness*. Unpublished doctoral dissertation, University of Texas at Austin, 1976.

Gibbons, F. X. Sexual standards and reactions to pornography: Enhancing behavioral consistency through self-focused attention. *Journal of Personality and Social Psychology*, 1978, *36*, 976–987.

Gibbons, F. X., & Wicklund, R. A. Selective exposure to self. *Journal of Research in Personality*, 1976, *10*, 98–106.

Gibbons, F. X., Wicklund, R. A., Karylowski, I., Rosenfield, D., &

Chase, T. C. *Altruistic responses to self-focused attention.* Unpublished manuscript, University of Texas at Austin, 1978.

Gibson, J. J. *The senses considered as perceptual systems.* Boston: Houghton Mifflin, 1966.

Goffman, E. *The presentation of self in everyday life* (Rev. ed.). New York: Doubleday, 1959.

Goffman, E. *Behavior in public places.* New York: Free Press, 1963.

Goldberg, L. R., & Slovic, P. Importance of test item content: An analysis of a corollary of the deviation hypothesis. *Journal of Counseling Psychology,* 1967, *14,* 462–472.

Goldsen, R. K., Rosenberg, M., Williams, R. M., & Suchman, E. A. *What college students think.* Princeton: Van Nostrand, 1960.

Goodstein, L. D., & Reinecker, V. M. Factors affecting self-disclosure: A review of the literature. In B. A. Maher (Ed.), *Progress in experimental personality research* (Vol. 7). New York: Academic Press, 1976.

Gordon, C. Self-conceptions: Configurations of content. In C. Gordon & K. J. Gergen (Eds.), *The self in social interaction.* New York: Wiley, 1968.

Gotay, C. C. *Helping behavior as a function of objective self-awareness and salience of the norm of helping.* Unpublished manuscript, University of Maryland, 1978.

Graham, D., Kabler, J., & Graham, F. Physiological response to suggestion of attitudes specific for hives and hypertension. *Psychosomatic Medicine,* 1962, *24,* 159–169.

Green, R. A., & Murray, E. J. Instigation to aggression as a function of self-disclosure and threat to self-esteem. *Journal of Consulting and Clinical Psychology,* 1973, *40,* 440–443.

Greenwald, A. G. *The totalitarian ego: Fabrication and revision of personal history.* Unpublished manuscript, Ohio State University, 1978.

Gross, A. E., Reimer, B. S., & Collins, B. E. Audience reactions as a determinant of the speaker's self-persuasion. *Journal of Experimental Social Psychology,* 1973, *9,* 246–256.

Gunzberger, D. W., Wegner, D. M., & Anooshian, L. Moral judgment and distributive justice. *Human Development,* 1977, *20,* 160–170.

Haan, N. *Coping and defending: Processes of self-environment organization.* New York: Academic Press, 1977.

Haney, C., Banks, W., & Zimbardo, P. Interpersonal dynamics in a simulated prison. *International Journal of Criminology and Penology,* 1973, *1,* 69–97.

Hartshorne, H., & May, M. A. *Studies in the nature of character.* New York: Macmillan, 1930.

Hass, R. G. A *test of the bidirectional focus of attention assumption of the theory of objective self-awareness*. Paper presented at the meeting of the Eastern Psychological Association, Philadelphia, April 1979.

Hess, R., & Torney, J. *The development of political attitudes in children*. London: Aldine, 1967.

Hiroto, D. S., & Seligman, M.E.P. Generality of learned helplessness in man. *Journal of Personality and Social Psychology*, 1975, 31, 311–327.

Hoffman, M. L. Empathy, role taking, guilt, and development of altruistic motives. In T. Lickona (Ed.), *Moral development and behavior*. New York: Holt, 1976.

Holmes, D. S. Compensation for ego threat: Two experiments. *Journal of Personality and Social Psychology*, 1971, 18, 234–237.

Hormuth, S. E. Self-awareness and drive theory: Comparing internal standards and dominant responses. In *Recent Developments in objective self-awareness theory*. Symposium presented at the meeting of the American Psychological Association, Toronto, August, 1978.

Horner, M. S. Toward an understanding of achievement-related conflicts in women. *Journal of Social Issues*, 1972, 28, 157–175.

Ickes, W., Layden, M. A., & Barnes, R. D. Objective self-awareness and individuation: An empirical link. *Journal of Personality*, 1978, 46, 146–161.

Jacobs, L., Berscheid, E., & Walster, E. Self-esteem and attraction. *Journal of Personality and Social Psychology*, 1971, 17, 84–91.

James, W. *Principles of psychology*. New York: Holt, 1890.

James, W. *Psychology: The briefer course*. New York: Holt, 1910.

James, W. The self. In C. Gordon & J. Gergen (Eds.), *The self in social interaction*. New York: Wiley, 1968. (Originally published, 1890.)

Jaynes, C. *The effects of self-degradation and self-aggrandizement on liking*. Unpublished honors thesis, University of Texas at Austin, 1978.

Jeffrey, D. B. A comparison of the effects of external control and self-control on the modification and maintenance of weight. *Journal of Abnormal Psychology*, 1974, 83, 404–410.

Jellison, J. M. *I'm sorry, I didn't mean to, and other lies we love to tell*. New York: Chatham Square Press, 1977.

Jellison, J. M. *Self presentation—A behavioristic approach*. Paper presented at the meeting of the American Psychological Association, Toronto, August 1978.

Jellison, J. M., & Arkin, R. Social comparison of abilities. In J. M.

Suls & R. L. Miller (Eds.), *Social comparison processes*. Washington, D.C.: Hemisphere, 1977.

Jellison, J. M., & Davis, D. Relationships between perceived ability and attitude extremity. *Journal of Personality and Social Psychology*, 1973, *27*, 430–436.

Jellison, J. M., & Gentry, K. W. A self-presentation interpretation of the seeking of social approval. *Personality and Social Psychology Bulletin*, 1978, *4*, 227–230.

Jellison, J. M., Jackson-White, R., Bruder, R. A., & Martyna, W. Achievement behavior: A situational behavior. *Sex Roles*, 1975, *1*, 375–390.

Jellison, J. M., & Riskind, J. A social comparison of abilities interpretation of risk taking behavior. *Journal of Personality and Social Psychology*, 1970, *15*, 375–390.

Jensen, R. E., & Moore, S. G. The effect of attribute statements on cooperativeness and competitiveness in school-age boys. *Child Development*, 1977, *48*, 305–307.

Jones, E. E., & Archer, R. L. Are there special effects of personalistic self-disclosure? *Journal of Experimental Social Psychology*, 1976, *12*, 180–193.

Jones, E. E., & Berglas, S. Control of attributions about the self through self-handicapping strategies: The appeal of alcohol and the role of underachievement. *Personality and Social Psychology Bulletin*, 1978, *4*, 200–206.

Jones, E. E., Gergen, K. J., Gumpert, P., & Thibaut, J. W. Some conditions affecting the use of ingratiation to influence performance evaluation. *Journal of Personality and Social Psychology*, 1965, *1*, 613–625.

Jones, E. E., Gergen, K. J., & Jones, R. G. Tactics of ingratiation among leaders and subordinates in a status hierarchy. *Psychological Monographs*, 1963, *77*(3, Whole No. 566).

Jones, E. E., & Nisbett, R. E. *The actor and the observer: Divergent perceptions of the causes of behavior*. Morristown, N.J.: General Learning Press, 1971.

Jones, E. E., & Sigall, H. The bogus pipeline: A new paradigm for measuring affect and attitude. *Psychological Bulletin*, 1971, *76*, 245–254.

Jones, E. E., & Wortman, C. *Ingratiation: An attributional approach*. Morristown, N.J.: General Learning Press, 1973.

Jones, R. A., Sensenig, J., & Haley, J. V. Self-descriptions: Configurations of content and order effects. *Journal of Personality and Social Psychology*, 1974, *30*, 36–45.

Jones, S. C. Self and interpersonal evaluations: Esteem theories versus consistency theories. *Psychological Bulletin*, 1973, *79*, 185–199.

Jones, S. C., & Schneider, D. J. Certainty of self-appraisal and reactions to evaluations from others. *Sociometry*, 1968, *31*, 395–403.

Jourard, S. M. *The transparent self*. Princeton, N.J.: Van Nostrand, 1964.

Jourard, S. M. *Self-disclosure: An experimental analysis of the transparent self*. New York: Wiley, 1971. (a)

Jourard, S. M. *The transparent self* (2nd ed.). Princeton, N.J.: Van Nostrand, 1971. (b)

Jourard, S. M., & Lasakow, P. Some factors in self-disclosure. *Journal of Abnormal and Social Psychology*, 1958, *56*, 91–98.

Jourard, S. M., & Resnick, J. L. The effect of high-revealing subjects on the self-disclosure of low-revealing subjects. *Journal of Humanistic Psychology*, 1970, *10*, 84–93.

Kelley, H. H. *Attribution in social interaction*. New York: General Learning Press, 1972.

Kelly, G. A. *The psychology of personal constructs*. New York: Norton, 1955.

Kelman, H. C. Processes of opinion change. *Public Opinion Quarterly*, 1961, *25*, 57–78.

Kerckhoff, A., & Back, K. *The June bug: A study of hysterical contagion*. New York: Appleton, 1968.

Kidder, L., Bellettirie, G., & Cohn, E. S. Secret ambitions and public performances: The effects of anonymity on reward allocations by men and women. *Journal of Experimental Social Psychology*, 1977, *13*, 70–80.

Kiesler, C. A. *The psychology of commitment: Experiments linking behavior to belief*. New York: Academic Press, 1971.

Kiesler, C. A., Nisbett, R. E., & Zanna, M. P. On inferring one's beliefs from one's behavior. *Journal of Personality and Social Psychology*, 1969, *11*, 321–327.

Koffka, K. *Principles of Gestalt psychology*. New York: Harcourt, 1935.

Kohlberg, L. Moral stages and moralization. In T. Lickona (Ed.), *Moral development and behavior*. New York: Holt, 1976.

Krantz, D. S. The social context of obesity research: Another perspective on its place in the field of social psychology. *Personality and Social Psychology Bulletin*, 1978, *4*, 177–184.

Kuiper, N. A., & Rogers, T. B. The encoding of personal information: Self-other differences. *Journal of Personality and Social Psychology*, 1979, *37*, 499–514.

Langer, E. J. The illusion of control. *Journal of Personality and Social Psychology*, 1975, *32*, 311–328.

Langer, E. J. Rethinking the role of thought in social interaction. In J. H. Harvey, W. Ickes, & R. F. Kidd (Eds.), *New directions in attribution research* (Vol. 2). Hillsdale, N.J.: Erlbaum, 1978.

Langer, E. J., & Rodin, J. The effects of choice and enhanced personal responsibility for the aged: A field experiment in an institutional setting. *Journal of Personality and Social Psychology*, 1976, *34*, 191–198.

Latané, B., & Darley, J. M. *The unresponsive bystander: Why doesn't he help?* New York: Appleton, 1968.

Lazarus, R., Opton, E. M., Nomikos, M. S., & Rankin, N. O. The principle of shortcircuiting of threat: Further evidence. *Journal of Personality*, 1965, *33*, 622–635.

Lefcourt, H. M. *Locus of control.* Hillsdale, N.J.: Erlbaum, 1976.

Lepper, M. R. Dissonance, self-perception, and honesty in children. *Journal of Personality and Social Psychology*, 1973, *25*, 56–74.

Lepper, M. R., & Greene, D. Turning play into work: Effects of adult surveillance and extrinsic rewards on children's intrinsic motivation. *Journal of Personality and Social Psychology*, 1975, *31*, 479–486.

Lepper, M. R., & Greene, D. Overjustification research and beyond: Toward a means-ends analysis of intrinsic and extrinsic motivation. In M. R. Lepper & D. Greene (Eds.), *The hidden costs of reward.* Hillsdale, N.J.: Erlbaum, 1978.

Lepper, M. R., Greene, D., & Nisbett, R. E. Undermining children's intrinsic interest with extrinsic reward: A test of the "overjustification" hypothesis. *Journal of Personality and Social Psychology*, 1973, *28*, 129–137.

Lerner, M. J. Observer's evaluation of a victim: Justice, guilt, and veridical perception. *Journal of Personality and Social Psychology*, 1971, *20*, 127–135.

Levinger, G. Reviewing the close relationship. In G. Levinger & H. L. Raush (Eds.), *Close relationships: Perspectives on the meaning of intimacy.* Amherst: University of Massachusetts Press, 1977.

Levinger, G., & Senn, D. J. Disclosure of feelings in marriage. *Merrill-Palmer Quarterly of Behavior and Development*, 1967, *13*, 237–249.

Lewin, K. *A dynamic theory of personality.* New York: McGraw-Hill, 1935.

Lewin, K. The social distance between individuals in the United States and Germany. In K. Lewin (Ed.), *Resolving social conflicts.* New York: Harper & Row, 1948.

Lewin, K. *Field theory and social science.* New York: Harper & Row, 1964.

Lewis, M., & Brooks, J. Self-knowledge and emotional development. In M. Lewis & L. Rosenblum (Eds.), *The development of affect.* New York: Plenum, 1978.

Liska, A. E. (Ed.). *The consistency controversy.* New York: Wiley, 1975.

Livesley, W. J., & Bromley, D. B. *Person perception in childhood and adolescence.* New York: Wiley, 1973.

Loevinger, J. The meaning and measurement of ego development. *American Psychologist,* 1966, *21,* 195–206.

Lord, C. G. *Schemas and images as memory aids: Two modes of processing social information.* Unpublished manuscript, Stanford University, 1978.

Mandler, G. *Mind and emotion.* New York: Wiley, 1975.

Manis, M. Social interaction and the self-concept. *Journal of Abnormal and Social Psychology,* 1955, *51,* 362–370.

Maracek, J., & Mettee, D. R. Avoidance of continued success as a function of self-esteem, level of esteem certainty, and responsibility for success. *Journal of Personality and Social Psychology,* 1972, *22,* 98–107.

Marañon, G. Contribution à l'étude de l'action emotive de l'adrenaline. *Revue Française d'Endocrinologie,* 1924, *2,* 301–325.

Markus, H. Self-schemata and processing information about the self. *Journal of Personality and Social Psychology,* 1977, *35,* 63–78.

Markus, H., Crane, M., & Siladi, M. *Cognitive consequences of androgyny.* Unpublished manuscript, University of Michigan, 1979.

Maslow, A. H. *Motivation and personality.* New York: Harper & Row, 1954.

Mayo, P. R. Self-disclosure and neurosis. *British Journal of Social and Clinical Psychology,* 1975, *43,* 13–19.

McCormick, T. F. *The development of attitudes and the mediation of self-focused attention.* Unpublished doctoral dissertation, University of Texas at Austin, 1977.

McGuire, W. J., McGuire, C. V., Child, P., & Fujioka, T. Salience of ethnicity in the spontaneous self-concept as a function of one's ethnic distinctiveness in the social environment. *Journal of Personality and Social Psychology,* 1978, *36,* 511–520.

McGuire, W. J., & Padawer-Singer, A. Trait salience in the spontaneous self-concept. *Journal of Personality and Social Psychology,* 1976, *33,* 743–754.

Mead, G. H. *Mind, self, and society.* Chicago: University of Chicago Press, 1934.

Mechanic, D. Social psychologic factors affecting the presentation of bodily complaints. *New England Journal of Medicine,* 1972, *286,* 1132–1139.

Medalia, N., & Larsen, O. Diffusion and belief in a collective delusion: The Seattle windshield pitting epidemic. *American Sociological Review,* 1958, *23,* 180–186.

Meichenbaum, D. *Cognitive behavior modification: An integrative approach.* New York: Plenum, 1977.

Meltzoff, A. N., & Moore, M. K. Imitation of facial and manual gestures by human neonates. *Science,* 1977, *198,* 75–78.

Merton, R. K. Patterns of influence: A study of interpersonal influence and communications behavior in a local community. In P. F. Lazarsfeld & F. N. Stanton (Eds.), *Communications research 1948–1949.* New York: Harper & Row, 1949.

Messick, S. The psychology of acquiescence: An interpretation of research evidence. In I. A. Berg (Ed.), *Response set in personality assessment.* Chicago: Aldine, 1967.

Milgram, S. *The individual in a social world: Essays and experiments.* Reading, Mass.: Addison-Wesley, 1977.

Miller, D. T., & Ross, M. Self-serving biases in the attribution of causality: Fact or fiction? *Psychological Review,* 1975, *82,* 213–225.

Miller, G. A., Galanter, E., & Pribram, K. *Plans and structure of behavior.* New York: Holt, 1960.

Miller, R. L., Brickman, P., & Bolen, D. Attribution versus persuasion as a means of modifying behavior. *Journal of Personality and Social Psychology,* 1975, *31,* 430–441.

Millham, J., & Jacobson, L. I. The need for approval. In H. London & J. E. Exner, Jr. (Eds.), *Dimensions of personality.* New York: Wiley, 1978.

Milton, G. A. *Five studies of the relation between sex role identification and achievement in problem solving* (Tech. Rep. No. 3). New Haven, Conn.: Yale University Press, 1958.

Milton, G. A. Sex differences in problem solving as a function of role appropriateness of the problem content. *Psychological Reports,* 1959, *5,* 705–708.

Mischel, W. *Personality and assessment.* New York: Wiley, 1968.

Mischel, W. Continuity and change in personality. *American Psychologist,* 1969, *24,* 1012–1018.

Mischel, W., Ebbesen, E. B., & Zeiss, A. R. Selective attention to the self: Situational and dispositional determinants. *Journal of Personality and Social Psychology,* 1973, *27,* 129–142.

Monson, T. C., & Snyder, M. Actors, observers, and the attribution process: Toward a reconceptualization. *Journal of Experimental Social Psychology,* 1977, *13,* 89–111.

Montemayor, R., & Eisen, M. The development of self-conceptions from childhood to adolescence. *Developmental Psychology,* 1977, *13,* 314–319.

Moore, L. M., & Baron, R. M. Effects of wage inequities on work attitudes and performance. *Journal of Experimental Social Psychology,* 1973, *9,* 1–16.

Moray, N. Attention in dichotic listening: Affective cues and the influence of instructions. *Quarterly Journal of Experimental Psychology*, 1959, *12*, 56–60.

Morse, S., & Gergen, K. J. Social comparison, self-consistency, and the concept of self. *Journal of Personality and Social Psychology*, 1970, *16*, 148–156.

Morton, T. L. Intimacy and reciprocity of exchange: A comparison of spouses and strangers. *Journal of Personality and Social Psychology*, 1978, *36*, 72–81.

Mowrer, O. H. Freudianism, behavior therapy, and self-disclosure. In E. Southwell & M. Merbaum (Eds.), *Personality: Readings in theory and research* (2nd ed.). Monterey, Calif.: Brooks/Cole, 1971.

Myers, D. G. Polarizing effects of social comparison. *Journal of Experimental Social Psychology*, 1978, *14*, 554–563.

Neisser, U. *Cognitive psychology*. New York: Appleton, 1967.

Neisser, U. *Cognition and reality: Principles and implications of cognitive psychology*. San Francisco: Freeman, 1976.

Newtson, D. Foundations of attribution: The perception of ongoing behavior. In J. Harvey, W. Ickes, & R. Kidd (Eds.), *New directions in attribution research* (Vol. 1). Hillsdale, N.J.: Erlbaum, 1976.

Nisbett, R., & Valins, S. Perceiving the causes of one's own behavior. In E. E. Jones, D. E. Kanouse, H. H. Kelley, R. E. Nisbett, S. Valins, & B. Weiner (Eds.), *Attribution: Perceiving the causes of behavior*. Morristown, N. J.: General Learning Press, 1971.

Nisbett, R. E., & Wilson, T. D. Telling more than we can know: Verbal reports on mental processes. *Psychological Review*, 1977, *84*, 231–259. (a)

Nisbett, R. E., & Wilson, T. D. The halo effect: Evidence for unconscious alteration of judgments. *Journal of Personality and Social Psychology*, 1977, *35*, 250–256. (b)

Ovsiankina, M. Untersuchungen zur Handlungs—Und Affektpsychologie: VI. Die Wiederaufnahme unterbrochener Handlungen. *Psychologische Forschung*, 1928, *11*, 302–379.

Pedersen, D. M., & Breglio, V. J. Personality correlates of actual self-disclosure. *Psychological Reports*, 1968, *22*, 495–501.

Pedersen, D. M., & Higbee, K. L. Personality correlates of self-disclosure. *Journal of Social Psychology*, 1969, *78*, 81–89.

Pennebaker, J. W. *Self-perception of emotion and specificity of physical symptoms*. Paper presented at the meeting of the American Psychological Association, New York, August 1979.

Pennebaker, J. W., & Skelton, J. A. Psychological parameters of physical symptoms. *Personality and Social Psychology Bulletin*, 1978, *4*, 524–530.

Pennebaker, J. W., & Skelton, J. A. *Cognitive processes influencing the interpretation of bodily states.* Unpublished manuscript, University of Virginia, 1979.

Peplau, L. A., & Perlman, D. *Blueprint for a social psychological theory of loneliness.* Paper presented at the Swansea Conference on Interpersonal Attraction and Love, Swansea, Wales, September 1977.

Phares, E. J. Locus of control. In H. London & J. E. Exner, Jr. (Eds.), *Dimensions of Personality.* New York: Wiley, 1978.

Piaget, J. *The construction of reality in the child.* New York: Basic Books, 1954.

Piaget, J. *The origins of intelligence in children.* New York: Norton, 1963.

Piaget, J. *The moral judgment of the child.* New York: Free Press, 1965.

Pryor, J. B., Comer, R. J., & Banks, W. C. *Causal attribution as a function of self-focused attention and attributional style.* Unpublished manuscript, Princeton University, 1976.

Pryor, J. B., Gibbons, F. X., Wicklund, R. A., Fazio, R. A., & Hood, R. Self-focused attention and self-report validity. *Journal of Personality,* 1977, *45,* 513–527.

Regan, D. T., & Totten, J. Empathy and attribution: Turning observers into actors. *Journal of Personality and Social Psychology,* 1975, *32,* 850–856.

Reis, H. T., & Gruzen, J. On mediating equity, equality, and self-interest: The role of self-presentation in social exchange. *Journal of Experimental Social Psychology,* 1976, *12,* 487–503.

Rickers-Ovsiankina, M. A. Social accessibility in three age groups. *Psychological Reports,* 1956, *2,* 283–294.

Rivera, A. N., & Tedeschi, J. T. Public versus private reactions to positive inequity. *Journal of Personality and Social Psychology,* 1976, *34,* 895–900.

Rodin, J. Research on eating behavior and obesity: Where does it fit in personality and social psychology? *Personality and Social Psychology Bulletin,* 1977, *3,* 333–355.

Rogers, C. R. *Client-centered therapy.* Boston: Houghton Mifflin, 1951.

Rogers, C. R. *On becoming a person: A therapist's view of psychotherapy.* Boston: Houghton Mifflin, 1961.

Rogers, T. B. Self-reference in memory: Recognition of personality items. *Journal of Research in Personality,* 1977, *11,* 295–305.

Rogers, T. B., Kuiper, N. A., & Kirker, W. S. Self-reference and the encoding of personal information. *Journal of Personality and Social Psychology,* 1977, *35,* 677–688.

Rohrberg, R. G., & Sousa-Poza, J. F. Alcohol, field dependence, and dyadic self-disclosure. *Psychological Reports,* 1976, *39,* 1151–1161.

Rorer, L. G. The great response style myth. *Psychological Bulletin,* 1965, *63,* 129–156.

Rosenthal, R. Interpersonal expectations: Effects of experimenter's hypothesis. In R. Rosenthal & R. L. Rosnow (Eds.), *Artifacts in behavioral research.* New York: Academic Press, 1969.

Ross, L. The intuitive psychologist and his shortcomings: Distortions in the attribution process. In L. Berkowitz (Ed.), *Advances in Experimental Social Psychology* (Vol. 10). New York: Academic Press, 1977.

Ross, L. Some afterthoughts on the intuitive psychologist. In L. Berkowitz (Ed.), *Cognitive theories in social psychology.* New York: Academic Press, 1978.

Ross, M., & Sicoly, F. Egocentric biases in availability and attribution. *Journal of Personality and Social Psychology,* 1979, *37,* 322–336.

Rotter, J. B. Generalized expectancies for internal versus external control of reinforcement. *Psychological Monographs,* 1966, *80*(1, Whole No. 609).

Rubin, Z. Disclosing oneself to a stranger: Reciprocity and its limits. *Journal of Experimental Social Psychology,* 1975, *11,* 233–260.

Rubin, Z., & Schenker, S. Friendship, proximity, and self-disclosure. *Journal of Personality,* 1978, *46,* 1–22.

Runge, T. E., & Archer, R. L. *Reactions to self-disclosure of public and private information.* Unpublished manuscript, University of Texas at Austin, 1979.

Rush, A. J., Khatami, M., & Beck, A. T. Cognitive and behavioral therapy in chronic depression. *Behavior Therapy,* 1975, *6,* 398–404.

Ryle, G. *The concept of mind.* London: Hutchinson, 1949.

Ryle, G. Self-knowledge. In H. Morick (Ed.), *Introduction to the philosophy of mind.* Glenview, Ill.: Scott, Foresman, 1970.

Salancik, G., & Conway, M. Attitude inferences from salient and relevant cognitive content about behavior. *Journal of Personality and Social Psychology,* 1975, *32,* 829–840.

Sarbin, T. R. A preface to a psychological analysis of the self. In C. Gordon & K. J. Gergen (Eds.), *The self in social interaction.* New York: Wiley, 1968.

Schachter, S. 1. Nicotine regulation in heavy and light smokers. *Journal of Experimental Psychology: General,* 1977, *106,* 5–12.

Schachter, S. Second thoughts on biological and psychological explanations of behavior. In L. Berkowitz (Ed.), *Cognitive theories in social psychology.* New York: Academic Press, 1978.

Schachter, S., & Rodin, J. *Obese humans and rats.* Hillsdale, N.J.: Erlbaum, 1974.

Schachter, S., & Singer, J. Cognitive, social and physiological determinants of emotional state. *Psychological Review,* 1962, 69, 379–399.

Scheier, M. F. Self-awareness, self-consciousness, and angry aggression. *Journal of Personality,* 1976, 44, 627–644.

Scheier, M. F., Buss, A. H., & Buss, D. M. Self-consciousness, self-report of aggressiveness, and aggression. *Journal of Research in Personality,* 1978, 12, 133–140.

Scheier, M. F., & Carver, C. S. Self-focused attention and the experience of emotion: Attraction, repulsion, elation, and depression. *Journal of Personality and Social Psychology,* 1977, 35, 624–636.

Scheier, M. F., Carver, C. S., & Gibbons, F. X. *Self-focused attention and reactions to fear: When standards and affect collide.* Unpublished manuscript, Carnegie-Mellon University, 1978.

Scheier, M. F., Carver, C. S., & Gibbons, F. X. Self-directed attention, awareness of bodily states, and suggestibility. *Journal of Personality and Social Psychology,* 1979, 37, 1576–1588.

Scheier, M. F., Fenigstein, A., & Buss, A. H. Self-awareness and physical aggression. *Journal of Experimental Social Psychology,* 1974, 10, 264–273.

Schulz, R. Effects of control and predictability on the psychological well-being of the institutionalized aged. *Journal of Personality and Social Psychology,* 1976, 33, 563–573.

Schwartz, S. H., & Gottlieb, A. Bystander reactions to a violent theft: Crime in Jerusalem. *Journal of Personality and Social Psychology,* 1976, 34, 1188–1199.

Seligman, M.E.P. *Helplessness: On depression, development, and death.* San Francisco: Freeman, 1975.

Sherif, M., & Hovland, C. *Social judgment.* New Haven, Conn.: Yale University Press, 1961.

Shibutani, T. *Society and personality: An interactionist approach to social psychology.* Englewood Cliffs, N.J.: Prentice-Hall, 1961.

Shrauger, J. S. Responses to evaluation as a function of initial self-perceptions. *Psychological Bulletin,* 1975, 82, 581–596.

Simmel, G. *The sociology of George Simmel* (K. H. Wolff, trans.). New York: Free Press, 1950.

Simner, M. L. Newborn's response to the cry of another infant. *Developmental Psychology,* 1971, 5, 136–150.

Skinner, B. F. *Verbal behavior.* New York: Appleton, 1957.

Skotko, V. P., & Langmeyer, D. The effects of interaction distance and gender on self-disclosure in the dyad. *Sociometry*, 1977, *40*, 178–182.

Snyder, M. Self-monitoring processes. In L. Berkowitz (Ed.), *Advances in experimental social psychology* (Vol. 12). New York: Academic Press, 1979.

Snyder, M., & Cunningham, M. R. To comply or not to comply: Testing the self-perception explanation of the "foot in the door" phenomenon. *Journal of Personality and Social Psychology*, 1975, *31*, 64–67.

Snyder, M., & Swann, W. B., Jr. Behavioral confirmation in social interaction: From social perception to social reality. *Journal of Experimental Social Psychology*, 1978, *14*, 148–162.

Snyder, M., Tanke, E. D., & Berscheid, E. Social perception and interpersonal behavior: On the self-fulfilling nature of social stereotypes. *Journal of Personality and Social Psychology*, 1977, *35*, 656–666.

Snyder, M. L., Stephan, W. G., & Rosenfield, D. Attributional egotism. In J. Harvey, W. Ickes, & R. F. Kidd (Eds.), *New directions in attribution research* (Vol. 2). Hillsdale, N.J.: Erlbaum, 1978.

Snyder, M. L. *Attributional ambiguity*. Unpublished manuscript, University of Texas at Austin, 1978.

Staub, E. *Positive social behavior and morality* (Vol. 1). New York: Academic Press, 1978.

Sternbach, R. *Principles of psychophysiology*. New York: Academic Press, 1966.

Storms, M. D. Videotape and the attribution process: Reversing actors' and observers' points of view. *Journal of Personality and Social Psychology*, 1973, *27*, 165–175.

Storms, M. D., & McCaul, K. D. Attribution processes and emotional exacerbation of dysfunctional behavior. In J. H. Harvey, W. J. Ickes, & R. F. Kidd (Eds.), *New directions in attribution research* (Vol. 1). Hillsdale, N.J.: Erlbaum, 1976.

Stotland, E. Exploratory studies of empathy. In L. Berkowitz (Ed.), *Advances in experimental social psychology*. (Vol. 4). New York: Academic Press, 1969.

Sullivan, H. S. *Conceptions of modern psychiatry*. New York: Norton, 1947.

Suls, J. M., & Miller, R. L. (Eds.). *Social comparison processes: Theoretical and empirical perspectives*. New York: Wiley, 1977.

Tavris, C., & Offir, C. *The longest war*. New York: Harcourt, 1977.

Taylor, C. What is human agency? In T. Mischel (Ed.), *The self*. Totowa, N.J.: Rowman & Littlefield, 1977.

Taylor, D. A., & Altman, I. *Intimacy-scaled stimuli for use in research on interpersonal exchange* (NMRI Tech. Rep. No. 9, MF022 .01.03-1002). Bethesda, Md.: Naval Medical Research Institute, May 1966.

Taylor, D. A., Altman, I., & Sorrentino, R. Interpersonal exchange as a function of rewards and costs and situational factors: Expectancy confirmation-disconfirmation. *Journal of Experimental Social Psychology*, 1969, *5*, 324–339.

Tedeschi, J. T., & Lindskold, S. *Social psychology: Interdependence, interaction, and influence.* New York: Wiley, 1976.

Turner, R. G. Self-consciousness and anticipatory belief change. *Personality and Social Psychology Bulletin*, 1977, *3*, 438–441.

Tversky, A., & Kahneman, D. Judgment under uncertainty: Heuristics and biases. *Science*, 1974, *184*, 1124–1131.

Valins, S. Cognitive effects of false heart-rate feedback. *Journal of Personality and Social Psychology*, 1966, *4*, 400–408.

Valins, S., & Nisbett, R. E. Attribution processes in the development and treatment of emotional disorder. In E. E. Jones, D. E. Kanouse, H. H. Kelley, R. E. Nisbett, S. Valins, & B. Weiner (Eds.), *Attribution: Perceiving the causes of behavior.* Morristown, N.J.: General Learning Press, 1971.

Vallacher, R. R. *Dimensions of the self and the perception of others.* Paper presented at the meeting of the Midwestern Psychological Association, Chicago, May 1975.

Vallacher, R. R., & Solodky, M. Objective self-awareness, standards of evaluation, and moral behavior. *Journal of Experimental Social Psychology*, 1979, *15*, 254–262.

Wallen, R. Ego-involvement as a determinant of selective forgetting. *Journal of Abnormal and Social Psychology*, 1942, *37*, 20–39.

Walster, E., Walster, G. W., & Bercheid, E. *Equity: Theory and research.* Boston: Allyn & Bacon, 1978.

Walz, G. R., & Johnston, J. A. Counselors look at themselves on videotape. *Journal of Counseling Psychology*, 1963, *10*, 232–236.

Wegner, D. M. *The development of morality.* Homewood, Ill.: Learning Systems, 1975.

Wegner, D. M. Attribute generality: The development and articulation of attributes in person perception. *Journal of Research in Personality*, 1977, *11*, 329–339.

Wegner, D. M., & Finstuen, K. Observers' focus of attention in the simulation of self-perception. *Journal of Personality and Social Psychology*, 1977, *35*, 56–62.

Wegner, D. M., & Giuliano, T. *The self-focusing effects of arousal.* Paper presented at the meeting of the Southwestern Psychological Association, San Antonio, Texas, April 1979.

Wegner, D. M., & Schaefer, D. The concentration of responsibility: An objective self awareness analysis of group size effects in helping situations. *Journal of Personality and Social Psychology*, 1978, 36, 147–155.

Wegner, D. M., & Vallacher, R. R. *Implicit psychology: An introduction to social cognition*. New York: Oxford University Press, 1977.

Weick, K. E. Systematic observational methods. In G. Lindzey & E. Aronson (Eds.), *Handbook of social psychology* (Vol. 2). Reading, Mass.: Addison-Wesley, 1968.

White, R. W. Motivation reconsidered: The concept of competence. *Psychological Review*, 1959, 66, 297–333.

Wicker, A. W. Attitude versus actions: The relationship between verbal and overt behavioral responses. *Journal of Social Issues*, 1969, 25, 41–78.

Wicker, A. W. An examination of the "other variables" explanation of attitude-behavior inconsistency. *Journal of Personality and Social Psychology*, 1971, 19, 18–30.

Wicklund, R. A. Objective self-awareness. In L. Berkowitz (Ed.), *Advances in experimental social psychology* (Vol. 8). New York: Academic Press, 1975.

Wicklund, R. A. Three years later. In L. Berkowitz (Ed.), *Cognitive theories in social psychology*. New York: Academic Press, 1978.

Wicklund, R. A. The influence of self on human behavior. *American Scientist*, 1979, 67, 187–193. (a)

Wicklund, R. A. Group contact and self-focused attention. In P. B. Paulus (Ed.), *Psychology of group influence*. Hillsdale, N.J.: Erlbaum, 1979. (b)

Wicklund, R. A., & Duval, S. Opinion change and performance facilitation as a result of objective self-awareness. *Journal of Experimental Social Psychology*, 1971, 7, 319–342.

Wiggins, J. S. *Personality and prediction: Principles of personality assessment*. Reading, Mass.: Addison-Wesley, 1973.

Wine, J. Test anxiety and direction of attention. *Psychological Bulletin*, 1971, 76, 92–104.

Worchel, S., & Teddlie, C. The experience of crowding: A two-factor theory. *Journal of Personality and Social Psychology*, 1976, 34, 30–40.

Wortman, C. B. Causal attributions and personal control. In J. H. Harvey, W. J. Ickes, & R. F. Kidd (Eds.), *New directions in attribution research* (Vol. 1). Hillsdale, N.J.: Erlbaum, 1976.

Wylie, R. *The self concept*. Lincoln, Neb.: University of Nebraska Press, 1974.

Zajonc, R. B. *Preferenda and discriminanda: Processing of affect.* Unpublished manuscript, University of Michigan, 1979.

Zanna, M. P., & Pack, S. J. On the self-fulfilling nature of apparent sex differences in behavior. *Journal of Experimental Social Psychology,* 1975, *11,* 583–591.

Zeller, A. F. An experimental analogue of repression: I. Historical summary. *Psychological Bulletin,* 1950, *47,* 39–51.

Zillman, D. Attribution and misattribution of excitatory reactions. In J. H. Harvey, W. J. Ickes, & R. F. Kidd (Eds.), *New directions in attribution research* (Vol. 2). Hillsdale, N.J.: Erlbaum, 1978.

Zimbardo, P. G. The human choice: Individuation, reason, and order versus deindividuation, impulse, and chaos. In W. J. Arnold & D. Levine (Eds.), *Nebraska Symposium on Motivation* (Vol. 17). Lincoln, Neb.: University of Nebraska Press, 1969.

Zimbardo, P. G. *Shyness: What is it, what to do about it.* Reading, Mass.: Addison-Wesley, 1977.

Author Index

Subject Index